Italian

lonely planet

phrasebooks
and
Karina Coates & Pietro Iagnocco

Italian audio phrasebook
1st edition – September 2009

Published by
Lonely Planet Publications Pty Ltd ABN 36 005 607 983
90 Maribyrnong St, Footscray, Victoria 3011, Australia

Lonely Planet Offices
Australia Locked Bag 1, Footscray, Victoria 3011
USA 150 Linden St, Oakland CA 94607
UK 2nd floor, 186 City Rd, London, EC1V 2NT

Cover illustration
Vespa Love by Daniel New

ISBN 9781741799293

10 9 8 7 6 5 4 3

Printed through Toppan Leefung Printing Limited
Printed in China

acknowledgments

Editors Annelies Mertens and Piers Kelly would like to thank the entire cast and crew that made this great debut possible …

Publishing manager Jim Jenkin who brought the whole production to life. Project manager Fabrice Rocher for keeping everything running backstage.

Series designer Yukiyoshi Kamimura for his great illustrations and cover design. Daniel New for the cover illustration. Virtuoso designer Patrick Marris for chipping in.

Karina Coates, Pietro Iagnocco and Susie Walker for their diligent translations of the libretto. The all-singing, all-dancing commissioning editor and translator Karina Coates successfully juggled many roles at once.

Thanks also to commissioning editor Karin Vidstrup Monk and the ensemble of fellow editors Ben Handicott, Meg Worby and Emma Koch. A round of applause to bilingual eagle eyes Adrienne Costanzo and Susie Walker for excellent proofing.

Special thanks to loyal layout designers Nicholas Stebbing, for carrying the project through to the end, Belinda Campbell, who filled in over the festive season, and Katie Cason and Sally Morgan who helped out at the last minute. Thanks to special projects managing cartographer Paolo Piaia and map editor Wayne Murphy for producing the language map.

Susie Walker would like to thank Luciano Furfaro, Amy Furfaro and contracted author, Mirna Cicioni, for their help with translating, transliterating and proofreading. Special thanks to Mirna for the creation of the Sustainable Travel section.

Karina would like to thank Pietro Iagnocco and the chorus of Lygon Street locals for the opportunities to rehearse.

make the most of this phrasebook ...

Anyone can speak another language! It's all about confidence. Don't worry if you can't remember your school language lessons or if you've never learnt a language before. Even if you learn the very basics (on the inside covers of this book), your travel experience will be the better for it. You have nothing to lose and everything to gain when the locals hear you making an effort.

finding things in this book

For easy navigation, this book is in sections. The Tools chapters are the ones you'll thumb through time and again. The Practical section covers basic travel situations like catching transport and finding a bed. The Social section gives you conversational phrases, pick-up lines, the ability to express opinions – so you can get to know people. Food has a section all of its own: gourmets and vegetarians are covered and local dishes feature. Safe Travel equips you with health and police phrases, just in case. Remember the colours of each section and you'll find everything easily; or use the comprehensive Index. Otherwise, check the two-way traveller's Dictionary for the word you need.

being understood

Throughout this book you'll see coloured phrases on the right-hand side of each page. They're phonetic guides to help you pronounce the language. You don't even need to look at the language itself, but you'll get used to the way we've represented particular sounds. The pronunciation chapter in Tools will explain more, but you can feel confident that if you read the coloured phrase slowly, you'll be understood.

using the audio

You'll notice the numbered tags (eg 32A) beside a selection of phrases in this book. The number refers to the audio track, the letter indicates the order it will be read in the audio track – so 'a' is first, 'b' is second etc. Use the audio to help master your own pronunciation, or use it on the road by transferring the MP3 files to your portable media player and letting it do some of the talking for you.

italian

- national language
- official language

EUROPE

For more details see the **introduction**.

English-speakers will find Italian a beautiful language to listen to and an easy one to start speaking. The expressive rhythm and melody of the language, which has lent itself to the epic poetry of Dante and the grand operas of Verdi, has fascinated visitors for centuries. When even a simple sentence can sound like an aria you'll find it difficult to resist striking up a conversation.

Of all the Romance languages – which include French, Spanish, Portuguese and Romanian – Italian claims the closest family relationship to Latin. Because English has been heavily influenced by Latin (particularly through its contact with French), there are many basic resemblances between the two languages.

at a glance ...

language name: Italian

name in language: *italiano*
ee·ta·*lya*·no

language family: Romance

key country: Italy

approximate number of speakers: 65 million

close relatives: French, Spanish, Portuguese

donations to English: Words to do with food, including spaghetti, broccoli and macaroni. Musical words like virtuoso, opera and viola. Architectural terms such as studio and stucco. Artistic words such as maestro and fresco.

Today, thanks to widespread migration and the enormous popularity of Italian culture and cuisine, most of us are also familiar with modern Italian words like *ciao, pasta,* and *bello.*

Outside Italy, Italian is spoken by minorities in Switzerland, Slovenia and France, and more recently by large communities of immigrants in Australia, Argentina and the US. Italian has official status in the Istrian peninsula of Croatia where Italian-speaking communities have existed since the Venetians began colonising parts of the Dalmatian coast during the twelfth century.

introduction

Another country where Italian is spoken is the African nation of Eritrea which remained a colony of Italy from 1880 until 1941. Today most Eritreans speak Italian only as a second language.

Around the world there are approximately 65 million Italian speakers, the majority of whom live in Italy. In Italy itself, most people also speak a local dialect. Dialects are spoken all over the country and some are so different from standard Italian as to be considered distinct languages in their own right. In fact, it wasn't until the nineteenth century that the Tuscan dialect – the language of Dante, Boccaccio, Petrarch and Macchiavelli – was chosen to become the standard language of the nation. Standard Italian is the official language of schools, media and administration, and is the form that will take you from the top of the boot to the very toe. All the language that we have provided here is in standard Italian.

This book gives you the words you need to get by, as well as all the fun, spontaneous phrases that lead to a better experience of Italy and its people. Need more encouragement? Remember, the contact you make through using Italian will make your travels unique. Local knowledge, new relationships and a sense of satisfaction are on the tip of your tongue, so don't just stand there, say something!

> abbreviations used in this book

f	feminine
inf	informal
m	masculine
sg	singular
pl	plural
pol	polite

The Italian sound system will be familiar to most English-speakers: almost all of the sounds you'll hear exist in English. You might notice some slight differences, particularly with the vowel sounds, but there's nothing to stop you having a go and being understood. Standard Italian pronunciation is given in this book – the same form that's used in education and the media.

vowel sounds

symbol	english equivalent	italian example
a	father	*pane*
e	red	*letto*
ee	bee	*vino*
o	pot	*molo*
oo	took	*frutta*

Vowel sounds are generally shorter than English equivalents. They also tend not to run together to form vowel sound combinations (diphthongs), though it can often sound that way to English-speakers. The following table presents four vowel sounds that roughly correspond to diphthongs in English:

symbol	english equivalent	italian example
ay	say	*vorrei*
ai	aisle	*mai*
oy	boy	*poi*
ow	cow	*ciao/autobus*

pronunciation

consonant sounds

symbol	english equivalent	italian example
b	**big**	*bello*
ch	**ch**illi	*centro*
d	**d**in	*denaro*
dz	li**ds**	*mezzo/zaino*
f	**f**un	*fare*
g	**g**o	*gomma*
j	**j**am	*cugino*
k	**k**ick	*cambio/quanto*
l	**l**oud	*linea*
ly	mi**lli**on	*figlia*
m	**m**an	*madre*
n	**n**o	*numero*
ny	ca**ny**on	*bagno*
p	**p**ig	*pronto*
r	**r**un (but stronger and rolled)	*ristorante*
s	**s**o	*sera*
sh	**sh**ow	*shopping*
t	**t**in	*teatro*
ts	hi**ts**	*grazie/sicurezza*
v	**v**an	*viaggio*
w	**w**in	*uomo*
y	**y**es	*italiano*
z	**z**oo	*casa*

As well as the pronunciation described above, Italian consonant sounds have an additional form that you'll notice: a stronger, almost emphatic, pronunciation. The actual sounds are basically the same, though meaning can be altered between a normal consonant sound and this double consonant sound. It's referred to as a 'double consonant' because usually if the word is written with a double consonant, that's the cue to use the stronger form.

TOOLS

10

Here are some examples where this 'double consonant' effect can make a difference:

sonno	*son·no*	**sleep**
sono	*so·no*	**I am**
pappa	*pap·pa*	**baby food**
papa	*pa·pa*	**pope**

Unlike the above examples, the phonetic guides in this book don't distinguish between the two forms. Refer to the written Italian beside each phonetic guide as the cue to making the consonant sounds a lilttle stronger. Even if you never distinguish them, you'll always be understood in context. Your audience will work out if you're talking about the pope or about baby food!

word stress

In Italian, you generally emphasise the second-last syllable of the word. When a written word has an accent marked on a vowel though, the stress is on that syllable. The characteristic sing-song that you hear in an Italian sentence is created by pronouncing the syllables evenly and rhythmically then swinging down on the last word.

The stressed syllable is always italicised in our pronunciation guide, so you can't go wrong with this, even if you can't remember the general rule!

plunge in!

Don't worry too much about pronunciation. Just listen to people around you. The pronunciation guides for every phrase account for the correct sounds and stressed syllables.

spellbound

The relationship between Italian sounds and their spelling is straightforward and consistent. The following rules will help you read the Italian that you come across in your travels:

c, g, sc	• before *a, o, u* and *h* they sound hard like the 'k' in 'kick', 'g' in 'go' and 'sc' in 'scooter' respectively	*bianco, dischetto, gomma, fresco,*
	• before *e* and *i* they sound soft like the 'ch' in 'chilli', 'j' in 'jam' and 'sh' in 'show' respectively	*centro, gelato, ascensore*
ci, gi sci	before *a, o, u,* the *i* is not pronounced	*ciao, giallo* and *prosciutto*
h	never pronounced	*traghetto*
j, w, k, x and y	only found in foreign words that have been adopted by Italian	*jogging, weekend, kosher, fax* and *yogurt*
z	pronounced as 'dz' or as 'ts'	*zaino grazie*
s	• pronounced as a 'z' between vowels	*casa*
	• as an 's' everywhere else	*sì, essere* and *scatola*
gli, gn	pronounced as 'lli' in 'million' and 'ny' in 'canyon' respectively	*figlia, bagno*

a/an

In Italian, 'a/an' takes the form of *un* or *una* depending on the gender of the thing, person or concept being talked about. (See also **gender**.)

I'd like a sandwich and an apple.

Vorrei un panino e   vo·*ray* oon pa·*nee*·no e
una mela.   oo·na *me*·la
(lit: I-would-like a sandwich and
an apple)

Two other forms, *uno* and *un'*, are used, depending on the first letter of the next word:

	with most nouns	exceptions	
masculine	un	uno	with nouns starting with *s* plus a consonant or starting with *z*, *gn*, *pn*, *ps*, *x* or *y*
feminine	una	un'	with nouns starting with a vowel

adjectives see describing things

any see some

articles see a/an and the

be

Italian has two words for the English verb 'be'.

Essere is generally used to describe ongoing characteristics:

I	am	happy	io	sono	felice
you sg inf	are	from Italy	tu	sei	d'Italia
you sg pol	are	an artist	Lei	è	artista
he/she/it	is	interesting	lui/lei	è	interessante
we	are	sad	noi	siamo	tristi
you pl	are	young	voi	siete	giovani
they	are	students	loro	sono	studenti

Stare describes temporary states or locations:

I	am	well	io	sto	bene
you sg inf	are	at home	tu	stai	a casa
you sg pol	are	sick	Lei	sta	male
he/she/it	is	better	lui/lei	sta	meglio
we	are	travelling	noi	stiamo	viaggiando
you pl	are	on holiday	voi	state	in vacanza
they	are	eating	loro	stanno	mangiando

comparing things

To compare one thing to another, use the words *più* (more) and *meno* (less) in the following ways:

più/meno ... di   pyoo/*me*·no ... dee
   (lit: more/less ... than)

You're less tired than me.
   Sei meno stanco di me.   say *me*·no *stan*·ko dee me
   (lit: you-are less tired than me)

il/la ... più/meno ...   eel/la ... pyoo/*me*·no ...
  (lit: the ... more/less ...)

You're the most beautiful woman in the world.
Sei la donna più   say la *do*·na pyoo
bella del mondo.   *be*·la del *mon*·do
  (lit: you-are the woman more
    beautiful of-the world)

describing things

Adjectives are usually placed after the noun in Italian:

a black cat
un gatto nero   oon *ga*·to *ne*·ro
  (lit: a cat black)

Exceptions to this rule include adjectives expressing quantity (many, few); possession (my, yours); and numbers (first).

Note that in the above example the adjective (*nero*) mirrors the masculine gender of the noun (*gatto*). The adjective endings change depending on the gender and number of the noun:

	singular	plural
masculine	-o	-i
feminine	-a	-e

Adjectives that end in -e in the singular, for example *felice* (happy), change their ending to -i in the plural, regardless of the noun's gender:

	singular	plural
masculine/feminine	-e	-i

the happy cats
i gatti felici   ee *ga*·tee fe·*lee*·chee
  (lit: the cats happy)

feminine see gender

gender

All nouns are considered either masculine or feminine. You can often guess a noun's gender using these handy tips:

often masculine	often feminine
• nouns referring to male people	• nouns referring to female people
• nouns ending in -o	• nouns ending in -a
• nouns ending in a consonant	• nouns ending in -ione
• nouns ending in -ore	

have

Possession can be shown in various ways in Italian. The easiest way is by using the verb *avere* (have):

I	have	a ticket	io	ho	un biglietto
you sg inf	have	a watch	tu	hai	un orologio
you sg pol	have	the bill	Lei	ha	il conto
he/she/it	has	a problem	lei/lui	ha	un problema
we	have	the key	noi	abbiamo	la chiave
you pl	have	a timetable	voi	avete	un orario
they	have	children	loro	hanno	dei bambini

masculine see gender

more than one

In general, words ending in -a in the singular end in -e in the plural, and words ending in -o or -e in the singular end in -i in the plural:

	singular			plural	
a person	*una persona*	oo·na per·so·na	three people	*tre persone*	tre per·so·ne
a ticket	*un biglietto*	oon bee·lye·to	two tickets	*due biglietti*	doo·e bee·lye·tee
a country	*un paese*	oon pa·e·se	five countries	*cinque paesi*	cheen·kwe pa·e·see

Remember, articles and adjectives mirror nouns in gender and number.

See also **a/an**, **describing things**, **some** and **the**.

perplexing plurals

Italian has some irregular plural forms – here are a couple:

il dio	eel *dee*·o	the god
i dei	ee day	the gods
la ala	la *a*·la	the wing
le ali	la *a*·lee	the wings

For added interest, some words are masculine in the singular and feminine in the plural:

il labbro	eel *la*·bro	the lip
le labbra	le *la*·bra	the lips

my & your

There are a number of words for 'my' and 'your' in Italian. Choose the correct form according to the gender and number of the noun:

	singular		plural	
	masculine 'ticket'	feminine 'room'	masculine 'coins'	feminine 'shoes'
my	*il mio biglietto*	*la mia camera*	*i miei spiccioli*	*le mie scarpe*
your sg inf	*il tuo biglietto*	*la tua camera*	*i tuoi spiccioli*	*le tue scarpe*
your sg pol	*il Suo biglietto*	*la Sua camera*	*i Suoi spiccioli*	*le Sue scarpe*
his/hers/its	*il suo biglietto*	*la sua camera*	*i suoi spiccioli*	*le sue scarpe*
our	*il nostro biglietto*	*la nostra camera*	*i nostri spiccioli*	*le nostre scarpe*
your pl	*il vostro biglietto*	*la vostra camera*	*i vostri spiccioli*	*le vostre scarpe*
their	*il loro biglietto*	*la loro camera*	*i loro spiccioli*	*le loro scarpe*

If the ownership of what is being talked about is obvious from the context, you can shorten the sentence as follows:

It's my ticket.
   È il mio biglietto.   e eel *mee*·o bee·*lye*·to
   (lit: it-is the my ticket)

It's mine.
   È il mio.   e eel *mee*·o
   (lit: it-is the my)

negative

To make a sentence negative, just add the word *non* (no) before
the verb:

I speak Italian.
  Parlo italiano.   *par*·lo ee·ta·*lya*·no
  (lit: I-speak Italian)

I don't speak Italian.
  Non parlo italiano.   non *par*·lo ee·ta·*lya*·no
  (lit: no I-speak Italian)

nouns see gender

number see more than one

planning ahead

The future tense is the easiest tense to learn in Italian, as all verbs
take the same endings. Take *viaggiare* (travel):

I		*io*	*viaggerò*
you sg inf		*tu*	*viaggerai*
you sg pol		*Lei*	*viaggerà*
he/she/it	will travel	*lui/lei*	*viaggerà*
we		*noi*	*viaggeremo*
you pl		*voi*	*viaggerete*
they		*loro*	*viaggeranno*

You can also express future plans by using the present tense with some indication of time referring to the future:

Tomorrow we're going to Rome.

> *Domani andiamo* do·*ma*·nee an·*dya*·mo
> *a Roma.* a *ro*·ma
> (lit: tomorrow we-go
> to Rome)

I'm back in three days.

> *Torno fra tre giorni.* *tor*·no fra tre *jor*·nee
> (lit: I-return within three days)

plural see **more than one**

pointing something out

You can point something out in Italian with *È* ... (it-is ...):

It's a local custom.

> *È una tradizione locale.* e *oo*·na tra·dee·*tsyo*·ne lo·*ka*·le
> (lit: it-is a custom local)

This could be made into a question with a rise in intonation at the end, as you would in English.

See also **this & that**.

polite forms see **pronouns**

possession see have, my & your, and somebody's

There are various ways to indicate possession in Italian. The easiest way is by using the verb *avere* (see **have**). You could also use possessive adjectives (see **my & your**) or, simplest of all, use the preposition *di* (of) followed by the possessor:

It's Lorenzo's backpack.
È lo zaino di Lorenzo.   e lo *dzai*·no dee lo·*ren*·dzo
(lit: it-is the backpack of Lorenzo)

To find out who's the owner of something, you can use the simple phrases *Di chi è ...?* (of who it-is ...?) for a single thing, or *Di chi sono ...?* (of who they-are ...?) for plural things:

Whose seat is this?
Di chi è questo posto?   dee kee e *kwe*·sto *pos*·to
(lit: of who it-is this place)

pronouns

Subject pronouns corresponding to 'I', 'you', 'he', 'she', 'it', 'we' and 'they' are often omitted, as verb endings make it clear who the subject is. Use them if you want to emphasise the subject.

singular		plural	
I	*io*	**we**	*noi*
you inf	*tu*	**you** inf	*voi*
you pol	*Lei*	**you** pol	*voi*
he/she/it	*lui/lei*	**they**	*loro*

The polite form of 'you' (singular) can be used when addressing strangers, older people or people with authority. When talking to family, children or peers you use the informal form *tu* (singular).

Do you live here?
Lei è di qui? pol   lay e dee kwee
(lit: he/she is of here)
Tu sei di qui? inf   too say dee kwee
(lit: you are of here)

question words

question words		
who	*chi*	kee
Who is it?	*Chi è?*	kee e
what	*che* *cosa*	ke ko·za
What work do you do?	*Che lavoro fa/fai?* pol/inf	ke la·vo·ro fa/fai
What do you study?	*Cosa studia/studi?* pol/inf	ko·za stoo·dya/ stoo·dee
which	*quale/i* sg/pl	kwa·le/kwa·lee
Which bus goes to Pisa?	*Quale autobus va a Pisa?*	kwa·le ow·to·boos va a pee·sa
What are the rates?	*Quali sono le tariffe?*	kwa·lee so·no le ta·ree·fe
when at what time	*quando* *a che ora*	kwan·do a ke o·ra
When was it built?	*Quando fu costruito?*	kwan·do foo kos·troo·ee·to
When's the next bus?	*A che ora passa il prossimo autobus?*	a ke o·ra pa·sa eel pro·see·mo ow·to·boos
where	*dove*	do·ve
Where can I buy a ticket?	*Dove posso comprare un biglietto?*	do·ve po·so kom·pra·re oon bee·lye·to
how	*come*	ko·me
How are you?	*Come stai?*	ko·me stai
how much how many	*quanto/a* m/f *quanti/e* m/f	kwan·to/a kwan·tee/kwan·te
How much does it cost?	*Quanto costa?*	kwan·to kos·ta
How many days?	*Quanti giorni?*	kwan·tee jor·nee
why	*perché*	per·ke
Why is it closed?	*Perché sta chiuso?*	per·ke sta kyoo·zo

some

There are a number of words for 'some' in Italian, literally translated as 'of the'. Choose the correct form based on the gender and number of what you're referring to:

	singular					plural		
	masculine			feminine		masculine		feminine
the	il	lo	l'	la	l'	i	gli	le
some	del	dello	dell'	della	dell'	dei	degli	delle

I'd like some antibiotics.
> *Vorrei degli*   vo·ray de·lyee
> *antibiotici.*   an·tee·bee·o·tee·chee
> (lit: I-would-like of-the
> antibiotics)

Bring me some water.
> *Mi porta dell'aqua.*   mee por·ta de·la·kwa
> (lit: me you-bring of-the-water)

the

There are a number of forms for 'the' in Italian, their use determined by the gender or number of the noun. Note the forms *lo* and *gli* are used before masculine words starting with *s* plus a consonant, or *z, gn, pn, ps, x* or *y*.

il treno	eel *tre*·no	**the train**
i treni	ee *tre*·nee	**the trains**
lo zaino	lo *dzai*·no	**the backpack**
gli zaini	lyee *dzai*·nee	**the backpacks**
la ricevuta	la ree·che·*voo*·ta	**the receipt**
le ricevute	le ree·che·*voo*·te	**the receipts**
l'uscita	loo·*shee*·ta	**the exit**
le uscite	le oo·*shee*·te	**the exits**

See also **gender** and **more than one**.

this & that

To refer to or to point out a person or object, use one of the following words for 'this/these' or that/those' before the noun:

singular		plural	
masculine	feminine	masculine	feminine
questo	questa	questi	queste
quel/quello	quella	quei/quegli/ quelli	quelle

Is this seat free?
   È libero questo posto?   e lee·be·ro kwe·sto pos·to
   (lit: it-is free this seat)

What's the local speciality?
   Qual'è la specialità   kwa·le la spe·cha·lee·ta
   di questa regione?   dee kwe·sta re·jo·ne
   (lit: which-it-is the speciality
    of this region)

These words can also be used on their own to mean 'this (one)', 'that (one)', or 'these' and 'those':

What's this called?
   Come si chiama questo?   ko·me see kya·ma kwe·sto
   (lit: how one calls this)

How much are these?
   Quanto costano questi/   kwan·to kos·ta·no kwe·stee/
   queste? m/f   kwe·ste
   (lit: how-much cost these)

verbs

I speak, read and understand Italian.

Parlo, scrivo   *par*·lo *skree*·vo
e capisco l'italiano.   e ka·*pee*·sko lee·ta·*lya*·no
(lit: I-speak, I-write and
   I-understand the-Italian)

Italian has three types of verbs: those ending in *-are* (eg, *parlare*, 'speak'), those ending in *-ere* (eg, *scrivere*, 'write') and those ending in *-ire* (eg, *capire*, 'understand'). The verb endings for each person (I, you, we, etc) are very similar for all three:

singular		plural	
I	*-o*	**we**	*-iamo*
you inf	*-i*	**you**	*-ate, -ete* or *-ite*
you pol he/she/it	*-a* (*-are* verbs) or *-e* (for *-ere* and *-ire* verbs)	**loro**	*-ano* (*-are* verbs) or *-ono* (for *-ere* and *-ire* verbs)

As any language, Italian has some irregular verbs. The most important ones are *essere*, *stare* and *avere* (see **be** and **have**).

word order

Generally, the word order of sentences is the same as in English (subject-verb-object):

We're waiting for the bus.

Noi aspettiamo l'autobus.   noy as·pe·*tya*·mo *low*·to·boos
(lit: we wait the-bus)

yes/no questions

When asking a question, simply make a statement, but raise your intonation towards the end of the sentence, as you would in English.

Do you speak English?
  Parli inglese?   *par·lee een·gle·ze*
  (lit: you-speak English)

You'll also frequently hear questions starting with *C'è ...* (There is ...) or *Ci sono ...* (There are ...).

Is there hot water?
  C'è acqua calda?   *che a·kwa kal·da*
  (lit: there-is water hot)

Are there any rooms?
  Ci sono camere?   *chee so·no ka·me·re*
  (lit: there are rooms?)

italian alphabet		
A a a	*B b* bee	*C c* chee
D d dee	*E e* e	*F f* e·fe
G g jee	*H h* a·ka	*I i* ee
L l e·le	*M m* e·me	*N n* e·ne
O o o	*P p* pee	*Q q* koo
R r e·re	*S s* e·se	*T t* tee
U u oo	*V v* voo	*Z z* tse·ta

language difficulties
le difficoltà di lingua

1A **Do you speak (English)?**
Parla/Parli (inglese)? pol/inf   *par·la/par·lee (een·gle·ze)*

Does anyone speak (English)?
C'è qualcuno che parla   che kwal·*koo*·no ke *par*·la
(inglese)?   (een·*gle*·ze)

1B **Do you understand?**
Capisce/Capisci? pol/inf   ka·*pee*·she/ka·*pee*·shee

1C **I understand.**
Capisco.   ka·*pee*·sko

1D **I don't understand.**
Non capisco.   non ka·*pee*·sko

I speak (Italian).
Parlo (italiano).   *par*·lo (ee·ta·*lya*·no)

I don't speak (Italian).
Non parlo (italiano).   non *par*·lo (ee·ta·*lya*·no)

I speak (English).
Parlo (inglese).   *par*·lo (een·*gle*·ze)

I speak a little.
Parlo un po'.   *par*·lo oon po

How do you ...?   *Come si ...?*   *ko*·me see ...
pronounce this   *pronuncia*   pro·*noon*·cha
     questo   *kwe*·sto
write 'arrivederci'   *scrive*   *skree*·ve
     'arrivederci'   a·ree·ve·*der*·chee

What does 'vietato' mean?
Che cosa vuol dire   ke *ko*·za vwol *dee*·re
'vietato'?   vye·*ta*·to

1E **Could you please repeat that?**
Può/Puoi ripeterlo   pwo/pwoy ree·*pe*·ter·lo
per favore? pol/inf   per fa·*vo*·re

1F **Could you please speak more slowly?**

Può/Puoi parlare più   pwo/pwoy par·*la*·re pyoo
lentamente per favore? pol/inf   len·ta·*men*·te per fa·*vo*·re

1G **Could you please write it down?**

Può/Puoi scriverlo   pwo/pwoy *skree*·ver·lo
per favore? pol/inf   per fa·*vo*·re

tongue twisters

The sing-song music of the Italian language lends itself
beautifully to tongue twisters or *scioglilingue*. You can
try to impress Italian acquaintances by casually slipping
out one of these:

**O schiavo con lo schiaccianoci che cosa schiacci?
Schiaccio sei noci del vecchio noce con lo
schiaccianoci.**
o *skya*·vo kon lo skya·cha·*no*·chee ke *ko*·za *skya*·chee
skya·cho say *no*·chee del *ve*·kyo *no*·che kon lo
skya·cha·*no*·chee
('Oh, slave with the nutcracker what are you
cracking? I am cracking six nuts from the old walnut
tree with the nutcracker.')

**Orrore, orrore, un ramarro verde su un muro
marrone!**
o·*ro*·re o·*ro*·re oon ra·*ma*·ro *ver*·de soo oon *moo*·ro
ma·*ro*·ne
('Horror, horror, a green lizard on a brown wall!')

**Trentatre Trentini entrarono a Trento, tutti e trentatre
trotterelando.**
tren·ta·*tre* tren·*tee*·nee en·*tra*·ro·no a *tren*·to *too*·tee
e·tren·ta·*tre* tro·te·re·*lan*·do
('Thirty-three Trentonians came into Trento, all
thirty-three trotting.')

numbers & amounts

cardinal numbers

			i numeri cardinali
	0	*zero*	dze·ro
3A	1	*uno*	oo·no
3A	2	*due*	doo·e
3A	3	*tre*	tre
3A	4	*quattro*	kwa·tro
3A	5	*cinque*	cheen·kwe
3A	6	*sei*	say
3A	7	*sette*	se·te
3A	8	*otto*	o·to
3A	9	*nove*	no·ve
3A	10	*dieci*	dye·chee
	11	*undici*	oon·dee·chee
	12	*dodici*	do·dee·chee
	13	*tredici*	tre·dee·chee
	14	*quattordici*	kwa·tor·dee·chee
	15	*quindici*	kween·dee·chee
	16	*sedici*	se·dee·chee
	17	*diciassette*	dee·cha·se·te
	18	*diciotto*	dee·cho·to
	19	*diciannove*	dee·cha·no·ve
3B	20	*venti*	ven·tee
	21	*ventuno*	ven·too·no
	22	*ventidue*	ven·tee·doo·e
3B	30	*trenta*	tren·ta
3B	40	*quaranta*	kwa·ran·ta
3B	50	*cinquanta*	cheen·kwan·ta
3B	60	*sessanta*	se·san·ta
3B	70	*settanta*	se·tan·ta
3B	80	*ottanta*	o·tan·ta
3B	90	*novanta*	no·van·ta
3B	100	*cento*	chen·to
	200	*duecento*	doo·e·chen·to

3C	1,000	*mille*	mee·le
	2,000	*duemila*	doo·e·mee·la
3D	1,000,000	*un milione*	oon mee·lyo·ne

ordinal numbers

numeri ordinali

1st	*primo/a* m/f	pree·mo/a
2nd	*secondo/a* m/f	se·kon·do/a
3rd	*terzo/a* m/f	ter·tso/a
4th	*quarto/a* m/f	kwar·to/a
5th	*quinto/a* m/f	kween·to/a

fractions

frazioni

a quarter	*un quarto*	oon kwar·to
a third	*un terzo*	oon ter·tso
a half	*mezzo*	me·dzo
three-quarters	*tre quarti*	tre kwar·tee
all	*tutto/a* m/f sg	too·to/a
	tutti/e m/f pl	too·tee/too·te
none	*niente*	nyen·te

useful amounts

quantità utili

How much?	*Quanto/a?* m/f	kwan·to/a
How many?	*Quanti/e?* m/f	kwan·tee/kwan·te
Please give me ...	*Può darmi ...,*	pwo dar·mee ...
	per favore.	per fa·vo·re
(just) a little	*(solo) un po'*	(so·lo) oon po
some	*alcuni/e* m/f	al·koo·nee/al·koo·ne
much	*molto/a* m/f	mol·to/a
many	*molti/e* m/f	mol·tee/mol·te
less	*di meno*	(dee) me·no
more	*di più*	(dee) pyoo

telling the time

leggere l'ora

When telling the time in Italian, 'It is ...' is expressed by *Sono le* followed by a number. However one o'clock is *È l'una*, and midday is *È mezzogiorno*. Note that in Italy the 24-hour clock is commonly used.

4A What time is it?	*Che ora è?*	ke o·ra e
4B It's one o'clock.	*È l'una.*	e *loo*·na
It's (two) o'clock.	*Sono le (due).*	so·no le (*doo*·e)
Five past (one).	*(L'una) e cinque.*	(*loo*·na) e cheen·kwe
Quarter past (one).	*(L'una) e un quarto.*	(*loo*·na) e oon *kwar*·to
Half past (one).	*(L'una) e mezza.*	(*loo*·na) e me·dza
Quarter to (eight).	*(Le otto) meno un quarto.*	(le o·to) me·no oon *kwar*·to
Twenty to (eight).	*(Le otto) meno venti.*	(le o·to) me·no ven·tee

am (in the morning)	*di mattina*	dee ma·tee·na
pm (in the afternoon)	*di pomeriggio*	dee po·me·ree·jo
in the evening	*di sera*	dee se·ra
at night	*di notte*	dee no·te
midday	*mezzogiorno*	me·dzo·jor·no
midnight	*mezzanotte*	me·dza·no·te
At what time ...?	*A che ora ...?*	a ke o·ra ...
At one.	*All'una.*	a·loo·na
At (six).	*Alle (sei).*	a·le (say)
At (7.57pm).	*Alle (19.57).*	a·le (dee·cha·no·ve e cheen·kwan·ta·se·te)

days of the week

5A	Monday	*lunedì*	loo·ne·*dee*
5A	Tuesday	*martedì*	mar·te·*dee*
5A	Wednesday	*mercoledì*	mer·ko·le·*dee*
5A	Thursday	*giovedì*	jo·ve·*dee*
5A	Friday	*venerdì*	ve·ner·*dee*
5A	Saturday	*sabato*	*sa*·ba·to
5A	Sunday	*domenica*	do·*me*·nee·ka

the calendar

il calendario

> months

5B	January	*gennaio*	je·*na*·yo
5B	February	*febbraio*	fe·*bra*·yo
5B	March	*marzo*	*mar*·tso
5B	April	*aprile*	a·*pree*·le
5B	May	*maggio*	*ma*·jo
5B	June	*giugno*	*joo*·nyo
5B	July	*luglio*	*loo*·lyo
5B	August	*agosto*	a·*gos*·to
5B	September	*settembre*	se·*tem*·bre
5B	October	*ottobre*	o·*to*·bre
5B	November	*novembre*	no·*vem*·bre
5B	December	*dicembre*	dee·*chem*·bre

> dates

| What date is it today? | *Che giorno è oggi?* | ke *jor*·no e o·jee |
| It's (18 October). | *È (il diciotto) ottobre.* | e (eel dee·*cho*·to) o·*to*·bre |

> seasons

5C	summer	*estate*	es·*ta*·te
5C	autumn	*autunno*	ow·*too*·no
5C	winter	*inverno*	een·*ver*·no
5C	spring	*primavera*	pree·ma·*ve*·ra

present

il presente

now	*adesso*	a·*de*·so
this ...		
afternoon	*oggi pomeriggio*	o·jee po·me·*ree*·jo
morning	*stamattina*	sta·ma·*tee*·na
month	*questo mese*	*kwe*·sto me·ze
week	*questa settimana*	*kwe*·sta se·tee·*ma*·na
year	*quest'anno*	kwe·*sta*·no
weekend	*fine settimana*	*fee*·ne se·tee·*ma*·na
6C today	*oggi*	o·jee
tonight	*stasera*	sta·*se*·ra

past

il passato

day before yesterday	*l'altro ieri*	*lal*·tro ye·ree
last night	*ieri notte*	ye·ree *no*·te
7A last week	*la settimana scorsa*	la se·tee·*ma*·na *skor*·sa
7B last month	*il mese scorso*	eel me·ze *skor*·so
7C last year	*l'anno scorso*	*la*·no *skor*·so
since (May)	*da (maggio)*	da (*ma*·jo)
(three days) ago	*(tre giorni) fa*	(tre *jor*·nee) fa
6B yesterday ...	*ieri ...*	ye·ree ...
afternoon	*pomeriggio*	po·me·*ree*·jo
evening	*sera*	*se*·ra
morning	*mattina*	ma·*tee*·na

future

il futuro

day after tomorrow	*dopodomani*	do·po·do·*ma*·nee
in (six days)	*fra (sei giorni)*	fra (say *jor*·nee)
8A next week	*la settimana prossima*	la se·tee·*ma*·na *pro*·see·ma

8B next month	*il mese*	eel *me*·ze
	prossimo	*pro*·see·mo
8C next year	*l'anno prossimo*	*la*·no *pro*·see·mo
6D tomorrow	*domani*	do·*ma*·nee
tomorrow evening	*domani sera*	do·*ma*·nee se·ra
tomorrow	*domani*	do·*ma*·nee
afternoon	*pomeriggio*	po·me·*ree*·jo
tomorrow morning	*domani*	do·*ma*·nee
	mattina	ma·*tee*·na
until (June)	*fino a (giugno)*	*fee*·no a (*joo*·nyo)

during the day

durante il giorno

4D afternoon	*pomeriggio* m	po·me·*ree*·jo
dawn	*alba* f	*al*·ba
day	*giorno* m	*jor*·no
4E evening	*sera* f	se·ra
midday	*mezzogiorno* m	me·dzo·*jor*·no
midnight	*mezzanotte* f	me·dza·*no*·te
4C morning	*mattina* f	ma·*tee*·na
night	*notte* f	*no*·te
sunrise	*alba* f	*al*·ba
sunset	*tramonto* m	tra·*mon*·to

golden years

You'll often hear the centuries referred to as follows, particularly when talking about periods of history and art:

Il Duecento (lit: the 200)	
eel doo·e·*chen*·to	13th century
Il Trecento (lit: the 300)	
eel tre·*chen*·to	14th century
Il Quattrocento (lit: the 400)	
eel kwa·tro·*chen*·to	15th century
Il Cinquecento (lit: the 500)	
eel cheen·kwe·*chen*·to	16th century

How much is it?
Quant'è?   kwan·*te*

How much is this?
Quanto costa questo?   kwan·to kos·ta kwe·sto

It's free.
È gratuito.   e gra·too·ee·to

It's ... euros.
È ... euro.   e ... e·oo·ro

Can you write down the price?
Può scrivere il prezzo?   pwo skree·ve·re eel *pre*·tso

Do you change money here?
Si cambiano i soldi qui?   see kam·bya·no ee sol·dee kwee

Do you accept ...?	Accettate ...?	a·che·*ta*·te ...
credit cards	la carta di credito	la *kar*·ta dee kre·dee·to
debit cards	la carta di debito	la *kar*·ta dee de·bee·to
travellers cheques	gli assegni di viaggio	lyee a·se·nyee dee vee·*a*·jo

I'd like to ...	Vorrei ...	vo·ray ...
cash a cheque	riscuotere un assegno	ree·*skwo*·te·re oo·na·se·nyo
change money	cambiare i soldi	kam·*bya*·re ee sol·dee
change a travellers cheque	cambiare un assegno di viaggio	kam·*bya*·re oo·na·se·nyo dee vee·*a*·jo
withdraw money	fare prelievi	fa·re pre·*lye*·vee

What's the ...?	Quant'è ...	kwan·te
commission	la commissione?	la ko·mee·syo·ne
exchange rate	il cambio?	eel kam·byo

I'd like ... please.	Vorrei ...,	vo·ray ...
	per favore.	per fa·vo·re
a receipt	una ricevuta	oo·na ree·che·voo·ta
my change	il mio resto	eel mee·o res·to
my money back	un rimborso	oon reem·bor·so

There's a mistake in the bill.

C'è un errore nel conto.   che oon e·ro·re nel kon·to

I don't want to pay the full price.

Non voglio pagare il   non vo·lyo pa·ga·re eel
prezzo intero.   pre·tso een·te·ro

Do I need to pay upfront?

Devo pagare   de·vo pa·ga·re
in anticipo?   ee·nan·tee·chee·po

Where's the nearest automatic teller machine?

Dov'è il Bancomat più   do·ve eel ban·ko·mat pyoo
vicino?   vee·chee·no

getting around

andare in giro

What time does the ... leave/arrive?	A che ora parte/arriva ...?	a ke o·ra par·te/a·ree·va ...
boat	*la nave*	la na·ve
bus	*l'autobus*	low·to·boos
ferry	*il traghetto*	eel tra·ge·to
hydrofoil	*l'aliscafo*	la·lees·ka·fo
metro	*la metropolitana*	la me·tro·po·lee·ta·na
plane	*l'aereo*	la·e·re·o
train	*il treno*	eel tre·no

12A What time's the first bus?
A che ora passa il primo autobus? m/f
a ke o·ra pa·sa eel *pree*·mo ow·to·boos

12B What time's the last bus?
A che ora passa l'ultimo autobus?
a ke o·ra pa·sa *lool*·tee·mo ow·to·boos

12C What time's the next bus?
A che ora passa il prossimo autobus?
a ke o·ra pa·sa eel *pro*·see·mo ow·to·boos

listen for ...

che *oo*·no *sho*·pe·ro
C'è uno sciopero.
There's a strike.

de·ve kam·*bya*·re a (*par*·ma)
Deve cambiare a (Parma).
You'll have to change at (Parma).

eel *tre*·no e kan·che·*la*·to
Il treno è cancellato.
The train is cancelled.

la·e·re·o e een ree·*tar*·do
L'aereo è in ritardo.
The plane is delayed.

When's the next flight to (Cagliari)?
A che ora parte il prossimo volo per (Cagliari)?
a ke o·ra par·te eel pro·see·mo vo·lo per (ka·lya·ree)

Can you tell me when we get to (Taranto)?
Mi sa dire quando arriviamo a (Taranto)?
mee sa dee·re kwan·do a·ree·vya·mo a (ta·ran·to)

I want to get off here.
Voglio scendere qui.
vo·lyo shen·de·re kwee

14A Is this seat free?
È libero questo posto?
e lee·be·ro kwe·sto pos·to

14B That's my seat.
Quel posto è mio.
kwel pos·to e mee·o

buying tickets

11A Where can I buy a ticket?
Dove posso comprare un biglietto?
do·ve po·so kom·pra·re oon bee·lye·to

11B Do I need to book?
Bisogna prenotare (un posto)?
bee·zo·nya pre·no·ta·re (oon pos·to)

Can I get a stand-by ticket?
Posso essere messo/a in lista d'attesa? m/f
po·so e·se·re me·so/a een lee·sta da·te·sa

11C I'd like to cancel my ticket, please.
Vorrei cancellare il mio biglietto, per favore.
vo·ray kan·che·la·re eel mee·o bee·lye·to per fa·vo·re

11D I'd like to change my ticket, please.
Vorrei cambiare il mio biglietto, per favore.
vo·ray kam·bya·re eel mee·o bee·lye·to per fa·vo·re

Two ... tickets (to Rome), please.	Due biglietti ... (per Roma), per favore.	doo·e bee·lye·tee ... (per ro·ma) per fa·vo·re
1st-class	di prima classe	dee pree·ma kla·se
2nd-class	di seconda classe	dee se·kon·da kla·se
child's	per bambini	per bam·bee·nee
one-way	di sola andata	dee so·la an·da·ta
return	di andata e ritorno	dee an·da·ta e ree·tor·no
student's	per studenti	per stoo·den·tee

I'd like a/an ... seat, please.	Vorrei un posto ..., per favore.	vo·ray oon pos·to ... per fa·vo·re
aisle	sul corridoio	sool ko·ree·do·yo
non-smoking	per non fumatori	per non foo·ma·to·ree
smoking	per fumatori	per foo·ma·to·ree
window	vicino al finestrino	vee·chee·no al fee·nes·tree·no

Is there (a) ...?	C'è ...?	che ...
air-conditioning	l'aria condizionata	la·rya kon·dee·tsyo·na·ta
blanket	una coperta	oo·na ko·per·ta
toilet	un gabinetto	oon ga·bee·ne·to
video	un video-registratore	oon vee·de·o·re·jee·stra·to·re

I'd like a sleeping berth.
Vorrei una cuccetta, per favore.   vo·ray oo·na koo·che·ta per fa·vo·re

How much is it?
Quant'è?   kwan·te

Do I need to pay a supplement?
Devo pagare un supplemento?   de·vo pa·ga·re oon soo·ple·men·to

13A How long does the trip take?
Quanto ci vuole?   kwan·to chee vwo·le

13B Is it a direct route?

È un itinerario diretto? e oon ee·tee·ne·*ra*·ryo dee·*re*·to

13C How long will it be delayed?

Di quanto ritarderà? dee kwan·to ree·tar·de·*ra*

What time do I have to check in?

A che ora devo presentarmi a ke o·ra *de*·vo pre·zen·*tar*·mee
per l'accettazione? per la·che·ta·*tsyo*·ne

For phrases about getting through customs and immigration,
see **border crossing**, page 49.

luggage

i bagagli

16A My luggage has been damaged.

Il mio bagaglio è eel *mee*·o ba·*ga*·lyo
stato danneggiato. e *sta*·to da·ne·*ja*·to

16B My luggage has been lost.

Il mio bagaglio è eel *mee*·o ba·*ga*·lyo
stato perso. e *sta*·to *per*·so

16C My luggage has been stolen.

Il mio bagaglio è eel *mee*·o ba·*ga*·lyo
stato rubato. e *sta*·to roo·*ba*·to

I'd like ...	*Vorrei ...*	vo·*ray* ...
a luggage locker	*un armadietto*	oon ar·ma·*dye*·to
	per il bagaglio	per eel ba·*ga*·lyo
some coins	*della moneta*	*de*·la mo·*ne*·ta
some tokens	*dei gettoni*	day je·*to*·nee

bus, tram & metro

autobus, tram & metrò

Which bus goes to (Rome)?

Quale autobus va a (Roma)? *kwa*·le *ow*·to·boos va a (*ro*·ma)

Bus/Tram number (three).

Autobus/Tram numero (tre). *ow*·to·boos/tram *noo*·me·ro (tre)

How many stops to (the museum)?

Quante fermate   kwan·te fer·ma·te
mancano (al museo)?   man·ka·no (al moo·ze·o)

15A **Please tell me when we get to (the market).**

Mi dica per favore   mee *dee*·ka per fa·*vo*·re
quando arriviamo   kwan·do a·ree·*vya*·mo
(al mercato).   (al mer·ka·to)

signs

Fermata del Tram	fer·*ma*·ta del tram	**Tram Stop**
Fermata	fer·*ma*·ta	**Bus**
dell'autobus	de·*low*·to·boos	**Stop**
M	e·me	**Metropolitana**
Stazione della	sta·*tsyo*·ne de·la	**Metro Station**
Metropolitana	me·tro·po·lee·*ta*·na	
Uscita	oo·*shee*·ta	**Way Out**

train

15B **What station is this?**
Che stazione è questa?　　ke sta·*tsyo*·ne e *kwe*·sta

15C **What's the next station?**
Qual'è la prossima　　kwa·*le* la *pro*·see·ma
stazione?　　sta·*tsyo*·ne

Does this train stop at (Milan)?
Questo treno si ferma　　*kwe*·sto *tre*·no see *fer*·ma
a (Milano)?　　a (mee·*la*·no)

Do I need to change (trains)?
Devo cambiare (treno)?　　*de*·vo kam·*bya*·re (*tre*·no)

Where's the dining car?
Dov'è il vagone ristorante?　　do·*ve* eel va·*go*·ne rees·to·*ran*·te

Which carriage is ...?	*Quale carrozza è ...?*	kwa·le ka·*ro*·tsa e ...
1st class	*di prima classe*	dee *pree*·ma *kla*·se
for (Rome)	*per (Roma)*	per (*ro*·ma)

trainspotting

diretto　　dee·*re*·to
indicates you don't need to change trains to reach
your destination

espresso　　es·*pre*·so
stops only at major stations

Eurostar Italia (ES)　　e·oo·ro·*star* ee·*ta*·lya
very fast, Italy's answer to France's TGV

Inter City　　*een*·ter *see*·tee
runs between large cities

locale　　lo·*ka*·le
usually stops at all stations and can be very slow

rapido　　ra·*pee*·do
runs between large towns and cities; faster than the
espresso

boat

la nave

Are there life jackets?
Ci sono giubbotti di   chee *so*·no joo·*bo*·tee dee
salvataggio?   sal·va·*ta*·jo

What's the sea like today?
Com'è il mare oggi?   ko·*me* eel *ma*·re o·jee

I feel seasick.
Ho il mal di mare.   o eel mal dee *ma*·re

taxi

il tassì

17A **I'd like a taxi.**
Vorrei un tassì.   vo·*ray* oon ta·*see*

17B **I'd like a taxi at (9am).**
Vorrei un tassì alle   vo·*ray* oon ta·*see*
(nove di mattina).   a·le (*no*·ve dee ma·*tee*·na)

17C **Is this taxi free?**
È libero questo tassì?   e *lee*·be·ro *kwe*·sto ta·*see*

17D **How much is it to …?**
Quant'è per …?   kwan·*te* per …

18A **Please put the meter on.**
Usi il tassametro,   oo·zee eel ta·*sa*·me·tro
per favore.   per fa·*vo*·re

18B **Please take me to (this address).**
Mi porti a (questo   mee *por*·tee a (*kwe*·sto
indirizzo), per piacere.   een·dee·*ree*·tso) per pya·*che*·re

18C **Please slow down.**
Rallenti, per favore.   ra·*len*·tee per fa·*vo*·re

18D **Please wait here.**
Mi aspetti qui, per favore.   mee as·*pe*·tee kwee per fa·*vo*·re

18E **Please stop here.**
Si fermi qui, per favore.   see *fer*·mee kwee per fa·*vo*·re

transport

43

typical addresses

Borgo (B.go)	*bor·go*	district
Corso (C.so)	*kor·so*	main street/avenue
Largo (L.go)	*lar·go*	little square
Piazza (P.za)	*pya·tsa*	square
Strada (Str.)	*stra·da*	street
Via (V.)	*vee·a*	road/street
Viale (V.le)	*vee·a·le*	avenue/boulevard
Vicolo (V.lo)	*vee·ko·lo*	alley/lane

in Venice:		
Calle	*ka·le*	street
Campiello	*kam·pye·lo*	square with no church
Fondamenta	*fon·da·men·ta*	street
Riva	*ree·va*	street (lit: shore/bank)

in Genoa:		
Carrugio	*ka·roo·jo*	little street

in medieval cities:		
Contrà	*kon·tra*	street
Contrada	*kon·tra·da*	street

car & motorbike

la macchina & la moto

> car & motorbike hire

19A I'd like to hire a car.
Vorrei noleggiare
una macchina.
vo·ray no·le·ja·re
oo·na ma·kee·na

19B I'd like to hire a motorbike.
Vorrei noleggiare una moto. vo·ray no·le·ja·re oo·na mo·to

I'd like to hire a/an ...	*Vorrei noleggiare ...*	vo·ray no·le·ja·re ...
4WD	*un fuoristrada*	oon fwo·ree·stra·da
automatic/ manual (car)	*una macchina automatica/ manuale*	oo·na ma·kee·na ow·to·ma·tee·ka/ ma·noo·a·le

with/without ...	con/senza ...	kon/sen·tsa ...
air-conditioning	aria	a·rya
	condizionata	kon·dee·tsyo·na·ta
antifreeze	anticongelante	an·tee·kon·je·lan·te
a driver	un'autista	oo·now·tee·sta
snow chains	le catene da neve	le ka·te·ne da ne·ve

19D How much for daily hire?
Quanto costa al giorno?   kwan·to kos·ta al jor·no

19E How much for weekly hire?
Quanto costa alla   kwan·to kos·ta a·la
settimana?   se·tee·ma·na

> on the road

What's the city/country speed limit?
Qual'è il limite di   kwa·le eel lee·mee·te dee
velocità in   ve·lo·chee·ta een
città/campagna?   chee·ta/kam·pa·nya

20A Is this the road to ...?
Questa strada porta a ...?   kwe·sta stra·da por·ta a ...

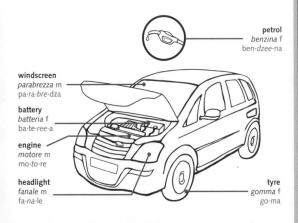

petrol
benzina f
ben·dzee·na

windscreen
parabrezza m
pa·ra·bre·dza

battery
batteria f
ba·te·ree·a

engine
motore m
mo·to·re

headlight
fanale m
fa·na·le

tyre
gomma f
go·ma

Where's a service station?
  Dov'è una stazione   do·*ve* oo·na sta·*tsyo*·ne
  di servizio?   dee ser·*vee*·tsyo

Please fill it up.
  Il pieno, per favore.   eel *pye*·no per fa·*vo*·re

I'd like (30) litres.
  Vorrei (trenta) litri.   vo·*ray* (*tren*·ta) *lee*·tree

road signs

Accesso	a·*che*·so	**24-Hour**
Permanente	per·ma·*nen*·te	**Access**
Alt	alt	**Stop**
Attenzione	a·ten·*tsyo*·ne	**Caution**
Autostrada	ow·to·*stra*·da	**Freeway**
Dare la	*da*·re la	**Give Way**
Precedenza	pre·che·*den*·tsa	
Deviazione	de·vya·*tsyo*·ne	**Detour**
Divieto di	dee·*vye*·to dee	**No Entry**
Accesso	a·*che*·so	
Divieto di	dee·*vye*·to dee	**No**
Sorpasso	sor·*pa*·so	**Overtaking**
Divieto di Sosta	dee·*vye*·to dee *sos*·ta	**No Parking**
Entrata	en·*tra*·ta	**Entrance**
Lavori in Corso	la·*vo*·ree een *kor*·so	**Roadworks**
Parcheggio	par·*ke*·jo	**Parking**
Passo Carrabile	*pa*·so ka·ra·bee·le	**Keep Clear**
Pedaggio	pe·*da*·jo	**Toll**
Pericolo	pe·*ree*·ko·lo	**Danger**
Rallentare	ra·len·*ta*·re	**Slow Down**
Rimozione	ree·mo·*tsyo*·ne	**Tow-Away**
Forzata	for·*tsa*·ta	**Zone**
Senso Unico	*sen*·so oo·nee·ko	**One Way**
Stop	stop	**Stop**
Uscita	oo·*shee*·ta	**Exit**

diesel	*gasolio/diesel* m	ga·zo·lyo/*dee*·zel
leaded petrol	*benzina* f *con piombo*	ben·*dzee*·na kon pyom·bo
LPG	*gasauto* m	ga·*zow*·to
unleaded petrol	*benzina* f *senza piombo*	ben·*dzee*·na sen·tsa pyom·bo

Please check the ...	*Può controllare ..., per favore?*	pwo kon·tro·*la*·re ... per fa·*vo*·re
oil	*l'olio*	*lo*·lyo
tyre pressure	*la pressione delle gomme*	la pre·*syo*·ne *de*·le *go*·me
water	*l'acqua*	*la*·kwa

(How long) Can I park here?
(Per quanto tempo) Posso parcheggiare qui?
(per *kwan*·to *tem*·po) *po*·so par·ke·*ja*·re kwee

Where do I pay?
Dove si paga?
do·ve see *pa*·ga

> problems

20B **I need a mechanic.**
Ho bisogno di un meccanico.
o bee·zo·nyo dee oon me·*ka*·nee·ko

The car/motorbike has broken down (at the intersection).
La macchina/moto si è guastata (all'incrocio).
la *ma*·kee·na/*mo*·to see e gwas·*ta*·ta (a·leen·*kro*·cho)

I had an accident.
Ho avuto un incidente.
o a·*voo*·to oon een·chee·*den*·te

The car/motorbike won't start.
La macchina/moto non parte.
la *ma*·kee·na/*mo*·to non *par*·te

20C **I have a flat tyre.**
Ho una gomma bucata.
o *oo*·na *go*·ma boo·*ka*·ta

I've lost my car keys.
Ho perso le chiavi della macchina.
o *per*·so le *kya*·vee *de*·la *ma*·kee·na

I've locked the keys inside the car.
Ho chiuso la macchina con   o *kyoo*·zo la *ma*·kee·na kon
le chiavi dentro.   le *kya*·vee *den*·tro

20D **I've run out of petrol.**
Ho esaurito la benzina.   o e·zow·*ree*·to la ben·*dzee*·na

Can you fix it (today)?
La può aggiustare   la pwo a·joo·*sta*·re
(oggi)?   (o·jee)

How long will it take?
Quanto ci vuole?   *kwan*·to chee *vwo*·le

---

listen for ...

de·vo or·dee·*na*·re eel *pe*·tso dee ree·*kam*·byo
   Devo ordinare il pezzo di   **I have to order that**
   ricambio.   **part.**

ke *tee*·po dee *ma*·kee·na/*mo*·to e
   Che tipo di macchina/   **What kind of car/**
   moto è?   **motorbike is it?**

---

bicycle

la bicicletta

19C **I'd like to hire a bicycle.**
Vorrei noleggiare   vo·ray no·le·*ja*·re
una bicicletta.   *oo*·na bee·chee·*kle*·ta

Where can I buy a second-hand bike?
Dove posso comprare una   *do*·ve *po*·so kom·*pra*·re *oo*·na
bicicletta di seconda   bee·chee·*kle*·ta dee se·*kon*·da
mano?   *ma*·no

I have a puncture.
Ho una gomma bucata.   o *oo*·na *go*·ma boo·*ka*·ta

How much is it per ...?	*Quanto costa ...?*	*kwan*·to *kos*·ta ...
afternoon	*per un pomeriggio*	per oon po·me·*ree*·jo
day	*al giorno*	al *jor*·no
hour	*all'ora*	a·*lo*·ra
morning	*per una mattina*	per *oo*·na ma·*tee*·na

PRACTICAL

10A I'm here on business.
Sono qui per affari. per a·*fa*·ree

10B I'm here on holiday.
Sono qui in vacanza. een va·*kan*·tsa

I'm here ...	*Sono qui ...*	*so*·no kwee ...
in transit	*in transito*	een *tran*·see·to
to visit	*per visitare*	per vee·zee·*ta*·re
relatives	*parenti*	pa·*ren*·tee

I'm here for ...	*Sono qui per ...*	*so*·no kwee per ...
(21) days	*(ventuno) giorni*	(ven·*too*·no) *jor*·nee
(two) months	*(due) mesi*	(*doo*·e) me·zee
(three) weeks	*(tre) settimane*	(tre) se·tee·*ma*·ne

I have a	*Ho un*	o oon
... permit.	*permesso di ...*	per·*me*·so dee ...
study	*studio*	*stoo*·dyo
work	*lavoro*	la·*vo*·ro

---

listen for ...

eel *soo*·o ...	*Il Suo ...,*	**Your ...,**
per fa·*vo*·re	*per favore.*	**please.**
pa·sa·*por*·to	*passaporto*	**passport**
vee·sto	*visto*	**visa**

vee·a·ja ...	*Viaggia ...?*	**Are you travelling ...?**
da *so*·lo/a	*da solo/a* m/f	**on your own**
een *groo*·po	*in gruppo*	**in a group**
kon fa·*mee*·lya	*con famiglia*	**with a family**

10C **I have nothing to declare.**
Non ho niente da   non o *nyen*·te da
dichiarare.   dee·kya·*ra*·re

10D **I have something to declare.**
Ho delle cose da dichiarare.   o *de*·le *ko*·ze da dee·kya·*ra*·re

I didn't know I had to declare it.
Non sapevo che dovevo   non sa·*pe*·vo ke do·*ve*·vo
dichiararlo.   dee·kya·*rar*·lo

Do you have this form in English?
Avete questo modulo   a·*ve*·te *kwe*·sto *mo*·doo·lo
in inglese?   een een·*gle*·ze

signs		
Controllo	kon·*tro*·lo	**Passport Control**
Passaporti	pa·sa·*por*·tee	
Dogana	do·*ga*·na	**Customs**
Immigrazione	ee·mee·gra·*tsyo*·ne	**Immigration**

finding accommodation

Where's a/an ...?	Dov'è ...?	do·ve ...
bed & breakfast	un bed e breakfast	oon bed e brek·fast
inn (budget hotel)	una locanda	oo·na lo·kan·da

26A Where's a guesthouse?
Dov'è una pensione?   do·ve oo·na pen·syo·ne

26B Where's a hotel?
Dov'è un albergo?   do·ve oo·nal·ber·go

26C Where's a youth hostel?
Dov'è un ostello della gioventù?   do·ve oo·nos·te·lo de·la jo·ven·too

26D Where's a camping ground?
Dov'è un campeggio?   do·ve oon kam·pe·jo

27A Can you recommend somewhere cheap?
Può consigliare qualche posto economico?   pwo kon·see·lya·re kwal·ke pos·to e·ko·no·mee·ko

27B Can you recommend somewhere luxurious?
Può consigliare qualche posto di lusso?   pwo kon·see·lya·re kwal·ke pos·to dee loo·so

27C Can you recommend somewhere nearby?
Può consigliare qualche posto vicino?   pwo kon·see·lya·re kwal·ke pos·to vee·chee·no

local talk

dive	bettola f	be·to·la
rat-infested	infestato/a m/f da topi	een·fes·ta·to/a da to·pee
top spot	luogo m molto frequentato	lwo·go mol·to fre·kwen·ta·to

booking ahead & checking in

prenotare in anticipo & registrazione

29A Do you have a single room?
Avete una camera singola?
a·ve·te oo·na ka·me·ra seen·go·la

29B Do you have a double room?
Avete una camera doppia con letto matrimoniale?
a·ve·te oo·na ka·me·ra do·pya kon le·to ma·tree·mo·nya·le

29C Do you have a twin room?
Avete una camera doppia a due letti?
a·ve·te oo·na ka·me·ra do·pya a doo·e le·tee

28A I'd like to book a room, please.
Vorrei prenotare una camera, per favore.
vo·ray pre·no·ta·re oo·na ka·me·ra per fa·vo·re

28B I have a reservation.
Ho una prenotazione.
o oo·na pre·no·ta·tsyo·ne

My name's ...
Mi chiamo ...
mee kya·mo ...

28C How much is it per night?
Quanto costa per una notte?
kwan·to kos·ta per oo·na no·te

28D How much is it per person?
Quanto costa per persona?
kwan·to kos·ta per per·so·na

For (three) nights/weeks.
Per (tre) notti/settimane.
per (tre) no·tee/se·tee·ma·ne

From (July 2) to (July 6).
Dal (due luglio) al (sei luglio).
dal (doo·e loo·lyo) al (say loo·lyo)

Can I see it?
Posso vederla?
po·so ve·der·la

It's fine. I'll take it.
Va bene. La prendo.
va be·ne. la pren·do

Do I need to pay upfront?
Devo pagare in anticipo?
de·vo pa·ga·re ee·nan·tee·chee·po

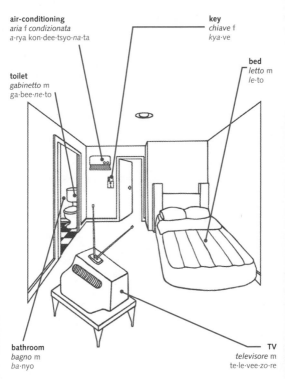

air-conditioning
aria f *condizionata*
a·rya kon·dee·tsyo·*na*·ta

key
chiave f
kya·ve

toilet
gabinetto m
ga·bee·*ne*·to

bed
letto m
le·to

bathroom
bagno m
ba·nyo

TV
televisore m
te·le·vee·*zo*·re

Can I pay ...?	*Posso pagare con ...?*	*po*·so pa·*ga*·re kon ...
by credit card	*la carta di credito*	la *kar*·ta dee *kre*·dee·to
with a travellers cheque	*un assegno di viaggio*	oo·na·*se*·nyo dee vee·*a*·jo

See also **banking**, page 79.

requests & queries

30A When's breakfast served?
A che ora è la prima colazione?
a ke o·ra e la pree·ma ko·la·tsyo·ne

30B Where's breakfast served?
Dove si prende la prima colazione?
do·ve see pren·de la pree·ma ko·la·tsyo·ne

30C Please wake me at (seven).
Mi svegli (alle sette), per favore.
mee sve·lyee (a·le se·te) per fa·vo·re

Can I get another ...?
Può darmi un altro/a ... m/f
pwo dar·mee oo·nal·tro/a

30D Do you have an elevator?
C'è un ascensore?
che oo·na·shen·so·re

30E Do you have a safe?
C'è una cassaforte?
che oo·na ka·sa·for·te

Can I use the ...?	*Posso usare ...?*	po·so oo·za·re ...
kitchen	*la cucina*	la koo·chee·na
laundry	*la lavanderia*	la la·van·de·ree·a
telephone	*il telefono*	eel te·le·fo·no

Do you have a ...?	*C'è ...?*	che ...
laundry service	*il servizio lavanderia*	eel ser·vee·tsyo la·van·de·ree·a
message board	*una bacheca*	oo·na ba·ke·ka
swimming pool	*una piscina*	oo·na pee·shee·na

Do you ... here?	*Si ... qui?*	see ... kwee
arrange tours	*organizzano le gite*	or·ga·nee·dza·no le jee·te
change money	*cambiano i soldi*	kam·bya·no ee sol·dee

Can I leave a message for someone?

Posso lasciare un messaggio per qualcuno?

po·so la·*sha*·re oon me·*sa*·jo per kwal·*koo*·no

Is there a message for me?

C'è un messaggio per me?

che oon me·*sa*·jo per me

I'm locked out of my room.

Mi sono chiuso/a fuori dalla mia camera. m/f

mee *so*·no *kyoo*·zo/a *fwo*·ree *da*·la *mee*·a *ka*·me·ra

The (bathroom) door is locked.

La porta (del bagno) è chiusa a chiave.

la *por*·ta (del *ba*·nyo) e *kyoo*·za a *kya*·ve

listen for ...

a *oo*·na pre·no·ta·*tsyo*·ne
Ha una prenotazione? — **Do you have a reservation?**

a oo·*za*·to eel *free*·go·bar
Ha usato il frigobar? — **Did you use the mini-bar?**

kwa·*le* eel *soo*·o *noo*·me·ro dee *ka*·me·ra
Qual'è il Suo numero di camera? — **What's your room number?**

la *kya*·ve e *a*·la ray·sep·*shon*
La chiave è alla reception. — **The key is at reception.**

mee dees·*pya*·che e kom·*ple*·to
Mi dispiace, è completo. — **I'm sorry, we're full.**

per *kwan*·te *no*·tee
Per quante notti? — **For how many nights?**

accommodation

55

complaints

The room is too ...	La camera è troppo ...	la ka·me·ra e tro·po ...
cold	fredda	fre·da
dark	scura	skoo·ra
expensive	cara	ka·ra
bright	luminosa	loo·mee·no·za
noisy	rumorosa	roo·mo·ro·za
small	piccola	pee·ko·la

31A The air-conditioning doesn't work.
L'aria condizionata   la·rya kon·dee·tsyo·na·ta
non funziona.   non foon·tsyo·na

31B The fan doesn't work.
Il ventilatore   eel ven·tee·la·to·re
non funziona.   non foon·tsyo·na

31C The toilet doesn't work.
Il gabinetto   eel ga·bee·ne·to
non funziona.   non foon·tsyo·na

This ... isn't clean.
Questo/a ... non è   kwe·sto/a ... no·ne
pulito/a. m/f   poo·lee·to/a

a knock at the door ...

Who is it?	Chi è?	kee e
Just a moment.	Un momento.	oon mo·men·to
Come in.	Avanti.	a·van·tee
Come back later, please.	Torni più tardi, per favore.	tor·nee pyoo tar·dee per fa·vo·re

checking out

32A **What time is checkout?**
A che ora si deve lasciar a ke o·*ra* see *de*·ve la·*shar*
libera la camera? lee·be·ra la *ka*·me·ra

Can I have a late checkout?
Posso liberare la *po*·so lee·be·ra·re la
camera più tardi? *ka*·me·ra pyoo tar·dee

32B **Can I leave my luggage here?**
Posso lasciare il mio *po*·so la·*sha*·re eel *mee*·o
bagaglio qui? ba·*ga*·lyo kwee

I'm leaving now.
Parto adesso. *par*·to a·*de*·so

36D **There's a mistake in the bill.**
C'è un errore nel conto. che oo·ne·*ro*·re nel *kon*·to

Can you call a taxi for me (for 11 o'clock)?
Può chiamarmi un tassì pwo kya·*mar*·mee oon ta·*see*
(per le undici)? (per le *oon*·dee·chee)

32C **Could I have my deposit, please?**
Posso avere la caparra, *po*·so a·*ve*·re la ka·*pa*·ra
per favore? per fa·*vo*·re

32D **Could I have my passport, please?**
Posso avere il mio *po*·so a·*ve*·re eel *mee*·o
passaporto, per favore? pa·sa·*por*·to per fa·*vo*·re

32E **Could I have my valuables, please?**
Posso avere i miei oggetti *po*·so a·*ve*·re ee myay
di valore, per favore? o·*je*·tee dee va·*lo*·re per fa·*vo*·re

I'll be back ... *Torno ...* *tor*·no ...
  in (three) days *fra (tre) giorni* fra (tre) *jor*·nee
  on (Tuesday) *(martedì)* (mar·te·*dee*)

I had a great stay, thank you.
  Sono stato/a   so·no sta·to/a
  benissimo/a, grazie. m/f   be·nee·see·mo/a gra·tsye

You've been terrific.
  È stato/a bravissimo/a. m/f   e sta·to/a bra·vee·see·mo/a

I'll recommend it to my friends.
  Lo consiglierò   lo kon·see·lye·ro
  ai miei amici.   ai myay a·mee·chee

camping

Where's the	*Dov'è ... più*	do·ve ... pyoo
nearest ...?	*vicino?*	vee·chee·no
campsite	*il campeggio*	eel kam·pe·jo
shop	*il negozio*	eel ne·go·tsyo
shower facility	*il servizio*	eel ser·vee·tsyo
	doccia	do·cha
Do you have ...?	*Avete ...?*	a·ve·te ...
electricity	*la corrente*	la ko·ren·te
shower facilities	*servizio doccia*	ser·vee·tsyo do·cha
a site	*un sito*	oon see·to
tents for hire	*tende da*	ten·de da
	noleggiare	no·le·ja·re
How much is it	*Quant'è per ...?*	kwan·te per ...
per ...?		
caravan	*roulotte*	roo·lot
person	*persona*	per·so·na
tent	*tenda*	ten·da
vehicle	*veicolo*	ve·ee·ko·lo
Can I ...?	*Si può ...?*	see pwo ...
park next to	*parcheggiare*	par·ke·ja·re
my tent	*accanto alla tenda*	a·kan·to a·la ten·da
pitch the tent	*piantare la*	pyan·ta·re la
here	*tenda qui*	ten·da kwee

26E Am I allowed to camp here?
Si può campeggiare qui? see pwo kam·pe·*ja*·re kwee

Who do I ask to stay here?
A chi chiedo permesso per a kee *kye*·do per·*me*·so per
stare qui? *sta*·re kwee

Where's the nearest toilet block?
Dove sono i servizi *do*·ve *so*·no ee ser·vee·tsee
igienici più vicini? ee·*je*·nee·chee pyoo vee·*chee*·nee

Is it coin-operated?
Funziona a gettoni? foon·*tsyo*·na a je·*to*·nee

Is the water drinkable?
L'acqua è potabile? *la*·kwa e po·*ta*·bee·le

Could I borrow (a mallet)?
Potrei prendere in po·*tray* pren·de·re een
prestito (un mazzuolo)? *pres*·tee·to (oon ma·*tswo*·lo)

renting

affittare

I'm here about the ... for rent.
Sono qui per il/la ... che *so*·no kwee per eel/la ... ke
date in affitto. m/f *da*·te ee·na·*fee*·to

Do you have	*Avete ...*	a·*ve*·te ...
a/an ... for rent?	*d'affittare?*	da·fee·*ta*·re
apartment	*un appartamento*	oo·na·*par*·ta·men·to
cabin	*una cabina*	oo·na ka·*bee*·na
house	*una casa*	oo·na *ka*·za
room	*una camera*	oo·na *ka*·me·ra
villa	*una villa*	oo·na *vee*·la

(partly) furnished	*(in parte)*	(een *par*·te)
	ammobiliato/a m/f	a·mo·bee·*lya*·to/a
unfurnished	*non*	no·na·mo·bee·*lya*·to/a
	ammobiliato/a m/f	

How much is it for ...?   *Quant'è per ...?*   kwan·*te* per ...

   (one) week   *(una) settimana*   (oo·na) se·tee·*ma*·na

   (two) months   *(due) mesi*   (*doo*·e) *me*·zee

Are bills extra?
Sono extra le bollette?   so·no ek·stra le bo·*le*·te

staying with locals

dalle persone del luogo

Can I stay at your place?
Posso stare da Lei/te? pol/inf   po·so *sta*·re da lay/te

Is there anything I can do to help?
Posso aiutare in   po·so a·yoo·*ta*·re een
qualche modo?   *kwal*·ke mo·do

I have my own ...	*Ho il mio proprio ...*	o eel *mee*·o *pro*·pryo ...
mattress	*materasso*	ma·te·*ra*·so
sleeping bag	*sacco a pelo*	*sa*·ko a *pe*·lo

Can I ...?	*Posso ...?*	po·so ...
bring anything for the meal	*portare qualcosa per il pasto*	por·*ta*·re kwal·*ko*·za per eel *pas*·to
do the dishes	*lavare i piatti*	la·*va*·re ee *pya*·tee
set/clear the table	*apparecchiare/ sparecchiare*	a·pa·re·*kya*·re/ spa·re·*kya*·re
take out the rubbish	*gettare la spazzatura*	je·*ta*·re la spa·tsa·*too*·ra

Thanks for your hospitality.
Grazie per la Sua/tua   *gra*·tsye per la soo·a/*too*·a
ospitalità. pol/inf   os·pee·ta·lee·*ta*

If you're dining with your hosts, see **eating out**, page 143, for additional phrases.

21A Where's (the bank)?
Dov'è (la banca)?   do·ve (la ban·ka)

21B What's the address?
Qual'è l'indirizzo?   kwa·le leen·dee·ree·tso

21C How do I get there?
Come ci si arriva?   ko·me chee see a·ree·va

21D How far is it?
Quant'è distante?   kwan·te dees·tan·te

21E Can you show me (on the map)?
Può mostrarmi   pwo mos·trar·mee
(sulla pianta)?   (soo·la pyan·ta)

I'm looking for (the public toilets).
Cerco (i servizi   cher·ko (ee ser·vee·tsee
igienici).   ee·je·nee·chee)

Which way's (the post office)?
Dove si trova (l'ufficcio   do·ve see tro·va (loo·fee·cho
postale)?   pos·ta·le)

22A It's far.	*È lontano.*	e lon·ta·no	
22B It's near.	*È vicino.*	e vee·chee·no	
22C here	*qui*	kwee	
22D there	*là*	la	
22E It's next to ...	*È accanto a ...*	e a·kan·to a ...	
22F opposite	*di fronte a*	dee fron·te a	
22G straight ahead	*sempre diritto*	sem·pre dee·ree·to	

It's ...   *È ...*   e ...

behind ...	*dietro ...*	dye·tro ...
in front of ...	*davanti a ...*	da·van·tee a ...
left	*a sinistra*	a see·nee·stra
on the corner	*all'angolo*	a lan·go·lo
right	*a destra*	a de·stra

23A Turn at the corner.
Giri all'angolo. — *jee·ree a·lan·go·lo*

23B Turn at the traffic lights.
Giri al semaforo. — *jee·ree al se·ma·fo·ro*

23C Turn left. | *Giri a sinistra.* | *jee·ree a see·nee·stra*
23D Turn right. | *Giri a destra.* | *jee·ree a de·stra*

24A	by bus	*con l'autobus*	kon *low*·to·boos
24B	by taxi	*con il tassì*	ko·neel ta·see
24C	by train	*con il treno*	ko·neel *tre*·no
24D	on foot	*a piedi*	a *pye*·dee

25A	north	*nord*	nord
25B	south	*sud*	sood
25C	east	*est*	est
25D	west	*ovest*	o·vest

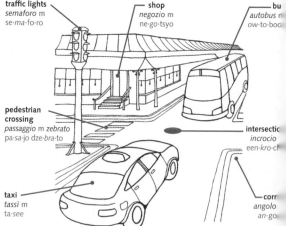

traffic lights
semaforo m
se·ma·fo·ro

shop
negozio m
ne·go·tsyo

bu[...]
autobus [...]
ow·to·boo[...]

pedestrian
crossing
passaggio m zebrato
pa·sa·jo dze·bra·to

intersectio[...]
incrocio
een·kro·ch[...]

taxi
tassì m
ta·see

corn[...]
angolo
an·go[...]

looking for ...

in cerca di ...

Where's (a travel agency)?
Dov'è (un'agenzia di viaggi)?
do·ve (oo·na·jen·*tsee*·a dee vee·*a*·jee)

33A **Where can I buy (a padlock)?**
Dove posso comprare (un lucchetto)?
do·ve po·so kom·*pra*·re (oon loo·*ke*·to)

For phrases on asking and giving directions, see **directions**, page 61 and for different types of shops, see the **dictionary**.

signs		
Aperto	a·*per*·to	**Open**
Chiuso	kyoo·zo	**Closed**
Spingere	speen·je·re	**Push**
Tirare	tee·*ra*·re	**Pull**

making a purchase

fare un acquisto

I'm just looking.
Sto solo guardando.
sto so·lo gwar·*dan*·do

33B **How much is this?**
Quanto costa questo?
kwan·to kos·ta kwe·sto

33C **Can you write down the price?**
Può scrivere il prezzo?
pwo skree·ve·re eel pre·tso

34A **I'd like to buy ...**
Vorrei comprare ...
vo·ray kom·*pra*·re ...

34B **Can I look at it?**
Posso dare un'occhiata?
po·so da·re oo·no·kya·ta

34C Do you have any others?

Ne avete altri?   ne a·ve·te al·tree

34D Does it have a guarantee?

Ha la garanzia?   a la ga·ran·tsee·a

Could I have it wrapped, please?

Può incartarlo,   pwo een·kar·tar·lo
per favore?   per fa·vo·re

Can I have it sent overseas?

Può spedirlo all'estero?   pwo spe·deer·lo a·les·te·ro

Can you order it for me?

Me lo può ordinare,   me lo pwo or·dee·na·re
per favore?   per fa·vo·re

Can I pick it up later?

Posso ritirarlo   po·so ree·tee·rar·lo
più tardi?   pyoo tar·dee

It's broken.

È rotto.   e ro·to

35A Do you accept credit cards?

Accettate la carta di   a·che·ta·te la kar·ta dee
credito?   kre·dee·to

35B Do you accept debit cards?

Accettate la carta di   a·che·ta·te la kar·ta dee
debito?   de·bee·to

35C Do you accept travellers cheques?

Accettate i travellers   a·che·ta·te ee tra·ve·lers
cheque?   chek

35D I'd like a bag, please.

Può darmi un sacchetto,   pwo dar·mee oon sa·ke·to
per favore?   per fa·vo·re

old-fashioned manners

The plural polite form has become virtually obsolete in modern Italian. If you want to show respect to more than one person, use *voi*. See **pronouns** in the **a–z phrasebuilder**.

35E I'd like a receipt, please.

Può darmi una ricevuta, per favore?

pwo *dar*·mee *oo*·na ree·che·*voo*·ta per fa·*vo*·re

35F I'd like my change, please.

Vorrei il mio resto, per favore.

vo·*ray* eel *mee*·o *res*·to per fa·*vo*·re

36A It's faulty.

È difettoso.

e dee·fe·*to*·zo

36B I'd like a refund, please.

Vorrei un rimborso, per favore.

vo·*ray* oon reem·*bor*·so per fa·*vo*·re

36C I'd like to return this, please.

Vorrei restituire questo/a, per favore. m/f

vo·*ray* res·tee·*twee*·re *kwe*·sto/a per fa·*vo*·re

local talk

bargain	*affare* m	a·*fa*·re
bargain hunter	*affarista* m	a·fa·*ree*·sta
rip-off	*fregatura* f	fre·ga·*too*·ra
specials	*occasioni* f pl	o·ka·*zyo*·nee
sales	*saldi* m pl	*sal*·dee

bargaining

contrattare

33D That's too expensive.

È troppo caro/a. m/f

e *tro*·po *ka*·ro/a

The price is very high.

Il prezzo è molto alto.

eel *pre*·tso e *mol*·to *al*·to

33E Can you lower the price?

Può farmi lo sconto?

pwo *far*·mee lo *skon*·to

Do you have something cheaper?

Ha qualcosa di meno costoso?

a kwal·*ko*·za dee *me*·no kos·*to*·zo

I'll give you ...

Le offro ...

le *o*·fro ...

clothes

37A Can I try it on?
Potrei provarmelo/a? m/f   po·*tray* pro·*var*·me·lo/a

37B It doesn't fit.
Non va bene.   non va *be*·ne

37C My size is (32).
Sono una tagli   *so*·no oo·na *ta*·lya
(trentadue).   (*tren*·ta·*doo*·e)

My size is ...	*Sono una taglia ...*	*so*·no oo·na *ta*·lya ...
large	*forte*	*for*·te
medium	*media*	*me*·dya
small	*piccola*	*pee*·ko·la

For different types of clothes, see the **dictionary**.

repairs

Can I have ...	*Posso far aggiustare*	*po*·so far a·joo·*sta*·re
repaired here?	*... qui?*	... kwee
my backpack	*il mio zaino*	eel *mee*·o *dzai*·no
my camera	*la mia macchina*	la *mee*·a ma·*kee*·na
	fotografica	fo·to·*gra*·fee·ka

When will my ...	*Quando saranno*	*kwan*·do sa·*ra*·no
be ready?	*pronti/e ...?* m/f pl	*pron*·tee/e ...
(sun)glasses	*i miei occhiali* m pl	ee myay o·*kya*·lee
	(da sole)	(da *so*·le)
shoes	*le mie scarpe* f pl	le *mee*·e *skar*·pe

don't touch!

In style-conscious Italy, though shop window displays may look good enough to eat, they're absolutely not to be touched. Disrupting a window display could jeopardise a shop's *bella figura* – that all-important Italian preoccupation with creating a good impression.

hairdressing

I'd like (a) ...	Vorrei ...	vo·ray ...
blow wave	una messa in piega a fon	oo·na me·sa een pye·ga a fon
colour	farmi tingere i capelli	far·mee teen·je·re ee ka·pe·lee
haircut	un taglio	oon ta·lyo
highlights	i colpi di sole	ee kol·pee dee so·le
layers	un taglio scalato	oon ta·lyo ska·la·to
my beard trimmed	una spuntatina alla barba	oo·na spoon·ta·tee·na a·la bar·ba
perm	una permanente	oo·na per·ma·nen·te
shave	una rasatura	oo·na ra·za·too·ra
straightening	farmi stirare i capelli	far·mee stee·ra·re ee ka·pe·lee
streaks	le mèches	le mesh
tips	i colpi di sole	ee kol·pee dee so·le
trim	una spuntatina	oo·na spoon·ta·tee·na

Do you do ...?	Fate ...	fa·te ...
facials	i trattamenti di bellezza (al viso)	ee tra·ta·men·tee dee be·le·tsa (al vee·zo)
massage	i massaggi	ee ma·sa·jee
waxing	la depilazione	la de·pee·la·tsyo·ne

Don't cut it too short.
Non li tagli troppo corti.   non lee ta·lyee tro·po kor·tee

Cut it all off!
Li tagli tutti!   lee ta·lyee too·tee

Please use a new blade.
Usi una lametta nuova, per favore.   oo·zee oo·na la·me·ta nwo·va per fa·vo·re

I should never have let you near me!
Non dovevo mai permetterLe di toccarmi!   non do·ve·vo mai per·me·ter·le dee to·kar·mee

For colours, see the **dictionary**.

books & reading

Is there a/an (English-language) bookshop?

C'è una libreria
(specializzata in
lingua inglese)?

che *oo*·na lee·bre·*ree*·a
(spe·cha·lee·*dza*·ta een
leen·gwa een·*gle*·ze)

Is there a/an (English-language) section?

C'è una sezione
(di lingua inglese)?

che *oo*·na se·*tsyo*·ne
(dee *leen*·gwa een·*gle*·ze)

Is there a/an (English-language) entertainment guide?

C'è una guida agli
spettacoli (in inglese)?

che *oo*·na *gwee*·da a·lyee
spe·*ta*·ko·lee (ee·neen·*gle*·ze)

Do you have a book by (Alberto Moravia)?

C'è un libro di
(Alberto Moravia)?

che oon *lee*·bro dee
(al·*ber*·to mo·*ra*·vee·a)

Do you have Lonely Planet guidebooks?

Avete le guide del
Lonely Planet?

a·*ve*·te le *gwee*·de del
lon·lee *pla*·net

Do you have a better phrasebook than this?

Avete un vocabolarietto
migliore di questo?

a·*ve*·te oon vo·ka·bo·la·*rye*·to
mee·*lyo*·re dee *kwe*·sto

listen for ...

lay *le*·je *lee*·bree een ee·ta·*lya*·no
*Lei legge libri in
italiano?*

**Do you read books
in Italian?**

no non ne a·*bya*·mo
No, non ne abbiamo.

No, we don't have any.

music

I'd like (a) ... *Vorrei ...* vo·ray ...
blank tape *una cassetta vuota* oo·na ka·se·ta vwo·ta
CD *un cidì* oon chee·dee
headphones *delle cuffia* de·le koo·fya

I heard a band called (Marlene Kuntz).
Ho sentito un gruppo o sen·tee·to oon groo·po
chiamato (Marlene Kuntz). kya·ma·to (mar·le·ne koonts)

I heard a singer called ...
Ho sentito un/una o sen·tee·to oon/oo·na
cantante chiamato/a ... m/f kan·tan·te kya·ma·to/a ...

What's his/her best recording?
Qual'è la sua migliore kwa·le la soo·a mee·lyo·re
incisione? een·chee·zyo·ne

Can I listen to this?
Potrei ascoltare questo? po·tray as·kol·ta·re kwe·sto

photography

Could you develop this film?
Potrebbe sviluppare po·tre·be svee·loo·pa·re
questo rullino? kwe·sto roo·lee·no

38A **Could you load my film?**
Potrebbe inserire il po·tre·be een·se·ree·re eel
mio rullino? mee·o roo·lee·no

38B **I need a B&W film for this camera.**
Vorrei un rullino in vo·ray oon roo·lee·no een
bianco e nero per questa byan·ko e ne·ro per kwe·sta
macchina fotografica. ma·kee·na fo·to·gra·fee·ka

38C **I need a colour film for this camera.**
Vorrei un rullino a vo·ray oon roo·lee·no a
colori per questa ko·lo·ree per kwe·sta
macchina fotografica. ma·kee·na fo·to·gra·fee·ka

I need a ...	Vorrei un rullino ...	vo·ray oon roo·lee·no ...
film for this	per questa macchina	per kwe·sta ma·kee·na
camera.	fotografica.	fo·to·gra·fee·ka
APS	da APS	da a·pee·e·se
(100) speed	da (cento) ASA	da (chen·to) a·za

How much is it to develop this film?

Quanto costa sviluppare   kwan·to kos·ta svee·loo·pa·re
questo rullino?   kwe·sto roo·lee·no

38D **When will it be ready?**

Quando sarà pronto?   kwan·do sa·ra pron·to

I need passport photos taken.

Vorrei delle foto tessera.   vo·ray de·le fo·to te·se·ra

I'm not happy with these photos.

Non mi piacciono   non mee pya·cho·no
queste foto.   kwe·ste fo·to

---

souvenirs

antiques	pezzi m d'antiquariato	pe·tsee dan·tee·kwa·rya·to
blown glass	vetro m soffiato	ve·tro so·fya·to
Carnevale masks	maschere f pl di Carnevale	ma·ske·re dee kar·ne·va·le
ceramics	ceramiche f pl	che·ra·mee·ke
embroidery	ricamo m	ree·ka·mo
glassware	vetrame m	ve·tra·me
handicrafts	ogetti m pl d'artigianato	o·je·tee dar·tee·ja·na·to
jewellery	gioielli m pl	jo·ye·lee
lace	merletto m	mer·le·to
leather goods	pelletterie f pl	pe·le·te·ree·e
marbled paper	carta f marmorizzata	kar·ta mar·mo·ree·tsa·ta
Murano glassware	vetri m pl di Murano	ve·tree dee moo·ra·no
paper goods	articoli m pl di carta	ar·tee·ko·lee dee kar·ta
pottery	ceramiche f pl	che·ra·mee·ke
woodcarvings	legno m intagliato	le·nyo een·ta·lya·to

post office

l'ufficio postale

39A I want to send a fax.
Vorrei mandare un fax. vo·ray man·*da*·re oon faks

39B I want to send a parcel.
Vorrei mandare vo·ray man·*da*·re
un pacchetto. oon pa·*ke*·to

39C I want to send a postcard.
Vorrei mandare vo·ray man·*da*·re
una cartolina. oo·na kar·to·*lee*·na

39D I want to buy an envelope.
Vorrei comprare una busta. vo·ray kom·*pra*·re oo·na *boo*·sta

39E I want to buy stamps.
Vorrei comprare vo·ray kom·*pra*·re
dei francobolli. day fran·ko·*bo*·lee

airmail	*via* f *aerea*	vee·a a·e·re·a
customs	*dichiarazione* f	dee·kya·ra·*tsyo*·ne
declaration	*doganale*	do·ga·*na*·le
domestic	*domestico/a* m/f	do·*mes*·tee·ko/a
express mail	*posta* f *prioritaria*	*pos*·ta pryo·ree·*ta*·rya
fragile	*fragile*	*fra*·jee·le
glue	*colla* f	*ko*·la
international	*internazionale*	een·ter·na·tsyo·*na*·le
mail box	*buca* f *delle lettere*	*boo*·ka de·le *le*·te·re
postcode	*codice* m *postale*	*ko*·dee·che pos·*ta*·le
registered mail	*posta* f	*pos*·ta
	raccomandata	ra·ko·man·*da*·ta
regular mail	*posta* f *ordinaria/*	*pos*·ta or·dee·*na*·rya/
	normale	nor·*ma*·le
sea mail	*via* f *mare*	vee·a *ma*·re

Please send it by airmail (to Denmark).

Lo mandi via aerea
(in Danimarca),
per favore.

lo man·dee vee·a a·e·re·a
(een da·nee·mar·ka)
per fa·vo·re

Please send it by regular mail (to Rome).

Lo mandi per posta
ordinaria (a Roma),
per favore.

lo man·dee per pos·ta
or·dee·na·rya (a ro·ma)
per fa·vo·re

It contains ...

Contiene ...

kon·tye·ne ...

Where's the poste restante section?

Dov'è il fermo posta?

do·ve eel fer·mo pos·ta

Is there any mail for me?

C'è posta per me?

che pos·ta per me

listen for ...

do·ve lo spe·dee·she
Dove lo spedisce?

Where are you sending it?

per pos·ta pryo·ree·ta·rya o nor·ma·le
Per posta prioritaria
o normale?

By express post or regular post?

phone

telefono

40A What's your phone number?

Qual'è il Suo/tuo
numero di telefono? pol/inf

kwa·le eel soo·o/too·o
noo·me·ro dee te·le·fo·no

40B Where's the nearest public phone?

Dov'è il telefono
pubblico più vicino?

do·ve eel te·le·fo·no
poo·blee·ko pyoo vee·chee·no

I want to make a (reverse-charge/ collect) call to ...	Vorrei fare una chiamata (a carico del destinatario) ...	vo·ray fa·re oo·na kya·ma·ta (a ka·ree·ko del des·tee·na·ta·ryo) ...
Belgium	in Belgio	een bel·jo
Naples	a Napoli	a na·po·lee

How much does ... cost?	*Quanto costa ...?*	kwan·to kos·ta ...
a (three)-minute call	*una telefonata di (tre) minuti*	oo·na te·le·fo·na·ta dee (tre) mee·noo·tee
each extra minute	*ogni minuto in più*	o·nyee mee·noo·to een pyoo

I want to speak for (three) minutes.
Vorrei parlare per (tre) minuti.
vo·ray par·la·re per (tre) mee·noo·tee

40C **I want to buy a phonecard.**
Vorrei comprare una scheda telefonica.
vo·ray kom·pra·re oo·na ske·da te·le·fo·nee·ka

The number is ...
Il numero è ...
eel noo·me·ro e ...

What's the area/country code for ...?
Qual'è il prefisso per ...?
kwa·le eel pre·fee·so per ...

It's engaged.
La linea è occupata.
la lee·ne·a e o·koo·pa·ta

I've been cut off.
È caduta la linea.
e ka·doo·ta la lee·ne·a

The connection's bad.
La linea non è buona.
la lee·ne·a no·ne bwo·na

Hello.
Pronto!
pron·to

It's ...
Sono ...
so·no ...

Can I speak to ...?
Posso parlare con ...?
po·so par·la·re kon ...

communications

73

Can I leave a message?
Posso lasciare un messaggio?   po·so la·*sha*·re oon me·*sa*·jo

Please tell him/her I called.
Gli/Le dica che ho   lyee/le *dee*·ka ke o
telefonato, per favore.   te·le·fo·*na*·to per fa·*vo*·re

I'll call back later.
Richiamerò più tardi.   ree·kya·me·*ro* pyoo *tar*·dee

My number is ...
Il mio numero è ...   eel *mee*·o *noo*·me·ro e ...

I don't have a contact number.
Non ho un numero fisso.   non o oon *noo*·me·ro *fee*·so

listen for ...

kon kee *par*·lo *Con chi parlo?*	Who's calling?
kon kee *vwo*·le par·*la*·re *Con chi vuole* *parlare?*	Who do you want (to speak to)?
lye·lo/*lye*·la pa·so *Glielo/Gliela passo.*	I'll put him/her on.
mee dees·*pya*·che (*loo*·ee/lay) non che *Mi dispiace, (lui/lei)* *non c'è.*	I'm sorry, (he/she) is not here.
mee dees·*pya*·che a sba·*lya*·to *noo*·me·ro *Mi dispiace, ha sbagliato* *numero.*	Sorry, wrong number.
oo·*na*·tee·mo *Un attimo.*	One moment.
see e kwee *Sì, è qui.*	Yes, he/she is here.

mobile/cell phone

I'd like a/an ...	Vorrei ...	vo·ray ...
adaptor plug	un adattatore	oo·na·da·ta·to·re
charger for my phone	un caricabatterie	oon ka·ree·ka·ba·te·ree·e
mobile/cell phone for hire	un cellulare da noleggiare	oon che·loo·la·re da no·le·ja·re
prepaid mobile/ cell phone	un cellulare prepagato	oon che·loo·la·re pre·pa·ga·to
recharge card for (Omnitel)	una ricarica telefonica per (Omnitel)	oo·na re·ka·ree·ka te·le·fo·nee·ka per (om·nee·tel)

40D I'd like a SIM card for your network.
Vorrei un SIM card per la — vo·ray oon seem kard per la
vostra rete telefonica. — vos·tra re·te te·le·fo·nee·ka

What are the rates?
Quali sono le tariffe? — kwa·lee so·no le ta·ree·fe

(30c) per (30) seconds.
(Trenta centesimi) per — (tren·ta chen·te·zee·mee)
(trenta) secondi. — per (tren·ta) se·kon·dee

the internet

41A Where's the local Internet cafe?
Dove si trova — do·ve see tro·va
l'Internet point? — leen·ter·net poynt

41B I'd like to get Internet access.
Vorrei usare Internet. — vo·ray oo·za·re een·ter·net

41C I'd like to use a printer.
Vorrei usare una — vo·ray oo·za·re oo·na
stampante. — stam·pan·te

I'd like to use a scanner.
Vorrei scandire. — vo·ray skan·dee·re

I'd like to check my email.
Vorrei controllare il — vo·*ray* kon·tro·*la*·re eel
mio email. — *mee*·e e·*mayl*

41D **How much is it per hour?**
Quanto costa all'ora? — kwan·to kos·ta a·*lo*·ra

How much per ...?	*Quanto costa ...?*	kwan·to kos·ta ...
(five) minutes	*per (cinque)*	per (*cheen*·kwe)
	minuti	mee·*noo*·tee
page	*a pagina*	a pa·jee·na

Do you have ...?	*Avete ...?*	a·*ve*·te ...
PCs	*i PC*	ee pee chee
Macs	*i Mac*	ee mak
a Zip drive	*uno ZIP drive*	*oo*·no zeep draiv

I need help with the computer.
Ho bisogna d'aiuto con — o bee·zo·nyo da·*yoo*·to
il computer. — ko·neel kom·*pyoo*·ter

It's crashed.
Si è bloccato. — see e blo·*ka*·to

I've finished.
Ho finito. — o fee·*nee*·to

---

phone frenzy

The voluble Italians have one of the highest rates of mobile phone ownership in the world. *Cellulari* or *telefonini* (lit: little telephones) are indeed an essential fashion accessory. When taking a train or bus expect cacophonic erruptions of mobile phones throughout the journey. Some Italian businessmen are observed to ritually reach for their *telefonini* on leaving the office to warn their wives to *buttare la pasta* (throw the pasta into the pot) for their imminent arrival.

I'm attending a ...	Sono qui per ...	so·no kwee per ...
conference	una conferenza	oo·na kon·fe·ren·tsa
course	un corso	oon kor·so
meeting	una riunione	oo·na ree·oo·nyo·ne
trade fair	una fiera	oo·na fye·ra
	commerciale	ko·mer·cha·le

I'm here with ...	Sono qui con ...	so·no kwee kon ...
my company	la mia azienda	la mee·a a·dzyen·da
my colleague	il mio collega m	eel mee·o ko·le·ga
	la mia collega f	la mee·a ko·le·ga
my colleagues	i miei	ee myay
	colleghi	ko·le·gee
(two) others	(due) altri	(doo·e) al·tree

I'm staying at (the Minerva hotel), room (309).
Alloggio al (Minerva),   a·lo·jo (al mee·ner·va),
camera (trecentonove).   ka·me·ra (tre·chen·to·no·ve)

I'm alone.
Sono solo/a. m/f   so·no so·lo/a

I'm here for (two) days/weeks.
Sono qui per (due)   so·no kwee per (doo·e)
giorni/settimane.   jor·nee/se·tee·ma·ne

Here's my business card.
Ecco il mio biglietto   e·ko eel mee·o bee·lye·to
da visita.   da vee·zee·ta

I have an appointment with (Mr Carlucci).
Ho un appuntamento   o oo·na·poon·ta·men·to
con (il Signor Carlucci).   kon (eel see·nyor kar·loo·chee)

That went very well.
È andato bene.   e an·da·to be·ne

Shall we go for a drink/meal?
Andiamo a bere/   an·dya·mo a be·re/
mangiare qualcosa?   man·ja·re kwal·ko·za

Where's the ...?	Dov'è ...?	do·ve ...
business centre	il business centre	eel beez·nees sen·ter
conference	la conferenza	la kon·fe·ren·tsa
meeting	la riunione	la ree·oo·nyo·ne
I need ...	Ho bisogno di ...	o bee·zo·nyo dee ...
a computer	un computer	oon kom·pyoo·ter
a connection to the Net	una connessione Internet	oo·na ko·ne·syo·ne een·ter·net
an interpreter	un/un'interprete m/f	oo·neen·ter·pre·te
more business cards	più biglietti da visita	pyoo bee·lye·tee da vee·zee·ta
some space to set up	un posto dove sistemare	oon pos·to do·ve sees·te·ma·re
to send an email/fax	mandare un email/fax	man·da·re oon e·mayl/faks
I'm expecting a ...	Aspetto ...	a·spet·o ...
call	una telefonata	oo·na te·le·fo·na·ta
fax	un fax	oon faks
data projector	proiettore m	pro·ye·to·re
flip chart	lavagna f con fogli	la·va·nya kon fo·lyee
overhead projector	lavagna f luminosa	la·va·nya loo·mee·no·sa
whiteboard	lavagna f bianca	la·va·nya byan·ka

the language of Italian business

Italian business culture is formal and hierarchical. First names are not used between executives and subordinates and using the right personal and professional titles may help you clinch that deal! Business is not usually discussed over a meal, but when you do dine with Italian colleagues or business partners wait for them to initiate any discussions about business. Also, as a visitor you'll be expected to be *in orario* (on time). Don't get touchy though about being kept waiting.

banking
in banca

Where can I ...?	Dove posso ...?	do·ve po·so ...
arrange a transfer	*trasferire soldi*	tras·fe·ree·re sol·dee
get a cash	*prelevare con*	pre·le·va·re kon
advance	*carta di credito*	kar·ta dee kre·dee·to

42A What time does the bank open?
A che ora apre la banca?　　a ke o·ra a·pre la ban·ka

42B Where's an ATM?
Dov'è un Bancomat?　　do·ve oon ban·ko·mat

42C Where's a foreign exchange office?
Dov'è un cambio?　　do·ve oon kam·byo

43A I'd like to cash a cheque.
Vorrei riscuotere　　vo·ray ree·skwo·te·re
un assegno.　　oo·na·se·nyo

43B I'd like to change a travellers cheque.
Vorrei cambiare　　vo·ray kam·bya·re
un travellers cheque.　　oon tra·ve·lers chek

43C I'd like to change money.
Vorrei cambiare denaro.　　vo·ray kam·bya·re de·na·ro

43D I'd like to withdraw money.
Vorrei fare un prelievo.　　vo·ray fa·re oon pre·lye·vo

The automatic teller machine took my card.
Il Bancomat ha　　eel ban·ko·mat a
trattenuto la mia　　tra·te·noo·to la mee·a
carta di credito.　　kar·ta dee kre·dee·to

I've forgotten my PIN.
Ho dimenticato il　　o dee·men·tee·ka·to eel
mio codice PIN.　　mee·o ko·dee·che peen

Can I use my credit card to withdraw money?
Si può usare la carta　　see pwo oo·za·re la kar·ta
di credito per fare　　dee kre·dee·to per fa·re
prelievi?　　pre·lye·vee

43E **What's the exchange rate?**
Quant'è il cambio? kwan·*te* eel *kam*·byo

What's the commission?
Quant'è la commissione? kwan·*te* la ko·mee·*syo*·ne

What's the charge for that?
Quanto costa? kwan·to kos·ta

Can I have smaller notes?
Mi può dare banconote mee pwo *da*·re ban·ko·*no*·te
più piccole? pyoo *pee*·ko·le

Has my money arrived yet?
È arrivato il mio denaro? e a·ree·*va*·to eel *mee*·o de·*na*·ro

How long will it take to arrive?
Quanto tempo ci vorrà kwan·to *tem*·po chee vo·*ra*
per il trasferimento? per eel tras·fe·ree·*men*·to

For other useful phrases, see **money**, page 35.

For other useful phrases, see **money**, page 35.

listen for ...		
eel *soo*·o ...	*il Suo ...*	**your ...**
do·koo·*men*·to	*documento*	**ID**
dee·den·tee·*ta*	*d'identità*	
pa·sa·*por*·to	*passaporto*	**passport**
fra ...	*Fra ...*	**In ...**
(*kwa*·tro) jor·nee	*(quattro) giorni*	**(four)**
la·vo·ra·*tee*·vee	*lavorativi*	**working days**
oo·na se·tee·*ma*·na	*una settimana*	**one week**
pwo ... per	*Può ..., per*	**Please ...**
fa·*vo*·re	*favore?*	
feer·*ma*·re kwee	*firmare qui*	**sign here**
skree·ver·lo	*scriverlo*	**write it down**
che oon pro·*ble*·ma ko·neel *soo*·o *kon*·to		
C'è un problema con il	**There's a problem**	
Suo conto.	**with your account.**	
non po·*sya*·mo *far*·lo		
Non possiamo farlo.	**We can't do that.**	

I'd like a/an ...	*Vorrei ...*	vo·ray ...
audio set	*un auricolare*	oo·now·ree·ko·la·re
catalogue	*un catalogo*	oon ka·ta·lo·go
guide (person)	*una guida*	oo·na gwee·da
guidebook in English	*una guida in inglese*	oo·na gwee·da ee·neen·gle·ze

Do you have information on ... sights?	*Avete delle informazioni su posti ...?*	a·ve·te de·le een·for·ma·tsyo·nee soo pos·tee ...
cultural	*culturali*	kool·too·ra·lee
local	*locali*	lo·ka·lee
religious	*religiosi*	re·lee·jo·zee
unique	*particolari*	par·tee·ko·la·ree

44A I'd like a local map.
Vorrei una cartina della zona.
vo·ray oo·na kar·tee·na de·la dzo·na

44B I'd like to see ...
Vorrei vedere ...
vo·ray ve·de·re ...

44C What's that?
Cos'è?
ko·ze

Who made it?
Chi l'ha fatto?
kee la fa·to

How old is it?
Quanti anni ha?
kwan·tee a·nee a

Could you take a photograph of me?
Può farmi una foto?
pwo far·mee oo·na fo·to

44D Can I take a photograph (of you)?
Posso fare una foto (di Lei)? po·so fa·re oo·na fo·to (dee lay)

I'll send you the photograph.
Le spedirò la foto. le spe·dee·ro la fo·to

signs

Entrata	en·tra·ta	**Entrance**
Gabinetti	ga·bee·ne·tee	**Toilets**
Informazioni	een·for·ma·tsyo·nee	**Information**
Ingresso	een·gre·so	**Entrance**
Ingresso	een·gre·so	**Free Admission**
Gratuito	gra·too·ee·to	
Messa in	me·sa een	**Service in**
Corso	kor·so	**Progress**
Non Calpestare	non kal·pe·sta·re	**Keep Off the**
l'Erba	ler·ba	**Grass**
Non Entrare	no·nen·tra·re	**No Entry**
Proibito	pro·ee·bee·to	**Prohibited**
Servizi	ser·vee·tsee	**Public**
Pubblici	poo·blee·chee	**Toilets**
Uscita	oo·shee·ta	**Exit**
Uscita di	oo·shee·ta dee	**Emergency**
Sicurezza	see·koo·re·tsa	**Exit**
Vietato	vye·ta·to	**Prohibited**
Vietato	vye·ta·to	**No Eating or**
Consumare	kon·soo·ma·re	**Drinking**
Cibi o	chee·bee o	**Allowed**
Bevande	be·van·de	
Vietato Entrare	vye·ta·to en·tra·re	**No Entry**
Vietato	vye·ta·to	**Do Not Take**
Fotografare	fo·to·gra·fa·re	**Photographs**
Vietato Fumare	vye·ta·to foo·ma·re	**No Smoking**
Vietato l'Ingresso	vye·ta·to leen·gre·so	**No Admittance**
Vietato Toccare	vye·ta·to to·ka·re	**Do Not Touch**
Vietato Usare	vye·ta·to oo·za·re	**Do Not Use**
Flash	flesh	**Flash**

getting in

45A **What time does it open?**
A che ora apre? a ke o·ra a·pre

45B **What time does it open/close?**
A che ora chiude? a ke o·ra kyoo·de

45C **What's the admission charge?**
Quant'è il prezzo d'ingresso? kwan·te eel pre·tso deen·gre·so

It costs (seven euros).
Costa (sette Euro). kos·ta (se·te e·oo·ro)

45D **Is there a discount for children?**
C'è uno sconto per che oo·no skon·to per
bambini? bam·bee·nee

45E **Is there a discount for students?**
C'è uno sconto per che oo·no skon·to per
studenti? stoo·den·tee

Is there a	C'è uno	che oo·no
discount for ...?	sconto per ...?	skon·to per ...
groups	gruppi	groo·pee
pensioners	pensionati	pen·syo·na·tee

tours

Can you	Può consigliare	pwo kon·see·lya·re
recommend a ...?	una ...?	oo·na ...
boat-trip	gita in barca	jee·ta een bar·ka
tour	gita	jee·ta
	turistica	too·ree·stee·ka

46A **When's the next daytrip?**
A che ora parte la prossima a ke o·ra par·te la pro·see·ma
escursione in giornata? es·koor·syo·ne een jor·na·ta

46B **When's the next excursion?**
A che ora parte la prossima a ke o·ra par·te la pro·see·ma
escursione? es·koor·syo·ne

46C Is food included?

È incluso il vitto?   e een·*kloo*·zo eel *vee*·to

46D Is transport included?

È incluso il trasporto?   e een·*kloo*·zo eel tras·*por*·to

46E How long is the tour?

Quanto dura la gita?   *kwan*·to *doo*·ra la *jee*·ta

46F What time should we be back?

A che ora dovremmo   a ke *o*·ra dov·*re*·mo
ritornare?   ree·tor·*na*·re

Be back here at (seven).

Torni qui alle (sette).   *tor*·nee kwee *a*·le (*se*·te)

I'm with them.

Sono con loro.   *so*·no kon *lo*·ro

I've lost my group.

Ho perso il mio gruppo.   o *per*·so eel *mee*·o *groo*·po

---

local talk

What's (Rome) like?

Com'è (Roma)?   ko·*me* (*ro*·ma)

There's (not) ...	*(Non) C'è ...*	(non) che ...
lots of	*molta*	*mol*·ta
culture	*cultura*	kool·*too*·ra
a lot to see	*molto da*	*mol*·to da
	vedere	ve·*de*·re
fabulous	*una vita*	oo·na *vee*·ta
nightlife	*notturna*	no·*toor*·na
	favolosa	fa·vo·*lo*·sa
a great	*un buon*	oon bwon
restaurant/	*ristorante/*	rees·to·*ran*·te/
hotel	*albergo*	al·*ber*·go
There are ...	*(Non) Ci sono ...*	(non) chee *so*·no ...
(no) rip-off	*imbroglioni*	eem·bro·*lyo*·nee
merchants		
(not) too	*troppi*	*tro*·pee
many tourists	*turisti*	too·*ree*·stee

travellers' latin

While a knowledge of Italian will help you in your travels through the Italy of today, it's a knowledge of Latin that will help you to understand the Italy of the past. Here are a few common words and phrases that will help you make sense of some inscriptions and dedications you'll come across while sightseeing:

AED	*aedilis*	aedile (magistrate)
ANN	*annos/anni*	years
COL	*colonia*	colony
COS	*consul*	consul
COSS	*consules*	consuls
C R	*cives Romani*	Roman citizens
CVR	*curavit*	attended to/took care of
D	*dat/dedit*	he gives/he gave
DEC	*decreto*	by decree
DED	*dedit*	gave
D M	*dis manibus*	to the spirits of the dead
EX S C	*ex senatus consulto*	by a decree of the Senate
F	*feci/faciundum/ filii/filia*	did/to be done/ son/daughter
FID	*fidelis*	faithful
IMP	*imperator*	general/emperor
I O M	*Iuppiter Optimus Maximus*	Jupiter Best (and) Greatest
P C	*Patres conscripti*	senators
P(ONT) M(AX)	*Pontifex Maximus*	chief priest
P R	*Populus Romanus*	the People of Rome
R	*Romanus*	Roman
REST	*restituit*	restored
R P	*res publica*	state/republic
S C	*senatus consulto*	by decree of the Senate
S P Q R	*Senatus Populusque Romanus*	the Senate and the People of Rome

traveller's latin

some common names:

AVG	*Augustus*	SP	*Spurius*
L	*Lucius*	CN	*Gnaeus*
Q	*Quintus*	MAM	*Mamius*
A	*Aulus*	T	*Titus*
M	*Marcus*	D	*Decimus*
S	*Servius*	P	*Publius*
C	*Gaius*	TI	*Tiberius*
M'	*Manius*		

numbers:

I	1	VI	6	L	50
II	2	VII	7	C	100
III	3	VIII	8	D	500
IV or IIII	4	IX	9	M	1000
V	5	X	10		

Here are some rules to help you work out the bigger numbers. In general, a smaller number to the left of a larger number should be subtracted from that number (eg IX = 9 and XL = 40), whereas a smaller number to the right of a larger number should be added to that number (eg XI = 11 and LX = 60):

MDCCCCLXXXV	1985
DCCCCXXV or CMXXV	925
MMIV	2004

disabled travellers
viaggiatori disabili

I'm disabled.
Sono disabile. so·no dee·za·bee·le

I need assistance.
Ho bisogno di assistenza. o bee·zo·nyo dee a·sees·ten·tsa

What services do you have for disabled people?
Di quali servizi dee kwa·lee ser·vee·tsee
disponete per i dees·po·ne·te per ee
disabili? dee·za·bee·lee

Is there wheelchair access?
C'è un'entrata per che oo·nen·tra·ta per
sedie a rotelle? se·dye a ro·te·le

I have a hearing aid.
Ho un apparecchio o oo·na·pa·re·kyo
acustico. a·koos·tee·ko

I'm deaf.
Sono sordo/a. m/f so·no sor·do/a

Are guide dogs permitted?
Sono ammessi i cani so·no a·me·see ee ka·nee
guida? gwee·da

Could you help me cross this street?
Può aiutarmi pwo a·yoo·tar·mee
ad attraversare la strada? a·da·tra·ver·sa·re la stra·da

signs

Riservato	ree·ser·va·to ai	**Reserved for**
ai Disabili	dee·za·bee·lee	**the Disabled**

disabled travellers

87

How wide is the entrance?
Quant'è larga l'entrata?   kwan·te lar·ga len·tra·ta

Is there a lift?
C'è un ascensore?   che oo·na·shen·so·re

How many steps are there?
Quanti gradini ci sono?   kwan·tee gra·dee·nee chee so·no

Is there somewhere I can sit down?
C'è un posto dove sedersi?   che oon pos·to do·ve se·der·see

Could you call me a disabled taxi please?
Può chiamarmi un tassì   pwo kya·mar·mee oon ta·see
per i disabili?   per ee dee·za·bee·lee

access for the disabled	*accesso* m *per i disabili*	a·che·so per ee dee·za·bee·lee
Braille library	*biblioteca* f *braille*	bee·blyo·te·ka bray
disabled person	*disabile* m&f	dee·za·bee·le
guide dog	*cane* m *guida*	ka·ne gwee·da
ramp	*rampa* f	ram·pa
space (to move around)	*spazio* m	spa·tsyo
wheelchair	*sedia* f *a rotelle*	se·dya a ro·te·le

Is there a/an ...?	C'è ...?	che ...
baby change room	un bagno con fasciatoio	oon ba·nyo kon fa·sha·to·yo
child-minding service	un servizio di babysitter	oon ser·vee·tsyo dee be·bee·see·ter
children's menu	un menù per bambini	oon me·noo per bam·bee·nee
creche	un asilo nido	oo·na·see·lo nee·do
(English-speaking) babysitter	un/una babysitter (che parli inglese) m/f	oon/oo·na be·bee·see·ter (ke par·lee een·gle·ze)
family discount	uno sconto per famiglia	oo·no skon·to per fa·mee·lya
highchair	un seggiolone per bambini	oon se·jo·lo·ne per bam·bee·nee
park	un parco	oon par·ko
playground	un parco giochi	oon par·ko jo·kee
nearby	da queste parti	da kwe·ste par·tee
theme park	un parco a tema	oon par·ko a te·ma
toyshop	un negozio di giocattoli	oon ne·go·tsyo dee jo·ka·to·lee
I need a ...	Ho bisogno di ...	o bee·zo·nyo dee ...
baby seat	un seggiolino per bambini	oon se·jo·lee·no per bam·bee·nee
booster seat	un seggiolino di di sicurezza	oon se·jo·lee·no dee see·koo·re·tsa
potty	un vasino	oon va·zee·no
stroller	un passeggino	oon pa·se·jee·no

Do you mind if I breast-feed here?

Le dispiace se allatto il/la bimbo/a qui? m/f   le dees·pya·che se a·la·to eel/la beem·bo/a kwee

Are children allowed?
I bambini sono   ee bam·*bee*·nee *so*·no
ammessi?   a·*me*·see

Is this suitable for (two)-year-old children?
Questo è adatto per   *kwe*·sto e a·*da*·to per
bambini di (due)   bam·*bee*·nee dee (*doo*·e)
anni?   a·nee

kids' talk

When's your birthday?
Quand'è il tuo   kwan·*de* eel *too*·o
compleanno?   kom·ple·*a*·no

Do you go to school or to kindergarten?
Vai a scuola o all'asilo?   vai a *skwo*·la o a·la·*zee*·lo

What grade are you in?
Quale classe fai?   *kwa*·le *kla*·se fai

Do you like school?
Ti piace la scuola?   tee *pya*·che la *skwo*·la

Do you like sport?
Ti piace lo sport?   tee *pya*·che lo sport

What do you do after school?
Cosa fai dopo la scuola?   *ko*·za fai *do*·po la *skwo*·la

Do you learn English?
Stai imparando l'inglese?   stai eem·pa·*ran*·do leen·*gle*·ze

Do you have a pet at home?
Hai un animale   ai oon a·nee·*ma*·le
domestico a casa?   do·*mes*·tee·ko a *ka*·za

Do you want to play a game?
Vuoi giocare?   vwoy jo·*ka*·re

Show me how to play.
Fammi vedere come si   *fa*·mee ve·*de*·re *ko*·me see
gioca.   *jo*·ka

You're good at this game!
Sei bravo/a in questo   say *bra*·vo/a een *kwe*·sto
gioco! m/f   *jo*·ko

SOCIAL > meeting people
fare conoscenze

basics

l'essenziale

2A	Yes.	*Sì.*	see
2B	No.	*No.*	no
2C	Please.	*Per favore.*	per fa·vo·re
2D	Thank you. (very much)	*Grazie (mille).*	gra·tsye (mee·le)
2E	You're welcome.	*Prego.*	pre·go
2F	Sorry.	*Mi dispiace.*	mee dees·pya·che

2G Excuse me. (for attention or apology)
Mi scusi. pol — mee *skoo*·zee
Scusami. inf — *skoo*·za·mee

Excuse me. (when squeezing past someone)
Permesso. — per·*me*·so

greetings

i saluti

Although *ciao* is a common greeting, it's best not to use it when addressing strangers. Also note that in Italy the word *buonasera* (good evening) may be heard any time from early afternoon onwards.

47A	Hello.	*Buongiorno/Salve.* pol	bwon·*jor*·no/*sal*·ve
	Hi.	*Ciao.* inf	chow
	Good day.	*Buongiorno.*	bwon·*jor*·no
	Good morning.	*Buongiorno.*	bwon·*jor*·no
	Good afternoon.	*Buongiorno.*	bwon·*jor*·no
	Good evening.	*Buonasera.*	bwo·na·*se*·ra
	Good night.	*Buonanotte.*	bwo·na·*no*·te
	See you.	*Ci vediamo.*	chee ve·*dya*·mo
47B	See you later.	*A più tardi.*	a pyoo *tar*·dee
47C	Goodbye.	*Arrivederci.* pol	a·ree·ve·*der*·chee
	Bye.	*Ciao.* inf	chow

47D How are you?

Come sta? pol	ko·me sta
Come stai? inf	ko·me stai
Come state? pl pol&inf	ko·me sta·te

47E Good, thanks.

| Bene, grazie. | be·ne gra·tsye |

And you?

| E Lei/tu? pol/inf | e lay/too |

What's your name?

| 48A Come si chiama? pol | ko·me see kya·ma |
| 48B Come ti chiami? inf | ko·me tee kya·mee |

48C My name is ...

| Mi chiamo ... | mee kya·mo ... |

I'd like to introduce you to ...

| Le/Ti presento ... pol/inf | le/tee pre·zen·to ... |

48D I'm pleased to meet you.

| Piacere. | pya·che·re |

getting friendly

Italian has two forms for the singular 'you'. With family, friends, children or peers use the informal form *tu*. When addressing strangers, older people, or people whom you've just met, use the polite form *Lei*. When your newly-made friends feel it's time to swap to the more informal forms they might suggest:

Let's use the *tu* form.

| Diamoci del tu. | dya·mo·chee del too |

See also **pronouns** in the **a–z phrasebuilder**.

titles & addressing people

Italians will greatly appreciate your efforts to try to speak their language and you'll leave an even better impression if you use the correct titles and forms of address. So when in Rome ...

49A	Mr/Sir	*Signore*	see·*nyo*·re
49B	Mrs/Madam	*Signora*	see·*nyo*·ra
49C	Miss/Ms	*Signorina*	see·nyo·*ree*·na

Doctor (anyone with a university degree)
    Dottore/Dottoressa m/f   do·*to*·re/do·to·*re*·sa

Professor (high-school teacher or university lecturer)
    Professore/Professoressa m/f   pro·fe·*so*·re/pro·fe·so·*re*·sa

Director or Manager (anybody that runs anything)
    Direttore/Direttrice m/f   dee·re·*to*·re/dee·re·*tree*·che

making conversation

Nice weather, isn't it?
    Fa bel tempo, no?   fa bel *tem*·po no

How did (Juventus) go?
    Cos'ha fatto (la Juve)?   *ko*·za *fa*·to (la *yoo*·ve)

Do you live here?
    Lei è di qui? pol   lay e dee kwee
    Tu sei di qui? inf   too say dee kwee

Where are you going?
    Dove va/vai? pol/inf   *do*·ve va/vai

What are you doing?
    Che fa/fai? pol/inf   ke fa/fai

Are you waiting (for a bus)?
    Aspetta/Aspetti   as·*pe*·ta/as·*pe*·tee
    (un autobus)? pol/inf   (oo·*now*·to·boos)

What's this called?
Come si chiama questo?   ko·me see *kya*·ma *kwe*·sto

That's (beautiful), isn't it!
È (bello/a), no? m/f   e (*be*·lo/a) no?

50A **This is my son.**
Le/Ti presento mio   le/tee pre·*zen*·to *mee*·o
figlio. pol/inf   *fee*·lyo

50B **This is my daughter.**
Le/Ti presento mia   le/tee pre·*zen*·to *mee*·a
figlia. pol/inf   *fee*·lya

50C **This is my friend.**
Le/Ti presento il mio   le/tee pre·*zen*·to eel *mee*·o
amico. pol/inf m   a·*mee*·ko

Le/Ti presento la mia   le/tee pre·*zen*·to la *mee*·a
amica. pol/inf f   a·*mee*·ka

50D **This is my husband.**
Le/Ti presento mio   le/tee pre·*zen*·to *mee*·o
marito. pol/inf   ma·*ree*·to

50E **This is my wife.**
Le/Ti presento mia   le/tee pre·*zen*·to *mee*·a
moglie. pol/inf   *mo*·lye

Are you here on holiday?
È/Sei qui in vacanza? pol/inf   e/say kwee een va·*kan*·tsa

How long are you here for?
Quanto tempo si fermerà? pol   *kwan*·to *tem*·po see fer·me·*ra*
Quanto tempo ti fermerai? inf   *kwan*·to *tem*·po tee fer·me·*rai*

local talk		
Hey!	*Uei!*	way
What's up?	*Cosa mi racconta/*	*ko*·za mee ra·*kon*·ta/
	racconti? pol/inf	ra·*kon*·tee
What's the matter?	*Cosa c'è?*	*ko*·za che
Everything OK?	*Tutto a posto?*	*too*·ta *pos*·to
It's/I'm OK.	*Va/Sto bene.*	va/sto *be*·ne
Great!	*Fantastico!*	fan·*tas*·tee·ko
No problem.	*Non c'è problema.*	non che pro·*ble*·ma
Sure.	*Certo.*	*cher*·to
Maybe.	*Forse.*	*for*·se
No way!	*Assolutamente no!*	a·so·loo·ta·*men*·te no

I'm here ...	Sono qui ...	so·no kwee ...
for a holiday	in vacanza	een va·kan·tsa
on business	per affari	per a·fa·ree
to study	per motivi di studio	per mo·tee·vee dee stoo·dyo
with my family	con la mia famiglia	kon la mee·a fa·mee·lya
with my partner	con il mio compagno m	kon eel mee·o kom·pa·nyo
	con la mia compagna f	kon la mee·a kom·pa·nya

nationalities

le nazionalità

51A **Where are you from?**
Da dove viene/vieni? pol/inf   da do·ve vye·ne/vye·nee

51B **I'm from Singapore.**
Vengo da Singapore.   ven·go da seen·ga·po·re

I'm from ...	Vengo ...	ven·go ...
England	dall'Inghilterra	da·leen·geel·te·ra
New Zealand	dalla Nuova Zelanda	da·la nwo·va ze·lan·da
Switzerland	dalla Svizzera	da·la zvee·tse·ra
the US	dagli Stati Uniti	da·lyee sta·tee oo·nee·tee

For more countries, see the **dictionary**.

age

età

How old ...?	Quanti anni ...?	kwan·tee a·nee ...
is your son	ha Suo/tuo figlio pol/inf	a soo·o/too·o fee·lyo
is your daughter	ha Sua/tua figlia pol/inf	a soo·a/too·a fee·lya

51C How old are you?
Quanti anni ha/hai? pol/inf   kwan·tee a·nee a/ai

51D I'm (25) years old.
Ho (venticinque) anni.   o (ven·tee·cheen·kwe) a·nee

He's/She's ... years old.
Ha ... anni.   a ... a·nee

For your age, see **numbers**, page 29.

occupations & studies

i mestieri & gli studi

What's your occupation?
Che lavoro fa/fai? pol/inf   ke la·vo·ro fa/fai

I'm a/an ...	Sono ...	so·no ...
manual worker	manovale m&f	ma·no·va·le
office worker	impiegato/a m/f	eem·pye·ga·to/a
tradesperson	operaio/a m/f	o·pe·ra·yo/a
I work in ...	Lavoro nel campo ...	la·vo·ro nel kam·po ...
administration	dell'amministrazione	de·la·mee·nee·stra·tsyo·ne
public relations	delle relazioni pubbliche	de·le re·la·tsyo·nee poo·blee·ke
retail	della vendità al minuto	de·la ven·dee·ta al mee·noo·to
I'm ...	Sono ...	so·no ...
retired	pensionato/a m/f	pen·syo·na·to/a
unemployed	disoccupato/a m/f	dee·zo·koo·pa·to/a

Che vuoi?
ke vwoy
What do you want?

Chi se ne frega?
kee se ne fre·ga
Who gives a damn?

Va' al diavolo!
va al dya·vo·lo
Go to hell!

Disgraziato!
dees·gra·tsee·a·to
You're a disgrace!

È delizioso!
e de·lee·tsyo·zo
It's delicious!

Che rottura di palle!
ke ro·too·ra dee pa·le
You're breaking my balls!

I'm self-employed.
    Lavoro in proprio.   la·vo·ro een pro·pryo

What are you studying?
    Cosa studia/studi? pol/inf   ko·za stoo·dya/stoo·dee

I'm studying ...	*Sto studiando ...*	sto stoo·dyan·do ...
arts/humanities	*lettere*	le·te·re
business	*commercio*	ko·mer·cho
engineering	*ingegneria*	een·je·nye·ree·a

For more occupations and studies, see the **dictionary**.

family

la famiglia

Do you have (children)?
    Ha/Hai (bambini)? pol/inf   a/ai (bam·bee·nee)
I have (a partner).
    Ho (un/una compagno/a). m/f   o (oon/oo·na kom·pa·nyo/a)
This is (my mother).
    Le/Ti presento   le/tee pre·zen·to
    (mia madre). pol/inf   (mee·a ma·dre)

---

in the mouth of the wolf

An Italian will typically wish you good luck with the expression *In bocca al lupo!*, meaning 'In the mouth of the wolf!'. Make sure your answer is *Crepi!* (Die!) to ward off bad luck.

Break a leg!
    In bocca al lupo!   een bo·ka·loo·po
Response:
    Crepi!   kre·pee

Do you live with (your family)?

Abita con (la Sua famiglia)? pol	a·bee·ta kon (la *soo*·a fa·*mee*·lya)
Abiti con (la tua famiglia)? inf	a·bee·tee kon (la *too*·a fa·*mee*·lya)

I live with (my parents).

Abito con (i miei genitori).	a·bee·to kon (ee myay je·nee·*to*·ree)

Are you married?

52A	*È sposato?* m pol	e spo·*za*·to
52B	*È sposata?* f pol	e spo·*za*·ta
52C	*Sei sposato?* m inf	say spo·*za*·to
52D	*Sei sposata?* f inf	say spo·*za*·ta

I live with someone.

Convivo.	kon·*vee*·vo

I'm separated.

Sono separato/a. m/f	*so*·no se·pa·*ra*·to/a

52E	I'm married.	*Sono sposato.* m	*so*·no spo·*za*·to
52F	I'm married.	*Sono sposata.* f	*so*·no spo·*za*·ta
52G	I'm married.	*Sono single.*	*so*·no *sin*·gle

For more kinship terms, see the **dictionary**.

body language

Italians are emotionally demonstrative so expect to see lots of cheek kissing among acquaintances, embraces between men who are good friends and lingering handshakes. Italian men may walk along arm-in-arm too, as may Italian women. Pushing and shoving in busy places is not considered rude, so don't be offended by it. Try to hold your ground amidst the scrimmage.

If you don't want to tread on any toes, be aware that respectful behaviour is expected in churches. Women should ideally cover their heads and avoid exposing too much flesh – wearing shorts or skimpy tops is considered disrespectful.

farewells

Tomorrow is my last day here.
Domani è il mio   do·*ma*·nee e eel *mee*·o
ultimo giorno qui.   ool·tee·mo *jor*·no kwee

53A **What's your address?**
Qual'è il tuo indirizzo?   kwa·*le* eel *too*·o een·dee·*ree*·tso

53B **What's your email address?**
Qual'è il tuo indirizzo   kwa·*le* eel *too*·o een·dee·*ree*·tso
di email?   dee e·mayl

53C **Here's my address.**
Ecco il mio indirizzo.   e·ko eel *mee*·o een·dee·*ree*·tso

53D **Here's my email address.**
Ecco il mio indirizzo   e·ko eel *mee*·o een·dee·*ree*·tso
di email.   dee e·mayl

Here's my ...	*Ecco il mio ...*	e·ko eel *mee*·o ...
What's your ...?	*Qual'è il tuo ...?*	kwa·*le* eel *too*·o ...
fax number	*numero di fax*	*noo*·me·ro dee faks
mobile number	*numero di*	*noo*·me·ro dee
	cellulare	che·loo·*la*·re
work number	*numero di*	*noo*·me·ro dee
	lavoro	la·*vo*·ro

If you ever visit	*Caso mai venissi*	*ka*·zo mai ve·*nee*·see
(Scotland) ...	*in (Scozia) ...*	een (*sko*·tsya) ...
come and visit us	*vieni a*	*vye*·ne a
	trovarci	tro·*var*·chee
you can stay	*puoi stare da me*	pwoy *sta*·re da me
with me		

It's been great meeting you.
È stato veramente un   e *sta*·to ve·ra·*men*·te oon
piacere conoscerti.   pya·*che*·re ko·*no*·sher·tee

Keep in touch!
Teniamoci in contatto!   te·*nya*·mo·chee een kon·*ta*·to

common interests

interessi comuni

What do you do in your spare time?
*Cosa fai nel tuo
tempo libero?*
ko·za fai nel *too*·o
tem·po *lee*·be·ro

54A Do you like ...?	*Ti piace ...?* sg	tee *pya*·che ...
54B Do you like ...?	*Ti piacciono ...?* pl	tee *pya*·cho·no ...
54C I like ...	*Mi piace ...* sg	mee *pya*·che ...
54D I like ...	*Mi piacciono ...* pl	mee *pya*·cho·no ...
54E I don't like ...	*Non mi piace ...* sg	non mee *pya*·che ...
54F I don't like ...	*Non mi piacciono ...* pl	non mee *pya*·cho·no ...
card games	*i giochi* pl *di carte*	ee *jo*·kee dee *kar*·te
cooking	*cucinare* sg	koo·chee·*na*·re
drawing	*disegnare* sg	dee·se·*nya*·re
films	*i film* pl	ee feelm
socialising	*socializzare* sg	so·cha·lee·*dza*·re

For more hobbies and types of sports, see **sports**, page 127, and the **dictionary**.

---

like it or not

In Italian, in order to say you like something, you say *mi piace* (lit: me it-pleases). If it's plural, use *mi piacciono* (lit: me they-please):

I like this band.
*Mi piace questo
gruppo.*
mee *pya*·che *kwe*·sto
groo·po

I like soap operas.
*Mi piacciono
le telenovelle.*
mee *pya*·cho·no
le te·le·no·*ve*·le

music

Do you like to ...?	Ti piace ...?	tee *pya*·che ...
dance	*ballare*	ba·*la*·re
go to concerts	*andare ai concerti*	an·*da*·re ai kon·*cher*·tee
listen to music	*ascoltare la musica*	as·kol·*ta*·re la *moo*·zee·ka
play an instrument	*suonare uno strumento*	swo·*na*·re oo·no stroo·*men*·to
sing	*cantare*	kan·*ta*·re

What bands do you like?
Quali gruppi   kwa·lee groo·pee
ti piacciono?   tee *pya*·cho·no

What music do you like?
Quale tipo di   kwa·le *tee*·po dee
musica ti piace?   moo·zee·ka tee *pya*·che

classical music	*musica* f *classica*	la *moo*·zee·ka *kla*·see·ka
electronic music	*musica* f *elettronica*	la *moo*·zee·ka e·le·*tro*·nee·ka
jazz	*musica* f *jazz*	*moo*·zee·ka jaz
metal	*musica* f *heavy metal*	*moo*·zee·ka *he*·vee *me*·tal
pop	*musica* f *pop*	*moo*·zee·ka pop
punk	*musica* f *punk*	*moo*·zee·ka punk
rock	*musica* f *rock*	*moo*·zee·ka rok
R&B	*rhythm and blues* m	reedem ent blooz
traditional music	*musica* f *tradizionale*	*moo*·zee·ka tra·dee·tsyo·*na*·le
world music	*musica* f *etnica*	*moo*·zee·ka *et*·nee·ka

Planning to go to a concert? See **buying tickets**, page 38 and **going out**, page 109.

cinema & theatre

I feel like going to a ...	*Ho voglia d'andare a ...*	o *vo*·lya dan·*da*·re a ...
ballet	*un balletto*	oon ba·*le*·to
comedy	*una commedia comica*	*oo*·na ko·*me*·dya *ko*·mee·ka
film	*vedere un film*	ve·*de*·re oon feelm
play	*teatro*	te·*a*·tro

What's showing at the cinema/theatre tonight?
Cosa danno al cinema/ teatro stasera?
ko·za *da*·no al *chee*·ne·ma/ te·a·tro sta·*se*·ra

Is it in English/Italian?
È in inglese/italiano?
e een een·*gle*·ze/ee·ta·*lya*·no

Does it have subtitles?
Ci sono i sottotitoli?
chee *so*·no ee so·to·*tee*·to·lee

Have you seen ...?
Hai visto ...?
ai *vee*·sto ...

Who's in it?
Chi sono i protagonisti?
kee *so*·no ee pro·ta·go·*nee*·stee

It stars ...
Il/La protagonista principale è ... m/f
eel/la pro·ta·go·*nee*·sta preen·chee·*pa*·le e ...

Did you like (the film)?
Ti è piaciuto (il film)?
tee e pya·*choo*·to eel feelm

I thought it was ...	*L'ho trovato/a ...* m/f	lo tro·*va*·to/a ...
excellent	*ottimo/a* m/f	*o*·tee·mo/a
long	*lungo/a* m/f	*loon*·go/a
OK	*passabile*	pa·*sa*·bee·le

I (don't) like ...	(Non) Mi piacciono ...	(non) mee pya·cho·no ...
action movies	i film d'azione	ee feelm da·tsyo·ne
animated films	i film animati	ee feelm a·nee·ma·tee
black comedy	i film tragicomici	ee feelm tra·jee·ko·mee·chee
comedies	le commedie comiche	le ko·me·dye ko·mee·ke
documentaries	i documentari	ee do·koo·men·ta·ree
drama	i film drammatici	ee feelm dra·ma·tee·chee
film noir	i film noir	ee feelm nwar
horror movies	i film d'orrore	ee feelm do·ro·re
period dramas	i drammi d'ambiente	ee dra·mee dam·byen·te
sci-fi	i film di fantascienza	ee feelm dee fan·ta·shen·tsa
short films	i film corti	ee feelm kor·tee
thrillers	i gialli	ee ja·lee
war movies	i film di guerra	ee feelm dee gwe·ra

feelings

i sentimenti

55A	Are you cold?	*Ha freddo?* pol	a fre·do
55B	Are you cold?	*Hai freddo?* inf	ai fre·do
55C	I'm cold.	*Ho freddo.*	o fre·do
55D	I'm not cold.	*Non ho freddo.*	non o fre·do
56A	Are you hot?	*Ha caldo?* pol	a kal·do
56B	Are you hot?	*Hai caldo?* inf	ai kal·do
56C	I'm hot.	*Ho caldo.*	o kal·do
56D	I'm not hot.	*Non ho caldo.*	non o kal·do
57A	Are you hungry?	*Ha fame?* pol	a fa·me
57B	Are you hungry?	*Hai fame?* inf	ai fa·me
57C	I'm hungry.	*Ho fame.*	o fa·me
57D	I'm not hungry.	*Non ho fame.*	non o fa·me
58A	Are you thirsty?	*Ha sete?* pol	a se·te
58B	Are you thirsty?	*Hai sete?* inf	ai se·te
58C	I'm thirsty.	*Ho sete.*	o se·te
58D	I'm not thirsty.	*Non ho sete.*	non o se·te
59A	Are you tired?	*Ha sonno?* pol	a so·no
59B	Are you tired?	*Hai sonno?* inf	ai so·no
59C	I'm tired.	*Ho sonno.*	o so·no
59D	I'm not tired.	*Non ho sonno.*	non o so·no
60A	Are you OK?	*Va tutto bene?*	va *tut*·to *be*·ne
60B	I'm not OK.	*Non va tutto bene.*	non va *tut*·to *be*·ne
60C	I'm OK.	*Va tutto bene.*	va *tut*·to *be*·ne

opinions

le opinioni

Did you like it?
   Ti è piaciuto/a? m/f   tee e pya·*choo*·to/a

What did you think of it?
   Che cosa ne pensi?   ke *ko*·za ne *pen*·see

It's ...	È ...	e ...
bizarre	*bizzarro/a* m/f	bee·*dza*·ro/a
boring	*noioso/a* m/f	no·*yo*·zo/a
great	*ottimo/a* m/f	o·*tee*·mo/a
interesting	*interessante*	een·te·re·*san*·te
OK	*passabile*	pa·*sa*·bee·le
weird	*strano/a* m/f	*stra*·no/a

mixed emotions

I'm a little sad.
Sono un po' triste.   so·no oon po *tree*·ste

I'm very content.
Sono molto contento/a. m/f   so·no *mol*·to kon·*ten*·to/a

I feel extremely lucky.
Mi sento   mee *sen*·to
fortunatissimo/a. m/f   for·too·na·*tee*·see·mo/a

politics & social issues

le questioni politiche & sociali

Italians don't shy away from discussing political and social issues and might be interested in knowing your opinion on all kinds of topics. Even *il campionato*, 'the soccer', takes on the dimensions of a serious political issue.

Who do you vote for?
Per chi vota Lei? pol	per kee *vo*·ta lay
Per chi voti? inf	per kee *vo*·tee

I support	*Sono per*	so·no per
the ... party.	*il partito ...*	eel par·*tee*·to ...
communist	*comunista*	ko·moo·*nee*·sta
conservative	*conservatore*	kon·ser·va·*to*·re
green	*verde*	*ver*·de
liberal (progressive)	*liberale*	lee·be·*ra*·le
labour	*laburista*	la·boo·*ree*·sta
socialist	*socialista*	so·cha·*lee*·sta

Do you agree with it?
È/Sei d'accordo con ...? pol/inf   e/say da·*kor*·do kon ...

I (don't) agree with ...
(Non) Sono d'accordo con ...   (non) *so*·no da·*kor*·do kon ...

Are you against ... ?
È/Sei contro ...? pol/inf   e/say *kon*·tro ...

Are you in favour of ...?
È/Sei a favore di ...? pol/inf   e/say a fa·*vo*·re dee ...

How do people feel about ...?
Cosa pensa la gente di ...?   ko·za *pen*·sa la *jen*·te dee ...

abortion	*aborto* m	a·*bor*·to
animal rights	*diritti* m pl	dee·*ree*·tee
	animali	a·nee·*ma*·lee
crime	*criminalità* f	kree·mee·na·lee·*ta*
discrimination	*discriminazione* f	dees·kree·mee·na·*tsyo*·ne
drugs	*droghe* f pl	*dro*·ge
the economy	*economia* f	e·ko·no·*mee*·a
education	*istruzione* f	ees·troo·*tsyo*·ne
the environment	*ambiente* m	am·*byen*·te
equal opportunity	*pari opportunità* f	pa·ree o·por·too·nee·*ta*
euthanasia	*eutanasia* f	e·oo·ta·na·*zee*·a
globalisation	*globalizzazione* f	glo·ba·lee·dza·*tsyo*·ne
human rights	*diritti* m pl *umani*	dee·*ree*·tee oo·*ma*·nee
immigration	*immigrazione* f	ee·mee·gra·*tsyo*·ne
inequality	*ineguaglianza* f	ee·ne·gwa·*lyan*·tsa
party politics	*politica* f	po·*lee*·tee·ka
	di partito	dee par·*tee*·to
privatisation	*privatizzazione* f	pree·va·tee·dza·*tsyo*·ne
racism	*razzismo* m	ra·*tseez*·mo
refugees	*profughi* m pl	*pro*·foo·gee
sexism	*sessismo* m	se·*seez*·mo
social welfare	*assistenza* f *sociale*	a·sees·*ten*·tsa so·*cha*·le
terrorism	*terrorismo* m	te·ro·*reez*·mo
unemployment	*disoccupazione* f	dee·zo·koo·pa·*tsyo*·ne

the environment

Is there a/an (environmental) problem here?

C'è un problema		che oon pro·*ble*·ma
(ambientale) qui?		(am·byen·*ta*·le) kwee

biodegradable	*biodegradabile*	bee·o·de·gra·*da*·bee·le
conservation	*conservazione* f	kon·ser·va·*tsyo*·ne
deforestation	*disboscamento* m	dees·bos·ka·*men*·to
drought	*siccità* f	see·chee·*ta*
hydroelectricity	*energia* f	e·ner·*jee*·a
	idroelettrica	ee·dro·e·*le*·tree·ka
irrigation	*irrigazione* f	ee·ree·ga·*tsyo*·ne
ozone layer	*strato* m *d'ozono*	*stra*·to do·*dzo*·no
pesticides	*pesticidi* m pl	pes·tee·*chee*·dee
pollution	*inquinamento* m	een·kwee·na·*men*·to
recycling	*programma* m	pro·*gra*·ma
programme	*di riciclaggio*	dee ree·chee·*kla*·jo
toxic waste	*rifiuti* m pl	ree·*fyoo*·tee
	tossici	*to*·see·chee

Is this a	*È ... protetto/a*	e ... pro·*te*·to/a
protected ...?	*questo/a?* m/f	*kwe*·sto/a
forest	*una foresta* f	oo·na fo·*res*·ta
park	*un parco* m	oon *par*·ko
species	*una specie* f	oo·na *spe*·che

local talk

No way!	*Per niente!*	per *nyen*·te
Shut up!	*Taci!*	*ta*·chee
That's (not) true!	*(Non) È vero!*	(non) e *ve*·ro
Unbelievable!	*Incredibile!*	een·kre·*dee*·bee·le
Yeah, right!	*Figuriamoci!*	fee·goo·*rya*·mo·chee
You're kidding!	*Scherzi!*	*sker*·tsee
If only!	*Magari!*	ma·*ga*·ree

where to go

dove andare

What's there to do in the evenings?
Cosa si fa di sera? ko·za see fa dee se·ra

What's on ...?	*Che c'è in programma ...?*	ke che een pro·gra·ma ...
locally	*in zona*	een dzo·na
this weekend	*questo finesettimana*	kwe·sto fee·ne·se·tee·ma·na
today	*oggi*	o·jee
tonight	*stasera*	sta·se·ra

61A Where can I find ...?
Dov'è ...? do·ve ...

61B Where can I find a gay venue?
Dov'è un locale gay? do·ve oon lo·ka·le ge

61C Where can I find a pub?
Dov'è un pub? do·ve oon pab

Where are the ...?	*Dove sono ...?*	do·ve so·no ...
bars	*dei locali*	day lo·ka·lee
cafes	*dei bar*	day bar
clubs	*dei clubs*	day kloobs
places to eat	*posti in cui mangiare*	pos·tee een koo·ee man·ja·re
Is there a local ... guide?	*C'è una guida ... in questa città?*	che oo·na gwee·da ... een kwe·sta chee·ta
entertainment	*agli spettacoli*	a·lyee spe·ta·ko·lee
film	*ai film*	ai feelm

What's the cover charge?
   Quant'è l'ingresso?   kwan·*te* leen·*gre*·so

It's free.
   È gratuito.   e gra·*too*·ee·to

it's not what it seems

Looking for a place to go in the wee hours? While you can have a *Nastro Azzurro* in a *birreria* and show off your moves in a *discoteca*, you'll be hard-pressed finding an Italian *bar* open after midnight:

bar m – is more like a snack bar where you can get coffee, tea and soft drinks but also alcoholic drinks, along with croissants, rolls and sandwiches. They open early in the morning and close somewhere between 10pm and midnight, depending on their location. They're mainly used by people dropping in for a quick coffee, consumed while standing at the counter – it costs more to sit down. Office workers tend to pop out or send out for a coffee from a *bar*.

osteria f – this is more of a sit-down eating place where people have wine with their meal.

pub m – a new and popular addition to the Italian night scene, inspired by English and Irish pubs. They usually stay open until around 3am.

birreria f – has a pub-like atmosphere but specialises in beer.

nite m – denotes a more elegant nightclub.

nightclub m – this English term is used and will be readily understood, but *il nite* is more common.

locale notturno m – this is the generic term for every type of night spot.

discoteca m – the most commonly frequented night spot for the under-30 age group.

I feel like going to ...	Ho voglia d'andare ...	o vo·lya dan·da·re ...
a bar	a un locale	a oon lo·ka·le
a cafe	a un bar	a oon bar
a coffee bar	a un caffè	a oon ka·fe
a nightclub	in un locale notturno	een oon lo·ka·le no·toor·no
a pub	a un pub	a oon pab

62A I feel like going to a concert.
Ho voglia d'andare a un concerto.
o vo·lya dan·da·re a oon kon·cher·to

62B I feel like going to the movies.
Ho voglia d'andare al cinema.
o vo·lya dan·da·re al chee·nee·ma

62C I feel like going to a party.
Ho voglia d'andare a una festa.
o vo·lya dan·da·re a oo·na fes·ta

62D I feel like going to the theatre.
Ho voglia d'andare al teatro. o vo·lya dan·da·re al te·a·tro

invitations

gli inviti

What are you doing ...?	Cosa fai/ fate ...? sg/pl	ko·za fai/ fa·te ...
this evening	stasera	sta·se·ra
this weekend	questo fine settimana	kwe·sto fee·ne se·tee·ma·na

Would you like to go (for a) ...?	Vuoi/Volete andare a ...? sg/pl	vwoy/vo·le·te an·da·re a ...
coffee	prendere un caffè	pren·de·re oon ka·fe
dancing	ballare	ba·la·re
drink	bere qualcosa	be·re kwal·ko·za
meal	mangiare qualcosa	man·ja·re kwal·ko·za
walk	fare una passeggiata	fa·re oo·na pa·se·ja·ta

My round.
Offro io. o·fro ee·o

Do you know a good restaurant?
Conosci/Conoscete un ko·*no*·shee/ko·*no*·she·te oon
buon ristorante? sg/pl bwon rees·to·*ran*·te

Do you want to come to a (jazz) concert with me?
Vuoi/Volete venire a vwoy/vo·*le*·te ve·*nee*·re a
un concerto (di oon kon·*cher*·to (dee
musica jazz)? sg/pl moo·zee·ka jaz)

We're having a party.
Facciamo una festa. fa·*chya*·mo oo·na *fes*·ta

You should come.
Dovresti/Dovreste dov·*res*·tee/dov·*res*·te
venire. sg/pl ve·*nee*·re

responding to invitations

come rispondere agli inviti

Sure!
Certo! *cher*·to

Yes, I'd love to.
Sì, mi piacerebbe. see mee pya·che·*re*·be

Where shall we go?
Dove andiamo? *do*·ve an·*dya*·mo

No, I'm afraid I can't.
No, temo di no. no *te*·mo dee no

What about tomorrow?
Domani che ne do·*ma*·nee ke ne
dici/dite? sg/pl *dee*·chee/*dee*·te

Sorry, I can't sing/dance.
Scusa. Non so *skoo*·za. non so
cantare/ballare. kan·*ta*·re/ba·*la*·re

arranging to meet

What time shall we meet?
A che ora ci vediamo?   a ke *o*·ra chee ve·*dya*·mo

Where will we meet?
Dove ci vediamo?   *do*·ve chee ve·*dya*·mo

I'll pick you up.
Ti/Vi vengo a prendere. sg/pl   tee/vee *ven*·go a *pren*·de·re

I'll be coming later. Where will you be?
Verrò più tardi.   ve·*ro* pyoo *tar*·dee.
Dove ti troverai? sg   *do*·ve tee tro·ve·*rai*
Dove vi troverete? pl   *do*·ve vee tro·ve·*re*·te

If I'm not there by (nine), don't wait for me.
Se non ci sono entro   se non chee *so*·no *en*·tro
(le nove), non aspettarmi.   (le *no*·ve) non as·pe·*tar*·mee

Let's meet at ...	*Incontriamoci ...*	een·kon·*trya*·mo·chee ...
(eight) o'clock	*alle (otto)*	a·le (*o*·to)
the entrance	*all'entrata*	a·len·*tra*·ta

OK!
D'accordo!　　　　　　　　　da·*kor*·do

I'll see you then.
Ci vediamo allora.　　　　　chee ve·*dya*·mo a·*lo*·ra

See you later.
A più tardi.　　　　　　　　a pyoo *tar*·dee

See you tomorrow.
A domani.　　　　　　　　　a do·*ma*·nee

I'm looking forward to it.
Non vedo l'ora.　　　　　　non *ve*·do *lo*·ra

Sorry I'm late.
Scusa. Sono in ritardo.　　*skoo*·za. *so*·no een ree·*tar*·do

Never mind.
Non importa.　　　　　　　non eem·*por*·ta

drugs

le droghe

I don't take drugs.
Non mi drogo.　　　　　　　non mee *dro*·go

I have ... occasionally.
Prendo ... ogni tanto.　　　*pren*·do ... o·nyee *tan*·to

Do you want to have a smoke?
Lo vuoi uno spinello?　　　lo vwoy *oo*·no spee·*ne*·lo

I'm high.
Sono stonato/a. m/f　　　　*so*·no sto·*na*·to/a

asking someone out

darsi appuntamenti

Would you like to do something (tonight)?
Vuoi fare qualcosa   vwoy *fa*·re kwal·*ko*·za
(stasera)?   (sta·*se*·ra)

Yes, I'd love to.
Sì, mi piacerebbe molto. see mee pya·che·*re*·be *mol*·to

No, I'm afraid I can't.
No, temo di no.   no *te*·mo dee no

Not if you were the last person on Earth!
Neanche se tu fossi   ne·*an*·ke se too *fo*·see
l'ultima persona   *lool*·tee·ma per·*so*·na
sulla terra!   *soo*·la *te*·ra

local talk

He/She gets around.
Si dà da fare.   see da da *fa*·re

Did you check out that guy/girl?
Hai adocchiato quello/a? ai a·do·*kya*·to *kwe*·lo/a

He's/She's a ...	È ...	e ...
babe	*un bel figo* m	oon bel *fee*·go
	una bella figa f	*oo*·na *be*·la *fee*·ga
bastard	*un bastardo*	oon bas·*tar*·do
bitch	*una cagna*	*oo*·na *ka*·nya
prick	*uno stronzo* m	*oo*·no *stron*·dzo
	una stronza f	*oo*·na *stron*·dza

pick-up lines

Would you like a drink?
Prendi qualcosa da bere?   pren·dee kwal·*ko*·za da *be*·re

Do you have a light?
Hai d'accendere?   ai da·*chen*·de·re

You're a fantastic dancer.
Balli benissimo.   ba·lee be·*nee*·see·mo

Shall we get some fresh air?
Andiamo a prendere un   an·*dya*·mo a *pren*·de·re oon
po' d'aria fresca?   po *da*·rya fres·ka

Can I take you for a ride (on my bike)?
Ti posso portare a fare   tee *po*·so por·*ta*·re a *fa*·re
un giro (in moto)?   oon *jee*·ro (een *mo*·to)

You have	*Hai ...*	ai ...
(a) beautiful ...		
body	*un bel fisico*	oon bel *fee*·zee·ko
eyes	*gli occhi belli*	lyee o·kee *be*·lee
hands	*le mani belle*	le *ma*·nee *be*·le
laugh	*un bel riso*	oon bel *ree*·zo
personality	*una bella*	oo·na *be*·la
	personalità	per·so·na·lee·*ta*
smile	*un bel sorriso*	oon bel so·*ree*·zo

Can I ...?	*Posso ...?*	*po*·so ...
dance with you	*ballare con te*	ba·*la*·re kon te
sit here	*sedermi qui*	se·*der*·mee kwee
take you home	*accompagnarti*	a·kom·pa·*nyar*·tee
	a casa	a *ka*·za

rejections

I'm here with my boyfriend.
*Sono qui con il mio
ragazzo.*
so·no kwee kon eel *mee*·o
ra·*ga*·tso

I'm here with my girlfriend.
*Sono qui con la mia
ragazza.*
so·no kwee kon la *mee*·a
ra·ga·tsa

Excuse me, I have to go now.
*Scusa. Adesso devo
andare.*
skoo·za. a·*de*·so de·vo
an·*da*·re

I'm sorry, but I don't feel like it.
*Mi dispiace ma non
ne ho voglia.*
mee dees·*pya*·che ma non
ne o *vo*·lya

Your ego is out of control.
*Il tuo ego è fuori
controllo.*
eel *too*·o e·go e *fwo*·ree
kon·*tro*·lo

I'm not interested.
Non mi interessa.
non mee een·te·*re*·sa

Leave me alone!
Lasciami in pace!
la·sha·mee een *pa*·che

Don't touch me!
Non mi toccare!
non mee to·*ka*·re

Let me through!
Lasciami passare!
la·sha·mee pa·*sa*·re

Get out of my face!
Levati dai piedi!
le·va·tee dai *pye*·dee

Fuck off!
Vaffanculo!
va·fan·*koo*·lo

---

mario or maria?

Throughout this book we have used the letters m or f to
indicate whether a word is masculine or feminine.
See also **gender** in the **a–z phrasebuilder**.

getting closer

You're very nice.
Sei molto simpatico/a. m/f   say mol·to seem·pa·tee·ko/a

You're great.
Sei fantastico/a. m/f   say fan·tas·tee·ko/a

Can I kiss you?
Ti posso baciare?   tee po·so ba·cha·re

Will you take me home?
Mi porti a casa?   mee por·tee a ka·za

Do you want to come inside for a while?
Vuoi entrare per un po'?   vwoy en·tra·re per oon po

sex

il sesso

I want to make love to you.
Voglio fare l'amore con te.   vo·lyo fa·re la·mo·re kon te

Do you have a condom?
Hai un preservativo?   ai oon pre·ser·va·tee·vo

I won't do it without protection.
Non lo farò senza   non lo fa·ro sen·tsa
protezione.   pro·te·tsyo·ne

I think we should stop now.
Penso che dovremmo   pen·so ke dov·re·mo
fermarci adesso.   fer·mar·chee a·de·so

Let's go to bed!
Andiamo a letto!   an·dya·mo a le·to

the birds and the bees

Be mindful of the word *finocchio*, which means both 'fennel' and 'queer' (homosexual). Likewise, *uccello* means 'bird' and 'dick'.

Kiss me.	Baciami.	ba·cha·mee
I want you.	Ti desidero.	tee de·see·de·ro
Do you like this?	Ti piace questo?	tee pya·che kwe·sto
I (don't) like that.	(Non) Mi piace quello.	(non) mee pya·che kwe·lo
Touch me here.	Toccami qui.	to·ka·mee kwee
Oh yeah!	Ah sì!	a see
Oh my god!	Oh dio mio!	o dee·o mee·o
Easy tiger!	Calma!	kal·ma
Come on!	Dai!	dai

harder	più forte	pyoo for·te
faster	più veloce	pyoo ve·lo·che
softer	più dolcemente	pyoo dol·che·men·te
slower	più lentamente	pyoo len·ta·men·te

I can't get it up. Sorry.
Non mi si raddrizza.   non mee see ra·dree·tsa.
Mi dispiace.   mee dees·pya·che

That was amazing.
È stato stupendo.   e sta·to stoo·pen·do

Can I stay over?
Posso restare la notte?   po·so res·ta·re la no·te

When can I see you again?
Quando possiamo   kwan·do po·sya·mo
rivederci?   ree·ve·der·chee

endearments

my love	amore mio	a·mo·re mee·o
my little fleshy thing	ciccino/a mio/a m/f	chee·chee·no/a mee·o/a
delicious one	delizia	de·lee·tsya
honey/sugar	dolcezza	dol·che·tsa
my joy	gioia mia	jo·ya mee·a
my darling	caro/a mio/a m/f	ka·ro/a mee·o/a
my little chook	pollastrello/a mio/a m/f	po·la·stre·lo/a mee·o/a
my treasure	tesoro mio	te·zo·ro mee·o

love

l'amore

I'm in love with you.
Sono innamorato/a di te. m/f   *so*·no ee·na·mo·*ra*·to/a dee te

I love you.
Ti amo.   tee *a*·mo

Do you love me?
Mi ami?   mee *a*·mee

I think we're good together.
Penso che stiamo   *pen*·so ke *stya*·mo
bene insieme.   *be*·ne een·*sye*·me

I want us to stay in touch.
Voglio che ci teniamo   *vo*·lyo ke chee te·*nya*·mo
in contatto.   een kon·*ta*·to

problems

i problemi

Are you seeing someone else?
Frequenti   fre·*kwen*·tee
qualcun'altro/a? m/f   kwal·koo·*nal*·tro/a

He's just a friend.
È solo un amico.   e *so*·lo oo·na·*mee*·ko

She's just a friend.
È solo un'amica.   e *so*·lo oo·na·*mee*·ka

I don't think it's working out.
Non credo che stia   non *kre*·do ke *stee*·a
funzionando fra noi due.   foon·tsyo·*nan*·do fra noy *doo*·e

We'll work it out.
Troveremo una soluzione.   tro·ve·*re*·mo *oo*·na so·loo·*tsyo*·ne

I never want to see you again.
Non voglio vederti mai più.   non *vo*·lyo ve·*der*·tee mai pyoo

I want to stay friends.
Voglio che restiamo amici.   *vo*·lyo ke res·*tya*·mo a·*mee*·chee

Italy is a paradise for art lovers and Italians are proud of the many treasures the country harbours. If art is your thing, you'll find plenty of people to talk to or to share your impressions with.

When's the gallery open?
Quando è aperta   kwan·do e a·*per*·ta
la galleria?   la ga·le·*ree*·a

When's the museum open?
Quando è aperto   kwan·do e a·*per*·to
il museo?   eel moo·*ze*·o

What kind of art are you interested in?
Che tipo di arte Le/ti   ke *tee*·po dee *ar*·te le/tee
interessa? pol/inf   een·te·*re*·sa

What do you think of ...?
Cosa ne pensa/   *ko*·za ne *pen*·sa/
pensi di ...? pol/inf   *pen*·see dee ...

It's a/an (futurist art) exhibition.
È una mostra di   e *oo*·na *mos*·tra dee
(arte futurista).   (*ar*·te foo·too·*ree*·sta)

I'm interested in ... art/architecture.	*Mi interessa l'arte/ l'architettura ...*	mee een·te·*re*·sa *lar*·te/ lar·kee·te·*too*·ra ...
baroque	*barocca*	ba·*ro*·ka
byzantine	*bizantina*	bee·dzan·*tee*·na
graphic	*grafica*	*gra*·fee·ka
impressionist	*impressionista*	eem·pre·syo·*nee*·sta
Gothic	*gotica*	*go*·tee·ka
modernist	*modernista*	mo·der·*nee*·sta
performance	*d'esibizione*	de·zee·bee·*tsyo*·ne
Renaissance	*rinascimentale*	ree·na·shee·men·*ta*·le
Romanesque	*romanica*	ro·*ma*·nee·ka

affresco m	a·*fres*·ko	fresco
arcata f	ar·*ka*·ta	series of arches
architrave m	ar·kee·*tra*·ve	lintel
arco m	*ar*·ko	arch
badia f	ba·*dee*·a	abbey
baldacchino m	bal·da·*kee*·no	canopy supported by columns over an altar
basilica f	ba·zee·lee·ka	in ancient Rome, an administration building • later a Christian church in the same style
battistero m	ba·tees·*te*·ro	baptistry
bottega f	bo·*te*·ga	(work)shop
contrafforte m	kon·tra·*for*·te	buttress
campanile m	kam·pa·*nee*·le	bell tower
cappella f	ka·*pe*·la	chapel • small room or altarpiece in a church
cattedrale f	ka·te·*dra*·le	cathedral
cenacolo m	che·*na*·ko·lo	supper room or refectory
chiesa f	*kye*·za	church
chiostro m	*kyos*·tro	cloister • covered walkway around a quadrangle
circo m	*cheer*·ko	oval or circular arena
cofano m	*ko*·fa·no	coffer • recessed panel in ceiling or vault
colonna f	ko·*lo*·na	column
colonnato m	ko·lo·*na*·to	a row of columns
cortile m	kor·*tee*·le	courtyard
cupola f	*koo*·po·la	dome (of cathedral)
cupolone m	koo·po·*lo*·ne	big dome
curia f	*koo*·rya	arcade of columns in a Venetian Byzantine palace
duomo m	*dwo*·mo	dome • cathedral
fascia f	*fa*·sha	frieze
fontana f	fon·*ta*·na	fountain
foro m	*fo*·ro	forum

fresco m	*fres*·ko	fresco
gargolla m	gar·*go*·la	gargoyle (carved creature, often a watersprout)
guglia f	*goo*·lya	spire
intarsio m	een·*tar*·syo	inlaid wood, marble or metal
intonaco m	een·*to*·na·ko	plaster surfacing of a wall
liagò m	lya·*go*	roofed terrace or enclosed balcony
loggia f	*lo*·ja	covered area on the side of a building • porch • small cottage garden
maestà f	ma·es·*ta*	Madonna and Child on a throne
navata f *centrale*	na·*va*·ta chen·*tra*·le	nave
pala f *d'altare*	*pa*·la dal·*ta*·re	altarpiece
palazzo m	pa·*la*·tso	large building
persiane f pl	per·*sya*·ne	louvre shutters
piazza f	*pya*·tsa	square
piazzale m	pya·*tsa*·le	large open square
pietà f	pye·*ta*	Virgin with dead Christ
ponte m	*pon*·te	bridge
portico m	*por*·tee·ko	covered walkway
putti m pl	*poo*·tee	cherubs
rilievo m	ree·*lye*·vo	relief
rocca f	*ro*·ka	fortress
sala f	*sa*·la	room or hall
sassi m pl	*sa*·see	houses carved out of rock
scale f pl	*ska*·le	stairs
scalinata f	ska·lee·*na*·ta	stairway
scavi m pl	*ska*·vee	excavations
terrazzo m	te·*ra*·tso	terrace • balcony
tondo m	*ton*·do	round painting
torre m	*to*·re	tower
trittico m	*tree*·tee·ko	triptych
vetrata f	ve·*tra*·ta	stained-glass window

art

123

artwork	*opera* f *d'arte*	o·pe·ra *dar*·te
curator	*conservatore/*	kon·ser·va·*to*·re/
	conservatrice m/f	kon·ser·va·*tree*·che
design	*disegno* m	dee·ze·nyo
engraving	*incisione* f	een·chee·*zyo*·ne
etching	*acquaforte* f	a·kwa·*for*·te
exhibition hall	*salone* m	sa·*lo*·ne
	d'esposizione	des·po·zee·*tsyo*·ne
installation	*installazione* f	een·sta·la·*tsyo*·ne
opening	*apertura* f	a·per·*too*·ra
painter	*pittore/pittrice* m/f	pee·*to*·re/pee·*tree*·che
painting (the art)	*pittura* f	pee·*too*·ra
painting (canvas)	*quadro* m	*kwa*·dro
period	*periodo* m	pe·*ree*·o·do
permanent	*collezione* f	ko·le·*tsyo*·ne
collection	*permanente*	per·ma·*nen*·te
print	*riproduzione* f	ree·pro·doo·*tsyo*·ne
sculptor	*scultore/*	skool·*to*·re/
	scultrice m/f	skool·*tree*·che
sculpture	*scultura* f	skool·*too*·ra
statue	*statua* f	*sta*·too·a
studio	*studio* m	*stoo*·dee·o
style	*stile* m	*stee*·le
tapestry	*tappezzeria* f	ta·pe·tse·*ree*·a
technique	*tecnica* f	*tek*·nee·ka

religion

la religione

What's your religion?
Di che religione è Lei? pol   dee ke re·lee·jo·ne e lay
Di che religione sei tu? inf   dee ke re·lee·jo·ne say too

I (don't) believe in God.
(Non) Credo in Dio.   (non) kre·do een dee·o

I'm (not) ...	*(Non) Sono ...*	(non) so·no ...
agnostic	*agnostico/a* m/f	a·nyos·tee·ko/a
atheist	*ateo/a* m/f	a·te·o/a
Buddhist	*buddista*	boo·dee·sta
Catholic	*cattolico/a* m/f	ka·to·lee·ko/a
Christian	*cristiano/a* m/f	krees·tya·no/a
Hindu	*indù*	een·doo
Jewish	*ebreo/a* m/f	e·bre·o/a
Muslim	*musulmano/a* m/f	moo·sool·ma·no/a
practising	*praticante*	pra·tee·kan·te
religious	*religioso/a* m/f	re·lee·jo·zo/a

I'd like to go to (the) ...	*Vorrei andare ...*	vo·ray an·da·re ...
church	*alla chiesa*	a·la kye·za
mosque	*alla moschea*	a·la mos·ke·a
synagogue	*alla sinagoga*	a·la see·na·go·ga
temple	*al tempio*	a·la tem·pyo

Can I ... here?	Posso ... qui?	po·so ... kwee
Where can I ...?	Dove posso ...?	do·ve po·so ...
attend mass	andare a messa	an·da·re a me·sa
go to church	andare in chiesa	an·da·re een kye·za
make confession	confessarmi	kon·fe·sar·mee
(in English)	(in inglese)	(een en·gle·ze)
pray	pregare	pre·ga·re
receive	ricevere la	ree·che·ve·re la
communion	comunione	ko·moo·nyo·ne

cultural differences

le differenze culturali

Is this a local or national custom?
È una tradizione   e oo·na tra·dee·tsyo·ne
locale o nazionale?   lo·ka·le o na·tsyo·na·le

I don't mind watching, but I'd rather not join in.
Non mi dispiace   non mee dees·pya·che
guardare ma preferisco   gwar·da·re ma pre·fe·rees·ko
non partecipare.   non par·te·chee·pa·re

I'll try it.
Lo proverò.   lo pro·ve·ro

I'm sorry, I didn't mean to do/say something wrong.
Mi dispiace, non   mee dees·pya·che non
volevo dire/fare   vo·le·vo dee·re/fa·re
qualcosa di sbagliato.   kwal·ko·za dee sba·lya·to

I'm sorry, it's against my ...	Mi dispiace, non è permesso dalla mia ...	mee dees·pya·che non e per·me·so da·la mee·a ...
beliefs	fede	fe·de
culture	cultura	kool·too·ra
religion	religione	re·lee·jo·ne

sporting interests

gli interessi sportivi

Do you like (sport)?
  Ti piace (lo sport)?   tee *pya*·che (lo sport)

Yes, very much.
  Sì, moltissimo.   see mol·*tee*·see·mo

Not really.
  Non molto.   non *mol*·to

I like watching it.
  Mi piace assistere.   mee *pya*·che a·*see*·ste·re

What sport do you play?
  Quale sport pratichi?   *kwa*·le sport *pra*·tee·kee

I play (soccer).
  Pratico (il calcio).   *pra*·tee·ko (eel *kal*·cho)

I follow (car racing).
  Seguo (l'automobilismo).   *se*·gwo (low·to·mo·bee·*leez*·mo)

For more sports, see the **dictionary**.

Who's your favourite sportsman?
  Chi è il tuo sportivo   kee e eel *too*·o spor·*tee*·vo
  preferito? m   pre·fe·*ree*·to

Who's your favourite sportswoman?
  Chi è la tua sportiva   kee e la *too*·a spor·*tee*·va
  preferita? f   pre·fe·*ree*·ta

Who's your favourite team?
  Qual'è la tua squadra   kwa·*le* la *too*·a *skwa*·dra
  preferita?   pre·fe·*ree*·ta

going to a game

Would you like to go to a game?
Ti piacerebbe andare
ad una partita?
tee pya·che·re·be an·da·re
a·doo·na par·tee·ta

Who are you supporting?
Per chi fai il tifo?
per kee fai eel tee·fo

Who's playing?
Chi gioca?
kee jo·ka

Who's winning?
Chi vince?
kee veen·che

How much time is left?
Quanto tempo manca?
kwan·to tem·po man·ka

What's the score?
Qual'è il punteggio?
kwa·le eel poon·te·jo

It's a draw.
Hanno pareggiato.
a·no pa·re·ja·to

The referee has disallowed it.
L'arbitro non l'ha
permesso.
lar·bee·tro non la
per·me·so

That was a ... game!	*Che partita ...!*	ke par·tee·ta ...
bad	*brutta*	broo·ta
boring	*noiosa*	no·yo·za
great	*fantastica*	fan·tas·tee·ka

sports talk

What a ...!	*Che ...!*	ke ...
goal	*gol*	gol
hit	*colpo*	kol·po
kick	*calcio*	kal·cho
pass	*passaggio*	pa·sa·jo
performance	*esecuzione*	e·se·koo·tsyo·ne

playing sport

Do you want to play?
Vuoi giocare?   vwoy jo·ka·re

Can I join in?
Posso giocare anch'io?   po·so jo·ka·re an·kee·o

Yes, that'd be great.
Sì, sarebbe bello.   see sa·re·be be·lo

I'm sorry, I can't.
Mi dispiace, non posso.   mee dees·pya·che non po·so

I have an injury.
Sono infortunato/a. m/f   so·no een·for·too·na·to/a

Where's the best place to jog around here?
Qual'è il miglior posto   kwa·le eel mee·lyor pos·to
per fare il footing   per fa·re eel foo·teeng
qui intorno?   kwee een·tor·no

Where's the nearest ...?	Dov'è ...?	do·ve ...
gym	*la palestra più vicina*	la pa·le·stra pyoo vee·chee·na
swimming pool	*la piscina più vicina*	la pee·shee·na pyoo vee·chee·na
tennis court	*il campo da tennis più vicino*	eel kam·po da te·nees pyoo vee·chee·no

What's the charge per ...?	Qual'è il prezzo richiesto ...?	kwa·le eel pre·tso ree·kye·sto ...
day	*per la giornata*	per la jor·na·ta
game	*per una partita*	per oo·na par·tee·ta
hour	*all'ora*	a·lo·ra
visit	*a visita*	a vee·see·ta

Can I hire a ...?	Posso noleggiare ...?	po·so no·le·ja·re ...
ball	*una palla*	oo·na pa·la
court	*un campo*	oon kam·po
racquet	*una racchetta*	oo·na ra·ke·ta

e·ra fwo·ree	*Era fuori.*	**That was out.**
eem·bro·lyo·ne/a	*Imbroglione/a!* m/f	**Cheat!**
gra·tsye de·la par·tee·ta	*Grazie della partita.*	**Thanks for the game.**
jo·kee be·ne	*Giochi bene.*	**You're a good player.**
pa·sa·la a me	*Passala a me!*	**Kick/Pass it to me!**
poon·to a me/te	*Punto a me/te.*	**Your/My point.**

Do I have to be a member to attend?
È necessario essere soci? e ne·che·sa·ryo e·se·re so·chee

Is there a women-only session?
Ci sono i corsi per sole donne? chee so·no ee kor·see per so·le do·ne

Where are the changing rooms?
Dove sono gli spogliatoi? do·ve so·no lyee spo·lya·to·ee

cycling

il ciclismo

Where does the race finish?
Dove finisce la gara? do·ve fee·nee·she la ga·ra

Where does it pass through?
Dove passa? do·ve pa·sa

Who's winning?
Chi vince? kee veen·che

How many kilometres is today's (leg)?
(La tappa) di oggi è di quanti chilometri? (la ta·pa) dee o·jee e dee kwan·tee kee·lo·me·tree

My favourite cyclist is ...
Il mio ciclista preferito è ... eel mee·o chee·klee·sta pre·fe·ree·to e ...

cyclist	ciclista m/f	chee·klee·sta
the (yellow) jersey	la maglia f (gialla)	ma·lya (ja·la)
leg (in race)	tappa f	ta·pa
mountain stage	tappa f in salita	ta·pa een sa·lee·ta
race	gara	ga·ra
the tour of Italy	il giro d'Italia	eel jee·ro dee·ta·lya
time trial	prova f	pro·va
	a cronometro	a kro·no·me·tro
winner (a leg)	vincitore/	veen·chee·to·re/
	vincitrice	veen·chee·tree·che
	(di tappa) m/f	(dee ta·pa)

For getting around by bike, see **transport**, page 48.

diving

fare immersioni

I'd like to ...	Vorrei ...	vo·ray ...
explore wrecks	esplorare relitti	es·plo·ra·re re·lee·tee
go scuba diving	fare immersioni	fa·re ee·mer·syo·nee
	subacquee	soo·ba·kwe·e
go snorkelling	fare immersioni	fa·re ee·mer·syo·nee
	in apnea	ee·nap·ne·a
join a diving tour	partecipare	par·te·chee·pa·re
	ad una gita	a·doo·na jee·ta
	d'immersione	dee·mer·syo·ne
hire diving gear	noleggiare	no·le·ja·re
	l'attrezzatura per	la·tre·tsa·too·ra per
	immersioni	ee·mer·syo·nee
	subacquee	soo·ba·kwe·e
hire snorkelling	noleggiare	no·le·ja·re
gear	l'attrezzatura	la·tre·tsa·too·ra per
	per immersioni	ee·mer·syo·nee
	in apnea	ee·nap·ne·a
learn to dive	imparare a fare	eem·pa·ra·re a fa·re
	immersioni	ee·mer·syo·nee
	subacquee	soo·ba·kwe·e

Where are some good diving sites?
Dove sono dei buoni   do·ve so·no day bwo·nee
posti per fare immersioni? pos·tee per fa·re ee·mer·syo·nee

Are there jellyfish?
Ci sono meduse?   chee so·no me·doo·ze

Where can I hire (flippers)?
Dove posso noleggiare   do·ve po·so no·le·ja·re
(pinne)?   (pee·ne)

extreme sports

Are you sure this is safe?
Sei sicuro che questo   say see·koo·ro ke kwe·sto
sia sicuro?   see·a see·koo·ro

Is the equipment secure?
È sicura l'attrezzatura? e see·koo·ra la·tre·tsa·too·ra

This is insane.
Questa è roba da matti. kwe·sta e ro·ba da ma·tee

abseiling	*discesa* f *a corda doppia*	dee·she·sa a kor·da do·pya
bungy-jumping	*bungee jumping* m	boon·jee joom·peeng
caving	*esplorazione* f *di caverne*	es·plo·ra·tsyo·ne dee ka·ver·ne
canoeing/rowing	*canottaggio* m	ka·no·ta·jo
canyoning	*torrentismo* m	to·ren·teez·mo
game fishing	*pesca ai pesci selvatici*	pes·ka ai pe·shee sel·va·tee·chee
mountain biking	*mountain biking* m	mown·tayn bai·keeng
paragliding	*parapendio* m	pa·ra·pen·dyo
parasailing	*parasailing* m	pa·ra·se·leeng
rock-climbing	*andare su roccia* f	an·da·re soo ro·cha

SOCIAL

skydiving	*paracadutismo* m	pa·ra·ka·doo·*teez*·mo
	acrobatico	ak·ro·*ba*·tee·ko
snowboarding	*surf* m *da neve*	soorf da *ne*·ve
trekking	*escursionismo* m	es·koor·syo·*neez*·mo
	a piedi	a *pye*·dee
white-water rafting	*rafting* m	raf·teeng

For words and phrases you might need while hiking or trekking, see **outdoors**, page 137, and **camping**, page 58.

soccer

il calcio

Who plays for (Sampdoria)?
Chi gioca per   kee *jo*·ka per
(la Sampdoria)?   (la samp·do·*ree*·a)

He's a great (player).
È un bravo (giocatore).   e oon *bra*·vo (jo·ka·*to*·re)

He played brilliantly in the match against (England).
Ha fatto un'ottima   a *fa*·to oo·*no*·tee·ma
partita contro   par·*tee*·ta kon·tro
(l'Inghilterra).   (leen·geel·*te*·ra)

Which team is at the top of the league?
Quale squadra è in   *kwa*·le *skwa*·dra e een
testa alla classifica?   *tes*·ta a·la kla·*see*·fee·ka

What a terrible team!
Che squadra schifosa!   ke *skwa*·dra skee·*fo*·za

ball	*pallone* m	pa·*lo*·ne
coach	*allenatore/*	a·le·na·*to*·re/
	allenatrice m/f	a·le·na·*tree*·che
corner	*angolo* m	*an*·go·lo
corner kick	*calcio* m *d'angolo*	*kal*·cho dan·go·lo
defensive player	*giocatore/*	jo·ka·*to*·re/
	giocatrice m/f	jo·ka·*tree*·che
	difensivo/a	de·fen·*see*·vo/a
expulsion	*espulsione* f	es·pool·*syo*·ne
fans	*tifosi* m pl	tee·*fo*·zee
foul	*fallo* m	*fa*·lo
free kick	*calcio* m	*kal*·cho
	di punizione	dee poo·nee·*tsyo*·ne

goal	*gol* m	gol
goal (place)	*porta* f	*por*·ta
goalkeeper	*portiere* m&f	por·*tye*·re
goal-scorer	*cannoniere* m	ka·no·*nye*·re
kick-off	*calcio* m *d'inizio*	*kal*·cho dee·*nee*·tsyo
league	*serie* f	*se*·rye
manager	*manager* m&f	*me*·na·je
mid-fielder	*centrocampista* m&f	chen·tro·kam·*pee*·sta
offside	*fuorigioco* m	fwo·ree·*jo*·ko
penalty (kick)	*rigore* m	ree·*go*·re
penalty area	*area* f *di rigore*	*a*·re·a dee ree·*go*·re
player	*giocatore/*	jo·ka·*to*·re/
	giocatrice m/f	jo·ka·*tree*·che
red card	*cartellino* m *rosso*	kar·te·*lee*·no *ro*·so
to score	*segnare*	se·*nya*·re
soccer player	*calciatore/*	kal·cha·*to*·re/
	calciatrice m/f	kal·cha·*tree*·che
striker	*attaccante/avanti* m	a·ta·*kan*·te/a·*van*·tee
supporters	*tifosi* m pl	tee·*fo*·zee
throw-in	*rimessa* f *laterale*	ree·*me*·sa la·te·*ra*·le
warning	*ammonizione* f	a·mo·nee·*tsyo*·ne
yellow card	*cartellino* m *giallo*	kar·te·*lee*·no *ja*·lo

a·*le*	*Alé!*	**Come on!**
for·tsa a·*dzoo*·ree	*Forza Azzurri!*	**Come on blues!**
		(the Italian team)
for·tsa ra·*ga*·tsee	*Forza ragazzi!*	**Come on boys!**

Off to see a match? You might also want to check out **going to a game**, page 128.

skiing

sci

I'd like to hire ...	*Vorrei noleggiare ...*	vo·ray no·le·*ja*·re ...
boots	*gli scarponi*	lyee skar·*po*·nee
	(da sci)	(da shee)
goggles	*gli occhiali di*	lyee o·*kya*·lee dee
	protezione	pro·te·*tsyo*·ne
poles	*i bastoncini*	ee bas·ton·*chee*·nee
skis	*gli sci*	lyee shee
a ski suit	*una tuta da sci*	*oo*·na *too*·ta da shee

Is it possible to go ... here/there?	*Si può ... qui/là?*	see pwo ... kwee/la
Alpine skiing	*fare lo sci*	*fa*·re lo shee
	alpino	al·*pee*·no
cross-country skiing	*fare lo sci*	*fa*·re lo shee
	di fondo	dee *fon*·do
snowboarding	*fare il surf*	*fa*·re eel soorf
	da neve	da *ne*·ve
tobogganing	*andare*	an·*da*·re
	in slitta	een *slee*·ta

How much is a pass?
Quant'è una tessera?   kwan·*te oo*·na *te*·se·ra

Can I take lessons?
Posso prendere lezioni?   *po*·so *pren*·de·re le·*tsyo*·nee

What level is that slope?
Qual'è il livello di
quella pista?

kwa·*le* eel lee·*ve*·lo dee
kwe·la *pee*·sta

Which are	*Quali sono le*	*kwa*·lee *so*·no le
the ... slopes?	*piste per ...?*	*pee*·ste per ...
advanced	*avanzati*	a·van·*tsa*·tee
beginner	*principianti*	preen·chee·*pyan*·tee
intermediate	*intermedi*	een·ter·*me*·dee

What are the	*In quali*	een *kwa*·lee
skiing conditions	*condizioni*	kon·dee·*tsyo*·nee
like ...?	*sono le piste ...?*	*so*·no le *pee*·ste ...
at (Cortina	*a (Cortina*	a (kor·*tee*·na
d'Ampezzo)	*d'Ampezzo)*	dam·*pe*·tso)
higher up	*più in alto*	pyoo ee·*nal*·to
on that run	*su quella pista*	soo *kwe*·la *pee*·sta

cable car	*funivia* f	foo·nee·*vee*·a
chairlift	*seggiovia* f	se·jo·*vee*·a
instructor	*maestro/a* m/f *di sci*	ma·es·tro/a dee shee
resort	*località* f	lo·ka·lee·*ta*
	sciistica	shee·ee·stee·ka
ski-lift	*sciovia* f	shee·o·*vee*·a
sled	*slittino* m	slee·*tee*·no
'white week'	*settimana* f	se·tee·*ma*·na
(skiing holiday)	*bianca*	*byan*·ka

swearing

God!	*Dio!*	*dee*·o
Christ!	*Cristo!*	*kree*·sto
Jesus!	*Gesù!*	je·*soo*
Goodness!	*Madonna!*	ma·*do*·na
Shit!	*Merda!*	*mer*·da
Damn!	*Maledizione!*	ma·le·dee·*tsyo*·ne
Fuck!	*Cazzo!*	*ka*·tso

hiking

escursionismo a piedi

Where can I ...?	*Dove posso ...?*	do·ve po·so ...
buy supplies	*comprare delle provviste*	kom·pra·re de·le pro·vee·ste
find out about	*informarmi*	een·for·mar·mee
hiking trails	*sulle piste per l'escursionismo a piedi*	soo·le pee·ste per les·koor·syo·neez·mo a pye·dee
find someone who knows this area	*trovare qualcuno che conosca la zona*	tro·va·re kwal·koo·no ke ko·no·ska la dzo·na
get a map	*trovare una carta*	tro·va·re oo·na kar·ta
hire hiking gear	*noleggiare l'attrezzatura per l'escursionismo a piedi*	no·le·ja·re la·tre·tsa·too·ra per les·koor·syo·neez·mo a pye·dee

Do we need to take ...?	*Dobbiamo portare ...?*	do·bya·mo por·ta·re ...
bedding	*qualcosa per dormire*	kwal·ko·za per dor·mee·re
food	*del cibo*	del chee·bo
water	*dell'acqua*	de·la·kwa
How ...?	*Quant'è ...?*	kwan·te ...
high is the climb	*alta la salita*	al·ta la sa·lee·ta
long is the hike	*lunga l'escursione*	loon·ga les·koor·syo·ne
long is the trail	*lungo il sentiero*	loon·go eel sen·tye·ro

Is the track ...?	La pista è ...?	la *pee*·sta e ...
(well-)marked	(ben) segnata	(ben) se·*nya*·ta
open	aperta	a·*per*·ta
scenic	panoramica	pa·no·*ra*·mee·ka

Which is the ... route?	Qual'è il percorso ...?	kwa·*le* eel per·*kor*·so ...
easiest	più facile	pyoo *fa*·chee·le
shortest	più corto	pyoo *kor*·to

Where's a/the ...?	Dov'è ...?	do·*ve* ...
camping site	un campeggio	oon kam·*pe*·jo
nearest village	il villaggio più vicino	eel vee·*la*·jo pyoo vee·*chee*·no

Where are the ...?	Dove sono ...?	*do*·ve *so*·no ...
showers	le docce	le *do*·che
toilets	i servizi igienici	ee ser·*vee*·tsee ee·je·nee·chee

Do we need a guide?
Occorre una guida? — o·*ko*·re oo·na gwee·da

Are there guided treks?
Ci sono delle escursioni guidate? — chee *so*·no *de*·le es·koor·*syo*·nee gwee·*da*·te

Is it safe?
È sicuro? — e see·*koo*·ro

Is there a hut there?
C'è un rifugio là? — che oon re·*foo*·jo la

When does it get dark?
Quando fa buio? — *kwan*·do fa *boo*·yo

Where have you come from?
Da dove è venuto/a? m/f pol — da *do*·ve e ve·*noo*·to/a
Da dove sei venuto/a? m/f inf — da *do*·ve say ve·*noo*·to/a

How long did it take?
Quanto ci è voluto?   kwan·to chee e vo·loo·to

Does this path go to (Ginostra)?
Questo sentiero va verso   kwe·sto sen·tye·ro va ver·so
(Ginostra)?   (jee·nos·tra)

Can we go through here?
Possiamo passare da qui?   po·sya·mo pa·sa·re da kwee

Is the water OK to drink?
Si può bere l'acqua?   see pwo be·re la·kwa

I'm lost.
Mi sono perso/a. m/f   mee so·no per·so/a

at the beach

alla spiaggia

Where's the ...	*Dov'è la*	do·ve la
beach?	*spiaggia ...?*	spya·ja ...
best	*migliore*	mee·lyo·re
nearest	*più vicina*	pyoo vee·chee·na
nudist	*nudista*	noo·dee·sta
public	*pubblica*	poo·blee·ka
Is it safe to ...	*Si può ... senza*	see pwo ... sen·tsa
here?	*pericolo?*	pe·ree·ko·lo
dive	*fare i tuffi*	fa·re ee too·fee
scuba dive	*fare le*	fa·re le
	immersioni	ee·mer·syo·nee
swim	*nuotare*	nwo·ta·re

outdoors

139

What time is ... tide?	A che ora è ... marea?	a ke o·ra e ... ma·re·a
high	l'alta	lal·ta
low	la bassa	la ba·sa

How much for a/an ...?	Quanto costa ...?	kwan·to ko·sta ...
deckchair	una sedia a sdraio	oo·na se·dya a zdra·yo
hut	una capanna	oo·na ka·pa·na
umbrella	un ombrello	oo·nom·bre·lo

weather

il tempo

9A **What's the weather like?**
Che tempo fa? ke *tem*·po fa

(Today) It's ...	(Oggi) È ...	(o·jee) e ...
Will it be ... tomorrow?	Domani sarà ...?	do·ma·nee sa·ra ...
cloudy	nuvoloso	noo·vo·lo·zo
fine	sereno	se·re·no
sunny	soleggiato	so·le·ja·to

SOCIAL

140

9B It's cold.	*Fa freddo.*	fa *fre*·do
9C It's hot.	*Fa caldo.*	fa *kal*·do
It's warm.	*Fa bel tempo.*	fa bel *tem*·po
It's freezing.	*Si gela.*	see *je*·la
9D It's raining.	*Piove.*	*pyo*·ve
It's windy.	*Tira vento.*	*tee*·ra *ven*·to
Will it be ... tomorrow?	*Domani ...?*	do·*ma*·nee ...
raining	*pioverà*	pyo·ve·*ra*
snowing	*nevicherà*	ne·vee·ke·*ra*
windy	*ci sarà vento*	chee sa·*ra* *ven*·to

flora & fauna

What (kind of) ... is that?	*Che (tipo di) ... è quello?*	ke (*tee*·po dee) ... e *kwe*·lo
animal	*animale*	a·nee·*ma*·le
flower	*fiore*	*fyo*·re
plant	*pianta*	*pyan*·ta
tree	*albero*	*al*·be·ro
Is it ...?	*È ...?*	e ...
common	*comune*	ko·*moo*·ne
dangerous	*pericoloso/a* m/f	pe·ree·ko·*lo*·zo/a
endangered	*in pericolo d'estinzione*	een pe·*ree*·ko·lo des·teen·*tsyo*·ne
poisonous	*velenoso/a* m/f	ve·le·*no*·zo/a
protected	*protetto/a* m/f	pro·*te*·to/a

What's it used for?
A che cosa serve?   a ke *ko·*za *ser·*ve

Can you eat it?
Si può mangiarlo?   see pwo man·*jar·*lo

mario or maria?

Throughout this book we have used the letters m or f to indicate whether a word is masculine or feminine. Where a word can be either masculine or feminine, the feminine ending is separated by a slash. For example, the two forms of the word for beautiful are written as *bello/a* m/f.

See also **gender** in the **a–z phrasebuilder**.

key language

	afternoon snack	*merenda* f	me·*ren*·da
63A	breakfast	*prima colazione* f	*pree*·ma ko·la·*tsyo*·ne
63C	dinner	*cena* f	*che*·na
63F	drink	*bere*	*be*·re
63E	eat		*mangiare* man·*ja*·re
63B	lunch	*pranzo* m	*pran*·dzo
63D	snack	*spuntino* m	spoon·*tee*·no

cheap and cheerful

There's no shortage of delicious, inexpensive food available in Italy. If you're on a modest budget, explore some of these easy eateries ...

bar/caffè   bar/ka·*fe*
serve drinks but also offer light meals such as bread rolls and snacks

osteria/trattoria   os·te·*ree*·a/tra·to·*ree*·a
provide simple food and some local specialities

paninoteca   pa·nee·no·*te*·ka
serves delicious sandwiches made with cheese and cold meats

tavola calda   *ta*·vo·la *kal*·da
a buffet offering local specialities, pizza, roasted meats and salads

pizzeria   pee·tse·*ree*·a
specialises in *pizza* and *calzoni* (a folded pizza dish), usually prepared in a woodfired oven

ristorante   ree·sto·*ran*·te
a more sophisticated eatery – expect a higher standard of service, a more expensive menu and a decent winelist

finding a place to eat

Can you recommend a ...	Potrebbe consigliare un ...	po·*tre*·be kon·see·*lya*·re oon ...
cafe	bar	bar
restaurant	ristorante	rees·to·*ran*·te
Where would you go for ...?	Dove andrebbe per ...	*do*·ve an·*dre*·be per ...
a business lunch	un pranzo d'affari	oon *pran*·dzo da·*fa*·ree
a cheap meal	un pasto economico	oon *pas*·to e·ko·*no*·mee·ko
a celebration	una celebrazione	*oo*·na che·le·bra·*tsyo*·ne
local specialities	le specialità locali	le spe·cha·lee·*ta* lo·*ka*·lee

listen for ...

bwon a·pe·*tee*·to *Buon appetito.*	**Enjoy your meal.**
do·ve vwo·le se·*der*·see *Dove vuole sedersi?*	**Where would you like to sit?**
e al kom·*ple*·to *È al completo.*	**We're fully booked.**
e·ko *Ecco!*	**Here you go!**
ko·me la vwo·le *ko*·ta *Come la vuole cotta?*	**How would you like that cooked?**
ko·za le *por*·to *Cosa Le porto?*	**What can I get for you?**
non a·*bya*·mo *ta*·vo·lee *Non abbiamo tavoli.*	**We have no tables.**
sya·mo kyoo·zee *Siamo chiusi.*	**We're closed.**

Caldo	*kal·*do	**Hot**
Donne	*do·*ne	**Women**
Freddo	*fre·*do	**Cold**
Gabinetti	ga·bee·*ne·*tee	**Toilets**
Prenotato	pre·no·*ta·*to	**Reserved**
Riservato	ree·ser·*va·*to	**Reserved**
Uomini	*wo·*mee·nee	**Men**

I'd like to reserve a table for ...	*Vorrei prenotare un tavolo per ...*	vo·*ray* pre·no·*ta·*re oon *ta·*vo·lo per ...
(two) people	*(due) persone*	(*doo·*e) per·*so·*ne
(eight) o'clock	*le (otto)*	le (*o·*to)

I'd like ..., please.	*Vorrei ..., per favore.*	vo·*ray* ... per fa·*vo·*re
a table for (four)	*un tavolo per (quattro)*	oon *ta·*vo·lo per (*kwa·*tro)
the menu	*il menù*	eel me·*noo*
the drink list	*la lista delle bevande*	la *lee·*sta *de·*le be·*van·*de
the (non-)smoking section	*(non) fumatori*	(non) foo·ma·*to·*ree

Do you have ...?	*Avete ...?*	a·*ve·*te ...
children's meals	*pasti per bambini*	*pas·*tee per bam·*bee·*nee
a menu in English	*un menù in inglese*	oon me·*noo* een een·*gle·*ze

Are you still serving food?

Servite ancora da mangiare?   ser·*vee·*te an·*ko·*ra da man·*ja·*re

How long is the wait?

Quanto si deve aspettare?   *kwan·*to see *de·*ve as·pe·*ta·*re

at the restaurant

I'd like the menu, please.
Vorrei il menù, per favore.   vo·ray eel me·noo per fa·vo·re

Is it self-serve?
È self-service?   e self·ser·vees

We're just having drinks.
Prendiamo solo da bere.   pren·dya·mo so·lo da be·re

66A **What would you recommend?**
Cosa mi consiglia?   ko·za mee kon·see·lya

I'll have what they're having.
Vorrei quello che stanno   vo·ray kwe·lo ke sta·no
mangiando loro.   man·jan·do lo·ro

I'd like a local speciality.
Vorrei una specialità   vo·ray oo·na spe·cha·lee·ta
di questa regione.   dee kwe·sta re·jo·ne

What's in that dish?
Quali ingredienti ci   kwa·li een·gre·dyen·tee chee
sono in questo piatto?   so·no een kwe·sto pya·to

Does it take long to prepare?
Ci vuole molto per   chee vwo·le mol·to per
prepararlo?   pre·pa·rar·lo

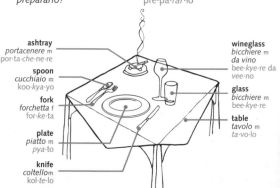

ashtray
portacenere m
por·ta·che·ne·re

spoon
cucchiaio m
koo·kya·yo

fork
forchetta f
for·ke·ta

plate
piatto m
pya·to

knife
coltello m
kol·te·lo

wineglass
bicchiere m
da vino
bee·kye·re da
vee·no

glass
bicchiere m
bee·kye·re

table
tavolo m
ta·vo·lo

146

look for ...

antipasti	an·tee·*pas*·tee	appetisers
zuppe	*tsoo*·pe	soups
primi (piatti)	*pree*·mee (*pya*·tee)	entrees
insalate	een·sa·*la*·te	salads
contorni	kon·*tor*·nee	side dishes
pasti leggeri	*pas*·tee le·*je*·ree	light meals
secondi (piatti)	se·*kon*·dee (*pya*·tee)	main courses
dolci	*dol*·chee	desserts
bevande	be·*van*·de	drinks
aperitivi	a·pe·ree·*tee*·vee	aperitifs
bibite	*bee*·bee·te	soft drinks
liquori	lee·*kwo*·ree	spirits
birre	*bee*·re	beers
vini della casa	*vee*·nee *de*·la *ka*·za	house wines
vini locali	*vee*·nee lo·*ka*·lee	local wines
vini frizzanti	*vee*·nee free·*tsan*·tee	sparkling wines
vini bianchi	*vee*·nee *byan*·kee	white wines
vini rossi	*vee*·nee *ro*·see	red wines
vini rosati	*vee*·nee ro·*za*·tee	roses
vini da dessert	*vee*·nee da de·*sert*	dessert wines
digestivi	dee·jes·*tee*·vee	digestifs

For more words you might see on a menu, see the **culinary reader**, page 161.

Is ... included in the bill?	*Il ... è compreso nel conto?*	eel ... e kom·*pre*·zo nel *kon*·to
the cover charge	*coperto*	ko·*per*·to
service	*servizio*	ser·*vee*·tsyo

Please bring ...	*Mi porta ..., per favore?*	mee *por*·ta ... per fa·*vo*·re
65D the bill	*il conto*	eel *kon*·to
a cloth	*uno strofinaccio*	*oo*·no stro·fee·*na*·cho
a glass	*un bicchiere*	oon bee·*kye*·re

Is there (any Parmesan cheese)?

C'è (del parmigiano)?   che (del par·mee·*ja*·no)

hot 'n' saucy

Pasta comes in all shapes and sizes from the standard *spaghetti* to potato *gnocchi* and bow-shaped *farfalle*. There are even more varieties of pasta sauce and each region boasts its own speciality. Here are just a few you might come across. Note that *alla* and *all'* mean 'in the style of'.

aglio e olio a·lyo e o·lyo
oil, garlic and sometimes chilli

al ragù al ra·goo
meat (minced veal or pork), vegetables, lemon peel and nutmeg

all'amatriciana a·la·ma·tree·cha·na
pig's cheek, lard, white wine, tomato, chilli and sheep's cheese

alla carbonara a·la kar·bo·na·ra
bacon, butter, eggs and sheep's cheese

alla partenopea a·la par·te·no·pe·a
mozzarella, tomato, bread crust, capers, olives, anchovies, basil, oil, chilli and salt

alla pescatora a·la pes·ka·to·ra
fish, tomato and sweet herbs

alla pommarola a·la po·ma·ro·la
tomato

alla puttanesca a·la poo·ta·nes·ka
garlic, anchovies, black olives, capers, tomato, oil and chilli

cacio e pepe ka·cho e pe·pe
black pepper and sheep's cheese

con il tonno kon eel to·no
with tuna

con le vongole kon le von·go·le
with clams

con tartufo di Norcia kon tar·too·fo dee nor·cha
with Norcia truffles

talking food

That was delicious!
Era squisito! — e·ra skwee·*zee*·to

My compliments to the chef.
Complimenti al cuoco! — kom·plee·*men*·tee al *kwo*·ko

I'm full.
Sono sazio/a. m/f — *so*·no *sa*·tsyo/a

I love ...	*Vado matto/a*	*va*·do *ma*·to/a
	per ... m/f	per ...
this dish	*questo piatto*	*kwe*·sto *pya*·to
the local	*la cucina*	la koo·*chee*·na
cuisine	*locale*	lo·*ka*·le

This is ...	*Questo/a è ...* m/f	*kwe*·sto/a e ...
(too) cold	*(troppo) freddo/a* m/f	(*tro*·po) *fre*·do/a
(too) hot	*(troppo) caldo/a* m/f	(*tro*·po) *kal*·do/a
spicy	*piccante*	pee·*kan*·te
superb	*delizioso/a* m/f	de·lee·*tsyo*·zo/a

breakfast

What's a typical breakfast?
Qual'è la prima — kwa·*le* la *pree*·ma
colazione tipica? — ko·la·*tsyo*·ne *tee*·pee·ka

bacon	*pancetta* f	pan·*che*·ta
bread	*pane* m	*pa*·ne
butter	*burro* m	*boo*·ro
cereal	*cereali* m pl	che·re·*a*·lee
croissant	*cornetto* m	kor·*ne*·to
eggs	*uova* f pl	*wo*·va
omelette	*frittata* f	free·*ta*·ta
milk	*latte* m	*la*·te
muesli	*muesli* m	*moos*·lee
pastry	*pasta* f	*pas*·ta
toast	*pane* m *tostato*	*pa*·ne tos·*ta*·to

methods of preparation

I'd like it ...	*Lo/La vorrei ...* m/f	lo/la vo·*ray* ...
I don't want	*Non lo/la*	non lo/la
it ...	*voglio ...* m/f	vo·lyo ...
boiled	*bollito/a* m/f	bo·*lee*·to/a
broiled	*cotto/a* m/f	*ko*·to/a
	a fuoco vivo	a *fwo*·ko vee·vo
deep-fried	*fritto/a* m/f *in*	*free*·to/a een
	abbondante olio	a·bon·*dan*·te o·lyo
fried	*fritto/a* m/f	*free*·to/a
grilled	*(cotto/a)* m/f *ai ferri*	(*ko*·to/a) ai *fe*·ree
medium	*non troppo*	non *tro*·po
	cotto/a m/f	*ko*·to/a
rare	*al sangue*	al *san*·gwe
re-heated	*riscaldato/a* m/f	rees·kal·*da*·to/a
steamed	*cotto/a* m/f *a vapore*	*ko*·to/a a va·*po*·re
well-done	*ben cotto/a* m/f	ben *ko*·to/a
with the	*con il*	kon eel
dressing	*condimento*	kon·dee·*men*·to
on the side	*a parte*	a *par*·te
without ...	*senza ...*	*sen*·tsa ...

in the bar

Excuse me!
  Scusi!   skoo·zee

I'll have (a glass of red wine).
  Prendo (un bicchiere di   pren·do (oon bee·*kye*·re dee
  vino rosso).   *vee*·no *ro*·so)

Same again, please.
  Un altro, per favore.   oon *al*·tro per fa·*vo*·re

No ice, thanks.
  Senza ghiaccio, grazie.   *sen*·tsa *gya*·cho *gra*·tsye

Straight, please.
Liscio, per favore.   lee·sho per fa·vo·re

66B I'll buy you a drink.
Ti offro da bere.   tee of·ro da be·re

66C What would you like?
Cosa prendi? inf   ko·za pren·dee

It's my round.
Offro io.   of·ro ee·o

You can get the next one.
La prossima la paghi tu.   la pro·see·ma la pa·gee too

Do you serve meals here?
Servite da mangiare qui?   ser·vee·te da man·ja·re kwee

nonalcoholic drinks

le bevande analcoliche

almond milk	*orzata* f	or·dza·ta
bitter cola	*chinotto* m	kee·no·to
fruit juice (bottled)	*succo* m *di frutta*	soo·ko dee froo·ta
fruit juice (fresh)	*spremuta* f	spre·moo·ta
grapefruit juice	*succo* m *di pompelmo*	soo·ko dee pom·pel·mo
lemonade/lemon squash	*limonata* f	lee·mo·na·ta
68B orange juice (bottled)	*succo* m *d'arancia*	soo·ko da·ran·cha
orange juice (fresh)	*spremuta* f *d'arancia*	spre·moo·ta da·ran·cha
orangeade	*aranciata* f	a·ran·cha·ta
68A soft drink	*bibita* f	bee·bee·ta
67A (cup of) tea	*(un) tè* m	(oon) te
67B (cup of) coffee	*(un) caffè* m	(oon) ka·fe
67C ... with milk	*... con latte*	... kon la·te
... without	*... senza/con*	... sen·tsa/kon
67D (sugar)	*(zucchero)*	(tsoo·ke·ro)

... water	*acqua* f ...	a·kwa ...
68C boiled	*bollita*	bo·*lee*·ta
68D mineral	*minerale*	mee·ne·*ra*·le
sparkling	*frizzante*	free·*tsan*·te
still	*naturale*	na·too·*ra*·le

coffee lovers

Italians often drink their coffee standing up at the bar, as many establishments charge extra for table service. Simply ask for a *caffè* and you'll receive an *espresso*, but don't order a *latte* unless you want a glass of milk. If you want to blend in, make sure you don't ask for coffee with milk in the afternoon.

caffè alla valdostana   ka·*fe* a·la val·dos·*ta*·na
   with *grappa*, lemon peel and spices

caffè americano   ka·*fe* a·me·ree·*ka*·no
   long and black

caffè corretto   ka·*fe* ko·*re*·to
   with a dash of liqueur

caffè doppio   ka·*fe do*·pyo
   long, strong and black

caffè macchiato   ka·*fe* ma·*kya*·to
   strong coffee with a drop of milk

caffè ristretto   ka·*fe* ree·*stre*·to
   super strong black coffee

caffellatte   ka·fe·*la*·te
   coffee with milk – usually only consumed at breakfast

cappuccino   ka·poo·*chee*·no
   coffee prepared with milk, served with a lot of froth and sprinkled with cocoa – considered a morning drink

espresso   es·*pre*·so
   short black coffee

ristretto   ree·*stre*·to
   very short black coffee

latte   *la*·te
   milk

alcoholic drinks

le bevande alcoliche

You shouldn't have too many problems getting what you want at the bar. Some Italian spirits have made their way into English (eg, *sambuca* and *grappa*) and similarly Italian has adopted the English names for classics like *gin*, *rum* and *whiskey*.

amaro (bitter liqueur)	*amaro* m	a·*ma*·ro
grappa (grape spirits)	*grappa* f	*gra*·pa
draught beer	*birra* f *a la spina*	*bee*·ra a la *spee*·na
brandy	*cognac* m	*ko*·nyak
champagne	*champagne* m	sham·*pa*·nye
cocktail	*cocktail* m	*kok*·tayl
wine	*vino* m	*vee*·no

69A a shot of ...	*un sorso di ...*	oon *sor*·so dee ...
a bottle of ... wine	*una bottiglia*	*oo*·na bo·*tee*·lya
	di vino ...	dee *vee*·no ...
a glass of ... wine	*un bicchiere*	oon bee·*kye*·re
	di vino ...	dee *vee*·no ...
dessert	*da dessert*	da de·*sert*
red	*rosso*	*ro*·so
rose	*rosato*	ro·*za*·to
sparkling	*spumante*	spoo·*man*·te
white	*bianco*	*byan*·ko
a ... of beer	*... di birra*	... dee *bee*·ra
glass	*un bicchiere*	oon bee·*kye*·re
pint	*una pinta*	*oo*·na *peen*·ta
bottle	*una bottiglia*	*oo*·na bo·*tee*·lya
jug	*una caraffa*	*oo*·na ka·*ra*·fa

one too many?

66D **Cheers!**
Salute!
sa·*loo*·te

Thanks, but I don't feel like it.
Grazie, ma non mi va.
gra·tsye ma non mee va

I don't drink alcohol.
Non bevo.
non *be*·vo

I'm tired, I'd better go home.
Sono stanco/a, è meglio
che vada a casa. m/f
so·no *stan*·ko/a e *me*·lyo
ke *va*·da a *ka*·za

Where's the toilet?
Dov'è il gabinetto?
do·ve eel ga·bee·*ne*·to

This is hitting the spot.
Ci voleva proprio!
chee vo·*le*·va *pro*·pryo

I'm feeling drunk.
Mi sento un po'
ubriaco/a. m/f
mee *sen*·to oon po
oo·bree·*a*·ko/a

Pull my finger!
Tirami il dito!
tee·ra·mee eel *dee*·to

I really, really love you.
Ti amo molto molto.
tee *a*·mo *mol*·to *mol*·to

I think I've had one too many.
Penso d'aver bevuto
troppo.
pen·so da·*ver* be·*voo*·to
tro·po

Can you call a taxi for me?
Mi puoi chiamare un
tassì?
mee pwoy kya·*ma*·re oon
ta·*see*

I don't think you should drive.
È meglio che non guidi.
e *me*·lyo ke non gwee·dee

I'm pissed.
Ho la ciucca.
o la *choo*·ka

I feel ill.
Mi sento male.
mee *sen*·to *ma*·le

key language

il vocabolario essenziale

cooked	*cotto/a* m/f	*ko·ta/a*
dried	*secco/a* m/f	*se·ko/a*
fresh	*fresco/a* m/f	*fres·ko/a*
frozen	*congelato/a* m/f	*kon·je·la·to/a*
raw	*crudo/a* m/f	*kroo·do/a*

shop till you drop

alimentari	a·lee·men·*ta*·ree	grocery store
caseificio	ka·ze·ee·*fee*·cho	creamery
enoteca	e·no·*te*·ka	wine shop
formaggeria	for·ma·je·*ree*·a	cheese shop (also sells other dairy products)
macelleria	ma·che·le·*ree*·a	butcher
mercato	mer·*ka*·to	market
pasticceria	pas·tee·che·*ree*·a	cake shop
pastificio	pas·tee·*fee*·cho	specialist pasta shop
pescheria	pes·ke·*ree*·a	fish shop
polleria	po·le·*ree*·a	poultry shop
salumeria	sa·loo·me·*ree*·a	delicatessen
tabacchi	ta·*ba*·kee	tobacconist
torrefazione	to·re·fa·*tsyo*·ne	coffee roasting house

buying food

How much?
Quanto/a? m/f   kwan·to/a

How much is (a kilo of cheese)?
Quanto costa (un chilo   kwan·to kos·ta (oon kee·lo
di formaggio)?   dee for·ma·jo)

70A What's the local speciality?
Qual'è la specialità   kwa·le la spe·cha·lee·ta
di questa regione?   dee kwe·sta re·jo·ne

70B What's that?
Cos'è?   ko·ze

Can I taste it?
Lo/La posso assaggiare? m/f   lo/la po·so a·sa·ja·re

Can I have a bag, please?
Posso avere un sacchetto,   po·so a·ve·re oon sa·ke·to
per favore?   per fa·vo·re

71A I'd like ...	*Vorrei ...*	vo·ray ...
100 grams	*un etto*	oo·ne·to
71B (200) grams	*(due) etti*	(doo·e) e·tee
a kilo	*un chilo*	oon kee·lo
71C (two) kilos	*(due) chili*	(doo·e) kee·lee
a bottle	*una bottiglia*	oo·na bo·tee·lya
a dozen	*una dozzina*	oo·na do·dzee·na
a jar	*un barattolo*	oon ba·ra·to·lo
a packet	*un sacchetto*	oon sa·ke·to
a piece	*un pezzo*	oon pe·tso
71D (three) pieces	*(tre) pezzi*	(tre) pe·tsee
a slice	*una fetta*	oo·na fe·ta
71E (six) slices	*(sei) fette*	(say) fe·te
a tin	*una scatola*	oo·na ska·to·la
some ...	*alcuni/e ...* m/f	al·koo·nee/al·koo·ne ...
that one	*quello/a* m/f	kwe·lo/a
this one	*questo/a* m/f	kwe·sto/a

Enough.	*Basta, grazie.*	*bas·ta gra·tsye*
A bit more.	*Un po' di più.*	oon po dee pyoo
Less.	*(Di) Meno.*	(dee) *me·*no

Do you have ...?	*Avete ...?*	a·*ve·*te ...
anything	*qualcosa di*	kwal·*ko·*za dee
cheaper	*meno costoso*	*me·*no kos·*to·*zo
other kinds	*altri tipi*	*al·*tree *tee·*pee

listen for ...

de·*see·*de·ra *al·*tro
Desidera altro? — Would you like anything else?

e (oo·na gor·gon·*dzo·*la)
È (una gorgonzola). — That's (a gorgonzola).

e e·zow·*ree·*to/a
È esaurito/a. m/f — There's none left.

e poy
E poi? — Anything else?

*ko·*za de·*see·*de·ra
Cosa desidera? — What would you like?

non ne ho
Non ne ho. — I don't have any.

*po·*so a·yoo·*tar·*la
Posso aiutarLa? — Can I help you?

*so·*no (*cheen·*kwe e·*oo·*ro)
Sono (cinque euro). — That's (five euros).

Where can I find	Dove posso trovare	do·ve po·so tro·va·re
the ... section?	il reparto ...?	eel re·par·to ...
dairy	dei latticini	day la·tee·chee·nee
frozen goods	dei surgelati	day soor·je·la·tee
fruit and	della frutta e	de·la froo·ta e
vegetable	verdura	ver·doo·ra
meat	della carne	de·la kar·ne
poultry	del pollame	del po·la·me

cooking utensils

utensili da cucina

Could I please borrow (a corkscrew)?

Posso prendere in   po·so pren·de·re een
prestito (un cavatappi),   pres·tee·to (oon ka·va·ta·pee)
per favore?   per fa·vo·re

Where's (a saucepan)?

Dov'è (un tegame)?   do·ve (oon te·ga·me)

For more cooking implements, see the **dictionary**.

ordering food

ordinare da mangiare

Is there a ...	*C'è un*	che oon
restaurant near	*ristorante ...*	rees·to·*ran*·te ...
here?	*qui vicino?*	kwee vee·*chee*·no
halal	*halal*	a·*lal*
kosher	*kasher*	ka·sher
72A vegetarian	*vegetariano*	ve·je·ta·*rya*·no

Do you have (vegetarian) food?
Avete piatti (vegetariani)?   a·*ve*·te pya·tee (ve·je·ta·*rya*·nee)

I'm vegan.
Sono vegetaliano/a. m/f   so·no ve·je·ta·*lya*·no/a

I don't eat (fish).
Non mangio (pesce).   non *man*·jo (*pe*·she)

Is it cooked with (oil)?
È cotto con (olio)?   e *ko*·to kon (*o*·lyo)

Is this ...?	*È ...?*	e ...
decaffeinated	*decaffeinato/a* m/f	de·ka·fey·*na*·to/a
cholesterol free	*senza*	*sen*·tsa
	colesterolo	ko·le·ste·*ro*·lo
free of animal	*senza prodotti*	*sen*·tsa pro·*do*·tee
produce	*animali*	a·nee·*ma*·lee
free range	*ruspante*	roos·*pan*·te
genetically	*geneticamente*	je·ne·tee·ka·*men*·te
modified	*modificato/a* m/f	mo·dee·fee·*ka*·to/a
gluten free	*senza glutine*	*sen*·tsa *gloo*·tee·ne
low fat/sugar	*a basso*	a *ba*·so
	contenuto	kon·te·*noo*·to
	lipidico/	lee·*pee*·dee·ko/
	glucosio	gloo·*ko*·zyo
organic	*biologico/a* m/f	bee·o·*lo*·jee·ko/a
salt free	*senza sale*	*sen*·tsa *sa*·le

Could you prepare a meal without ...?	Potreste preparare un pasto senza ...?	po·*tres*·te pre·pa·*ra*·re oon *pas*·to *sen*·tsa ...
butter	burro	*boo*·ro
72B eggs	uova	*wo*·va
meat/fish	brodo di carne/ pesce	*bro*·do dee *kar*·ne/ *pe*·she
72C stock		
pork	carne di maiale	*kar*·ne dee ma·*ya*·le
poultry	pollame	po·*la*·me
red meat	carne rossa	*kar*·ne *ro*·sa

special diets & allergies

diete speciali & allergie

I'm on a special diet.
  Seguo una dieta speciale.   se·gwo oo·na *dye*·ta spe·*cha*·le

I'm allergic to ...	Sono allergico/a ... m/f	*so*·no a·*ler*·jee·ko/a ...
dairy produce	ai latticini	ai la·tee·*chee*·nee
eggs	alle uova	*a*·le *wo*·va
fish	al pesce	al *pe*·she
gelatin	alla gelatina	*a*·la je·la·*tee*·na
gluten	al glutine	al *gloo*·tee·ne
honey	al miele	al *mye*·le
MSG	al glutammato monosodico	al gloo·ta·*ma*·to mo·no·so·*dee*·ko
nuts	alle noci	*a*·le *no*·chee
peanuts	alle arachidi	*a*·le a·*ra*·kee·dee
seafood	ai frutti di mare	ai *froo*·tee dee *ma*·re
shellfish	ai crostacei	ai kros·*ta*·che·ee

A number of dishes listed here are regionally specific.

A

abbacchio ⑩ a·ba·kyo *young lamb*
  — alla cacciatora a·la ka·cha·to·ra
*lamb casserole with spices, white
wine & anchovies*
  — a scottadito a·sko·ta·dee·to *lamb
cutlets fried in oil*

acciughe ① pl a·choo·ge *anchovies
(often preserved in salt)*

aceto ⑩ a·che·to *vinegar*

acquacotta ① a·kwa·ko·ta *soup
prepared with tomato, peppers,
celery, eggs, artichokes or
mushrooms*

acquapazza ① a·kwa·pa·tsa *'crazy
water' – a type of fish soup*

aglio ⑩ a·lyo *garlic*
  — e olio e o·lyo *garlic & olive oil
pasta sauce*

agnello ⑩ a·nye·lo *lamb*
  — ai funghi ai foon·gee *with
mushrooms*
  — al forno al for·no *with garlic &
sometimes potatoes*
  — da latte da la·te *very young milk-
fed lamb*

agnolini ⑩ pl a·nyo·lee·nee *round
pasta stuffed with stewed beef,
eggs, cheese & other ingredients*

agnolotti ⑩ pl **ripieni** a·nyo·lo·tee
ree·pye·nee *pasta stuffed with meat,
herbs, eggs & parmesan*

agro, all' ag·ro, al *with oil & lemon
dressing*

albicocca ① al·bee·ko·ka *apricot*

alborella ① al·bo·re·la *common
freshwater fish*

alici ① pl a·lee·chee *anchovies*
  — a crudo a kroo·do *raw, marinated
in oil & spices*

al dente al den·te *'to the tooth' –
describes cooked pasta & rice that
are still slightly hard*

all'/alla ... al/a·la *... in the style of ...*

alloro ⑩ a·lo·ro *bay leaf*

al sangue al san·gwe *rare (cooked)*

amaretti ⑩ pl a·ma·re·tee *almond
biscuits (macaroons)*

amatriciana a·ma·tree·cha·na, al
*spicy sauce with salami, tomato,
capsicums & cheese*

ananas ⑩ a·na·nas *pineapple*

anatra ① a·na·tra *duck*
  — al sale al sa·le *roast duck cooked
in a crust of salt*

angiulottus ⑩ an·joo·lo·toos *stuffed
square pasta served with meat sauce
or tomato sauce*

anguilla ① an·gwee·la *eel*

anice ⑩ a·nee·che *aniseed*

annoglia ① a·no·lya *dry-cured pork
sausage with chilli*

anolini ⑩ pl a·no·lee·nee *stuffed round
pasta with braised beef, cheese,
parmesan, egg & breadcrumbs*

aragosta ① a·ra·go·sta *lobster • crayfish*

arancia ① a·ran·cha *orange*

arancia, all' a·ran·cha, al *sprinkled or
baked with orange juice*

arancini ⑩ pl a·ran·chee·nee *rice-balls
stuffed with a meat mixture*

aranzada ① a·ran·tsa·da *almond nougat*

arborio ⑩ ar·bo·ryo *short-grain rice
used for risotto*

aringa ① a·reen·ga *herring*

arista ① a·ree·sta *loin – generally pork*
  — alla fiorentina a·la fyo·ren·tee·na
baked with spices

aromi ⑩ pl a·ro·mee *herbs*

arrabbiata, all' a·ra·bya·ta, al *'angry-
style' – with spicy sauce*

arrosticini ⓜ a·ros·tee·chee·nee
  skewered & roasted meat – often
  lamb
arrosto/a ⓜ/ⓕ a·ro·sto/a roasted
  — **alla griglia** a·la gree·lya barbecued
artigianale ar·tee·ja·na·le home-made
asiago ⓜ a·zya·go hard white cheese
asparagi ⓜ pl as·pa·ra·jee asparagus
aspro/a ⓜ/ⓕ as·pro/a sour

B

babà ⓜ ba·ba dessert containing
  sultanas
baccalà ⓜ ba·ka·la dried salted cod
  — **alla pizzaiola** a·la pee·tsa·yo·la
  with a tomato sauce
  — **mantecato** man·te·ka·to mixed to
  a puree
baci ⓜ pl ba·chee 'kisses' – type of
  chocolate • type of pastry or biscuit
bagnetto ⓜ **verde** ba·nye·to ver·de
  parsley & garlic sauce
barbabietola ⓕ bar·ba·bye·to·la
  beetroot
basilico ⓜ ba·zee·lee·ko basil
batsoà ⓜ bat·so·a boned, boiled &
  fried pig's trotters
battuto ⓜ ba·too·to soup or meat
  seasoning prepared with lard &
  vegetables
bavetta ⓕ ba·ve·ta long, thick pasta
bel paese ⓜ bel pa·e·ze soft, creamy
  cheese
besciamella ⓕ be·sha·me·la bechamel
  sauce
bescó·cc ⓜ bes·koch almond biscuits
  soaked in **grappa**
bianchetti ⓜ pl byan·ke·tee whitebait
  fried in oil
bianco ⓜ **d'uovo** byan·ko dwo·vo
  egg white
bigné ⓜ bee·nye cream puff
bigoli ⓜ pl bee·go·lee thick,
  wholemeal flour spaghetti
bisció'la ⓕ bee·sho·la cake with nuts,
  dried figs & raisins
biscotti ⓜ pl bees·ko·tee biscuits
biscó·cc ⓜ bees·koch see bescó·cc
bisi ⓜ pl bee·zee peas

bistecca ⓕ bees·te·ka steak
  — **alla fiorentina** a·la fyo·ren·tee·na
  tasty, thick loin steak with its bone
bitto ⓜ bee·to cow's milk cheese
blanc manger ⓜ blank man·je sweet
  white dessert with milk, sugar & vanilla
bocconcini ⓜ pl bo·kon·chee·nee tiny
  portions of **mozzarella** • can refer to
  anything bite-sized
boghe ⓕ pl in scabescio bo·ge een
  ska·be·sho marinated, floured fish,
  browned in oil
bollito bo·lee·to boiled
bollito (Bú'i) ⓜ bo·lee·to (boo·ee) mixed
  boiled meat with various sauces
bomba ⓕ di riso bom·ba dee ree·zo
  baked rice with stewed pigeon, eggs,
  mushrooms, truffles & sausage
bombas ⓕ bom·bas stewed veal
  meatballs
bonèt ⓜ bo·net baked pudding of
  macaroons, cocoa, coffee, **marsala** &
  rum
bostrengo ⓜ bos·tren·go cake
  prepared with boiled rice, chocolate,
  sugar, spices & pine nuts
boudin ⓜ boo·deen blood sausage
bra ⓑ bra mild cheese
braciola ⓕ bra·cho·la chop • cutlet
braciolone ⓜ **napoletano** bra·cho·lo·ne
  na·po·le·ta·no steak rolled & filled with
  bacon, provolone & other ingredients
branzi ⓜ pl bran·dzee soft table cheese
branzino ⓜ bran·dzee·no sea bass
brasato ⓜ bra·za·to beef marinated in red
  wine & spices, then stewed
brasare bra·za·re to cook slowly
brioche ⓕ bree·osh breakfast pastry
brochat ⓜ bro·shat sweet, thick cream
  made with milk, wine & sugar & eaten
  with rye bread
brodetto ⓜ **di pesce** bro·de·to dee pe·she
  fish soup
brodo ⓜ bro·do broth
brôs ⓜ broos creamy paste made by
  fermenting older cheese with herbs,
  spices & **grappa**
bruschetta ⓕ broos·ke·ta stale bread
  sliced, toasted, rubbed with garlic &
  flavoured with salt, pepper & olive oil

bruscitt ⓜ broo-*sheet* beef pieces cooked with red wine & served with polenta or mashed potatoes

brutti ma buoni ⓜ pl *broo*-tee ma *bwo*-nee 'ugly but good' – hazelnut macaroons

bucatini ⓜ pl boo-ka-*tee*-nee long hollow tubes of pasta

buccellato ⓜ **di Lucca** boo-che-*la*-to dee *loo*-ka traditional ring-shaped cake

budino ⓜ boo-*dee*-no milk-based pudding

bugie ⓕ pl boo-*jee*-e 'lies' – small ribbons of sweet pastry covered with icing sugar

burro ⓜ *boo*-ro butter

burtléina ⓕ boort-*lay*-na little omelette prepared with water, flour, lard & onion, served with salami

busecca ⓕ boo-ze-ka tripe

bussolà ⓜ **vicentino** boo-so-*la* vee-chen-*tee*-no sponge cake based dessert

C

caciotta ⓕ ka-*cho*-ta semi-soft mild cheese

cacciucco ⓜ **(alla livornese)** ka-*choo*-ko (a-la lee-vor-*ne*-ze) fish soup with at least five kinds of fish

cacio ⓜ *ka*-cho cheese in general • a creamy cheese

caciocavallo ⓜ ka-cho-ka-*va*-lo hard cow's milk cheese from southern Italy

cacioricotta ⓕ ka-cho-ree-*ko*-ta small round cheese made from cow/sheep/goat's milk curd

caciuni ⓜ pl ka-*choo*-nee big ravioli or puff pastry filled with egg yolks, cheeses, sugar & lemon peel

caffè ⓜ ka-*fe* coffee (also see page 152)

calamari ⓜ pl ka-la-*ma*-ree calamari • squid

calhiettes ⓕ **tradizionali** ka-*lyet* tra-dee-tsyo-*na*-lee mixture of raw, grated potatoes, left-over meat, minced lard, onion, flour & eggs mixed & boiled, normally used to prepare dumplings & omelettes

calzone ⓜ kal-*tso*-ne fried or baked flat bread made with two thin sheets of pasta stuffed with any number of ingredients

canederli ⓜ pl ka-ne-der-lee big dumplings made with stale bread, speck & other ingredients such as liver, cheese, spinach or dried prunes

cannaroni ⓜ pl ka-na-*ro*-nee large pasta tubes

cannella ⓕ ka-*ne*-la cinnamon

cannelloni ⓜ pl ka-ne-*lo*-nee tubes of pasta stuffed with spinach, minced roast veal, ham, eggs, parmesan & spices

cannoli ⓜ pl **(ripieni)** ka-*no*-lee (ree-*pye*-nee) sweet pastry tubes filled with a mixture of sugar, candied fruit, sweet ricotta & other ingredients

cantarelli ⓜ pl kan-ta-*re*-lee chanterelle mushrooms

cantucci ⓜ pl kan-*too*-chee crunchy, hard biscuits made with aniseed & almonds

capasante ⓕ pl ka-pa-*san*-te scallops

capocollo ⓜ ka-po-*ko*-lo dry-cured pork sausage washed with red wine

caponata ⓕ ka-po-*na*-ta starter prepared with vegetables cooked in oil & vinegar – served with olives, anchovies & capers

capelli ⓜ pl **d'angelo** ka-*pe*-lee *dan*-je-lo 'angel's hair' – long, thin strands of pasta

cappellacci ⓜ pl **di zucca** ka-pe-*la*-chee dee *tsoo*-ka small pasta, filled with pumpkin & parmesan

cappelletti ⓜ pl ka-pe-*le*-tee similar to **tortellini**, only larger

cappello ⓜ **da prete** ka-*pe*-lo da *pre*-te boiled lower part of the pig's trotter, served with salsa verde or mustard

capperi ⓜ pl *ka*-pe-ree capers

cappon ⓜ **magro** ka-*pon* *ma*-gro salad with vegetables, fish & shellfish, dressed with a rich green sauce

capra ⓕ *ka*-pra goat • goat's cheese

caprese ⓕ ka-*pre*-ze salad with tomato, basil & **mozzarella**

capretto ⓜ ka·pre·to kid (goat)

caprino ⓜ ka·pree·no tart goat cheese often mixed at the table into a paste

carbonada ⓕ kar·bo·na·da diced, salted beef cooked in red wine

carbonara kar·bo·na·ra, a·la pasta sauce with egg, cheese & pancetta

carciofi ⓜ pl kar·cho·fee artichokes

cardoncelli ⓜ pl kar·don·che·lee type of mushroom, similar to oyster mushrooms

carnaroli ⓜ pl kar·na·ro·lee short grain rice used for risotto

carne ⓕ kar·ne meat
— **equina** e·kwee·na horse meat
— **suina** swee·na pork
— **trita/tritata** tree·ta/tree·ta·ta mince meat

carota ⓕ ka·ro·ta carrot

carpa ⓕ kar·pa carp

carpaccio ⓜ kar·pa·cho very thin slices of raw meat

carpione ⓜ kar·pyo·ne fried fish preserved in a marinade of oil & spices

carta ⓕ **da musica** kar·ta da moo·zee·ka thin & very crunchy bread

cartoccio ⓜ kar·to·cho cooking method where fish, chicken or game are tightly wrapped in tinfoil & baked

càscà ⓕ **di carloforte** kas·ka dee kar·lo·for·te couscous with vegetables, minced meat & spices

càsonséi ⓜ pl ka·zon·say rectangles of pasta usually stuffed with parmesan, vegetables & sausage

cassata ⓕ ka·sa·ta ice cream or sponge cake stuffed with sweet ricotta, vanilla, chocolate, pistachios, candied fruit & liqueur

cassola ⓕ ka·so·la fish-soup with tomato sauce & herbs

casoncelli ⓜ pl ka·zon·che·lee pasta stuffed with meat and, depending on the region, spinach, eggs, raisins, almond biscuits, cheese or breadcrumbs

castagnaccio ⓜ ka·sta·nya·cho cake made with chestnut flour & sprinkled with pine nuts & rosemary

castagne ⓕ pl ka·sta·nye chestnuts

castelmagno ⓜ ka·stel·ma·nyo nutty blue cheese

casunzei ⓜ pl ka·zoon·say kind of ravioli stuffed with pumpkin or spinach, ham & cinnamon – served with smoked ricotta

caulada ⓕ kow·la·da cabbage-based soup with meat, mint & garlic

cavallucci ⓜ pl ka·va·loo·chee white sweets made with candied orange, nuts & spices

cavatelli ⓜ pl ka·va·te·lee small, round home-made pasta – often served with tomato sauce, oil & rocket

cavolo ⓜ ka·vo·lo cabbage

cavolfiore ⓜ ka·vol·fyo·re cauliflower

cazzimperio ⓜ ka·tseem·pe·ree·o fresh & crunchy vegetables dunked into a tasty sauce

cazzmar ⓜ kats·mar sliced sausage containing lamb's entrails, liver & giblets

cecenielli ⓜ pl che·che·nye·lee very small fish that can be fried or put on pizzas

ceci ⓜ pl che·chee chickpeas

cefalo ⓜ che·fa·lo mullet

cervello ⓜ cher·ve·lo brain

cervo ⓜ cher·vo venison

cevapcici ⓜ pl che·vap·chee·chee spicy fresh pork, beef or lamb sausages

chenella ⓕ ke·ne·la meatballs (sometimes fishballs)

chinulille ⓕ pl kee·noo·lee·le ravioli stuffed with sugar, ricotta, egg yolks, fried lemon & orange peel

chiodino ⓜ kyo·dee·no honey coloured fungus – mushroom that must be cooked

ciabatta ⓕ cha·ba·ta crisp, flat & long bread

cialzons ⓜ pl chal·tsons ravioli stuffed with ricotta, spinach, sultanas, chocolate & sometimes chicken & herbs

ciambelle ⓕ pl **al mosto** cham·be·le al mos·to ring-shaped cakes made with grape must

ciammotta ⓕ cha·mo·ta *mixed vegetable-fry*

cianfotta ⓕ chan·fo·ta *stew with vegetables, garlic & basil*

ciaudedda ⓕ chow·de·da *vegetable stew with artichokes, onions & potatoes*

ciavarro ⓜ cha·va·ro *spring soup made with cereals & legumes*

cibuddau ⓜ chee·boo·da·oo *onion-based dish*

cicala ⓕ chee·ka·la *crustacean*

ciccioli ⓜ pl chee·cho·lee *tasty pieces of crispy fat*

ciceri ⓜ pl **e tria** chee·che·ree e tree·a *dish of boiled chickpeas & pasta, served with onions*

cicirata ⓕ chee·chee·ra·ta *small, sweet balls fried & covered with honey*

ciliegia ⓕ chee·lee·e·ja *cherry*

cima ⓕ chee·ma *breast, normally veal*

cime ⓕ pl **di rapa** chee·me dee ra·pa *turnip tops*

cioccolato ⓜ cho·ko·la·to *chocolate*
— **fondente** fon·den·te *cooking chocolate*

cipollata ⓕ chee·po·la·ta *dish with pork, spare ribs, stale bread & a lot of white onion*

cipolle ⓕ pl chee·po·le *onions*
— **ripiene** ree·pye·ne *stuffed half onions*
— **selvatiche** sel·va·tee·ke *wild onions*

coccois ⓜ ko·ko·ees *flat bread made with salty cheese & crackling*

cocomero ⓜ ko·ko·me·ro *watermelon*

coda ⓕ ko·da *tail • angler fish*

cognà ⓕ ko·nya *apple, pear, fig & grape sauce*

coietas ⓕ pl ko·ye·tas *roulades made with savoy cabbage & meat sauce*

colombo/a ⓜ/ⓕ ko·lom·bo/a *dove • pigeon • type of cake*

conchiglie ⓕ pl kon·kee·lye *pasta shells*

condimento ⓜ kon·dee·men·to *dressing*

confetti ⓜ pl kon·fe·tee *sugar-coated almonds*

coniglio ⓜ ko·nee·lyo *rabbit*

conserva ⓕ kon·ser·va *preserve*
— **di pomodoro** dee po·mo·do·ro *traditional tomato sauce*

cornetto ⓜ kor·ne·to *breakfast pastry*

coscia ⓕ ko·sha *leg • haunch*

costata ⓕ kos·ta·ta *beef steak (rib)*
— **alla napoletana** a·la na·po·le·ta·na *with oil, tomato sauce, oregano, garlic & white wine*
— **di manzo alla pizzaiola** dee man·dzo a·la pee·tsa·yo·la *with garlic, oil, tomatoes & oregano*

costine ⓕ pl kos·tee·ne *ribs*
— **di maiale** dee ma·ya·le *pork spare ribs grilled on stone*

costoletta ⓕ kos·to·le·ta *veal cutlet*

cotechinata ⓕ ko·te·kee·na·ta *roulade of pig rind stuffed with garlic, parsley & lard cooked with tomato sauce*

cotechino ⓜ ko·te·kee·no *boiled pork sausage*
— **in galera** een ga·le·ra *'in prison' – meatloaf stuffed with a boiled cotechino*

cotoletta ⓕ ko·to·le·ta *(veal) cutlet usually breaded & fried*
— **alla bolognese** a·la bo·lo·nye·ze *breaded veal cutlet sauteed with butter & baked with cured ham & fresh parmesan*
— **alla milanese** a·la mee·la·ne·ze *veal loin steak breaded & fried in butter*

cotto/a ⓜ/ⓕ ko·to/ta *cooked*
ben — ben *well done*
non troppo — non tro·po *medium rare*
poco — po·ko *rare*

cozze ⓕ pl ko·tse *mussels*

crema ⓕ kre·ma *custard*
— **inglese** een·gle·ze

cren ⓜ kren *horseradish*

crescenza ⓕ kre·shen·tsa *fresh, soft cheese, see* **stracchino**

crespella ⓕ kres·pe·la *thin fritter*

crespelle ⓕ pl **bagnate** kres·pe·le ba·nya·te *with savoury filling served in chicken stock*

crocchette ① pl kro·ke·te *croquettes of mashed potatoes & various ingredients*

crostacei ⓜ pl kro·sta·chay *crustaceans*

crostata ① kro·sta·ta *fruit tart • crust*

crostini ⓜ pl kro·stee·nee *slices of bread toasted with savoury toppings*

crostoi ⓜ pl kro·stoy *little fritters with sweet or savoury fillings*

crostoli ⓜ pl kro·sto·lee *fried sweet pastry with icing sugar • small flat bread*

crucetta ① kroo·che·ta *sweet made with figs stuffed with nuts & arranged as a cross*

crudo/a ⓜ/① kroo·do/a *raw*

crumiri ⓜ pl kroo·mee·ree *type of dry biscuits*

crusca ① kroos·ka *bran*

culatello ⓜ **(di Busseto)** koo·la·te·lo (dee boo·se·to) *ham made of salted & spiced pig's rump*

culingiones ⓜ pl koo·leen·jo·nes *kind of ravioli stuffed with potatoes or chard, sheep's cheese, garlic & mint*

cupeta ① koo·pe·ta *nougat stuffed between two wafers*

cuscus ⓜ koos·koos *couscous*

cutturiddi ⓜ pl koo·too·ree·dee *lamb stew with chilli, tomatoes, small onions & celery*

D

di/d' ... dee/d ... *from ...*

datteri ⓜ pl da·te·ree *dates (fruit)*
— **di mare** dee ma·re *type of mussel*

della casa de·la ka·za *'of the house' – house speciality*

diavola, alla dya·vo·la, a·la *spicy dish*

diavolicchio ⓜ dya·vo·lee·kyo *dynamite chilli*

ditali(ni) ⓜ pl dee·ta·lee/dee·ta·lee·nee *small bits of pasta often used in soups*

dolce dol·che *dessert • sweet • soft*

dolcelatte ⓜ dol·che·la·te *soft mild blue cheese*

dolcetti ⓜ pl **di pasta di mandorle** dol·che·tee dee pas·ta dee man·dor·le *traditional sweets made with marzipan, sugar & egg whites*

E

erbazzone ⓜ er·ba·tso·ne *baked pasta stuffed with spinach, lard, spices, parmesan, eggs & parsley*
— **dolce** dol·che *sweet baked shortcrust pastry filled with boiled & chopped chards mixed with ricotta, sugar & almonds*

erbe ① pl er·be *herbs*

F

fagiano ⓜ fa·ja·no *pheasant*

fagioli ⓜ pl fa·jo·lee *beans – usually dried*

fagiolini ⓜ pl fa·jo·lee·nee *green beans*

false salsicce ① pl fal·se sal·see·che *'false sausages' – sausages made with lard & potatoes & coloured with beet*

farcito ⓜ far·chee·to *stuffed food*

farfalle ① pl far·fa·le *butterfly-shaped pasta*

farina ① fa·ree·na *flour*

farinata ① fa·ree·na·ta *thin, flat bread made from chickpea flour*

farro ⓜ fa·ro *spelt – an ancient grain*

fasoi ⓜ pl **col muset** fa·zoy kol myoo·zet *dish with dried beans, sausage, pork rind & spices*

fatto/a ⓜ/① fa·to/a *made*
— **a mano** a ma·no *made by hand*
— **in casa** een ka·za *home-made • made on the premises*

favata ① fa·va·ta *rustic dish of broad beans, lard, pork, sausages, tomatoes & herbs*

fave ① pl fa·ve *broad beans*

fegato ⓜ fe·ga·to *liver*

felino ⓜ fe·lee·no *type of salami*

ferri, ai fe·ree, ai *grilled on an open fire*

fesa ① fe·za *northern Italian word for veal*

fetta ① fe·ta *a slice of meat, cheese, etc*

fettuccine ① pl fe·too·chee·ne *long ribbon-shaped pasta*
— **alla romana** a·la ro·ma·na *'Roman-style' – served with meat sauce, mushrooms & sheep's cheese*

fiadoni ⑩ pl **alla trentina** fya·do·nee a·la tren·tee·na *little sweets stuffed with almonds, honey, cinnamon & rum*

fiandolein ① fyan·do·layn *'egg flip' made with yolks, milk, sugar & lemon peel*

fico ⑩ fee·ko *fig*

filoncino ⑩ fee·lon·chee·no *breadstick*

finanziera ① fee·nan·tsye·ra *sweetbreads, mushrooms & chicken livers in a creamy sauce*

finocchio ⑩ fee·no·kyo *fennel*

fior di latte ⑩ fyor dee la·te *fresh & very soft cheese • a gelato flavour*

fiori ⑩ pl fyo·ree *flowers – some, especially zucchini flowers, are commonly eaten*
 — di zucca farciti dee tsoo·ka far·chee·tee *stuffed, fried zucchini or squash flowers*

focaccia ① fo·ka·cha *flat bread often filled/topped with cheese, ham, vegetables & other ingredients*

foglia ① **d'alloro** fo·lya da·lo·ro *bay leaf*

fondo ⑩ fon·do *stock*

fondua ① fon·doo·a *fontina cheese melted with butter & eggs & topped with thin slices of truffle*

fontina ① fon·tee·na *sweet & creamy cheese, similar to Gruyère*

formaggio ⑩ for·ma·jo *cheese*

forno, al for·no, al *cooked in an oven*

fragole ① pl fra·go·le *strawberries*

freddo/a ⑩/① fre·do/a *cold (temperature)*

fresco/a ⑩/① fres·ko/a *fresh*

fregola ① fre·go·la *type of couscous*

fregnacce ① pl fre·nya·che *thin rolled pancakes stuffed with meat*

frisceu ⑩ free·she·oo *fritters with lettuce, whitebait, zucchini, liver, brain, dried cod, pumpkin, etc*

frisedde ① pl free·ze·de *big ring-shaped cakes, boiled, baked then served with tomatoes, oil, salt & oregano*

fritole ① pl free·to·le *fritters containing sultanas, pine nuts, candied lemon & liqueur*

frittata ① free·ta·ta *thick omelette slice, served hot or cold*

frittatensuppe ① pl free·ta·ten·soo·pe *thin omelettes cut into strips & served with meat stock*

frittatine ① pl **di farina al miele di fichi** free·ta·tee·ne dee fa·ree·na al mye·le dee fee·kee *pancakes folded & stuffed with fig honey*

frittelle ① pl free·te·le *fritters*

frittelloni ⑩ pl free·te·lo·nee *boiled spinach tortellini sauteed with butter, sultanas & cheese, then fried in lard*

fritto/a ⑩/① free·to/a *fried*

fritto ⑩ **misto** free·to mees·to *a mixture of various ingredients, depending on the region & time of year, fried in olive oil (some versions contain offal)*
 — abruzzese a·broo·tse·ze *diced artichokes & boiled fennel, breaded & fried*

frumento ⑩ froo·men·to *wheat*

frutta ① froo·ta *fruit*
 — secca se·ka *dried fruit*

frutti ⑩ pl **di mare** froo·tee dee ma·re *sea food*

fugazza ① foo·ga·tsa *very rich, tasty sweet pastry*

funghi ⑩ pl foon·gee *mushrooms*

fusilli ⑩ pl foo·zee·lee *corkscrew shaped pasta*

G

galani ⑩ pl ga·la·nee *layered strips of fried pastry sprinkled with icing sugar*

gallina ① ga·lee·na *chicken • hen*

gambero ⑩ gam·be·ro *prawn • shrimp*

gamberoni ⑩ pl gam·be·ro·nee *prawns*

gambon ⑩ gam·bon *pig's leg, boned, pressed & matured*

garagoli ⑩ pl ga·ra·go·lee *shellfish similar to periwinkles*

garganelli ⑩ pl gar·ga·ne·lee *short pasta served with various sauces*

gattò ⑩ **di patate e salsiccia** ga·to dee pa·ta·te e sal·see·cha *baked meatloaf made with mashed potato, eggs, ham & cheeses*

gelato ⓜ je·la·to *ice cream*

genovese, alla je·no·ve·ze, a·la *sauce including olive oil, garlic & herbs*

gerstensuppe ⓜ ger·sten·soo·pe *barley-soup with onions, parsley, spices & speck*

gianduiotto ⓜ jyan·doo·yo·to *hazelnut chocolate*

giardiniera ⓕ jar·dee·nye·ra *pickled vegetables*

girello ⓜ jee·re·lo *round cut of meat*

gnocchi ⓜ pl nyo·kee *small dumplings – most commonly potato dumplings*

gnocchetti ⓜ pl nyo·ke·tee *small shell-shaped pasta*

gnocco ⓜ **di pane (al prosciutto)** nyo·ko dee pa·ne (al pro·shoo·to) *pieces of bread fried in a mixture of butter, eggs, milk (& ham)*

goregone go·re·go·ne *freshwater lake fish*

gorgonzola ⓕ gor·gon·dzo·la *spicy, sweet, creamy blue vein cow's milk cheese*

grana ⓕ **(padano)** gra·na (pa·da·no) *hard cheese, also refers to cheeses such as* **parmigiano**

granchio ⓜ gran·kyo *crab*

granita ⓕ gra·nee·ta *finely crushed flavoured ice*

granseola ⓕ gran·se·o·la *spider crab*

grano ⓜ gra·no *wheat*

gran(o)turco ⓜ gra·n(o)·toor·ko *maize*

grappa ⓕ gra·pa *distilled grape must*

grissini ⓜ pl gree·see·nee *breadsticks*

guanciale ⓜ gwan·cha·le *cheek, usually pig's*

gubana ⓕ goo·ba·na *sweet pastry*

I

impanada ⓕ eem·pa·na·da *savoury tart stuffed with vegetables & many kinds of meat & fish*

impepata ⓕ **di cozze** eem·pe·pa·ta dee ko·tse *fish-based dish prepared with mussels & lemon*

infarinata ⓕ een·fa·ree·na·ta *polenta as a soup, or fried in strips, with various meat & vegetable combinations*

insalata ⓕ een·sa·la·ta *salad*
— **caprese** ka·pre·ze *with* **mozzarella**, *tomato & basil*
— **di carne cruda** dee kar·ne kroo·da *with raw minced meat*

involtini ⓜ pl een·vol·tee·nee *stuffed rolls of meat or fish*
— **di carne** dee kar·ne *small veal slices, rolled up, stuffed, pierced on kebabs & baked or grilled*
— **siciliani** see·chee·lya·nee *meat rolled in breadcrumbs, stuffed with egg, ham & cheese*

J

jota ⓕ yo·ta *soup with beans, milk, & polenta • soup with beans, potatoes, sauerkraut & smoked pork rinds*

L

laganelle ⓕ pl **e fagioli** la·ga·ne·le e fa·jo·lee *sheets of pasta served in a bean soup*

lamponi ⓜ pl lam·po·nee *raspberries*

lasagne ⓕ pl la·za·nye *flat sheets of egg pasta*
— **alla bolognese** a·la bo·lo·nye·ze *baked lasagne with meat sauce, bechamel & parmesan*

lattuga ⓕ la·too·ga *lettuce*

lavarelli ⓜ pl la·va·re·lee *fresh water whitefish*

lecca-lecca ⓕ le·ka le·ka *lollipop*

lenticchie ⓕ pl len·tee·kye *lentils*

lepre ⓕ lep·re *hare*

lesso/a ⓜ/ⓕ le·so *boiled*

liscio/a ⓜ/ⓕ lee·sho/a *smooth – describes pasta with a smooth surface*

lianeddè ⓜ pl lya·ne·de *noodles with chickpeas or rabbit sauce*

lievito ⓜ lye·vee·to *yeast*

limone ⓜ lee·mo·ne *lemon*

lingua ⓕ leen·gwa *tongue*

linguine ⓕ pl leen·gwee·ne *long thin ribbons of pasta*

luccio ⓜ loo·cho *pike*

luganega ① loo·ga·ne·ga pork sausage

luganiga di verze ① loo·ga·nee·ga dee ver·dze cabbage sausage stuffed with mince, cheese, eggs & breadcrumbs

lumache ① pl loo·ma·ke snails

luppoli ⑩ pl loo·po·lee hops

M

maccaruni ⑩ pl di casa con ragù ma·ka·roo·nee dee ka·za kon ra·goo small pasta tubes served with tomato & meat sauce

maccheroni ⑩ pl make·ro·nee can refer to any tube pasta
— **alla chitarra** a·la kee·ta·ra square spaghetti, generally served with a meat sauce
— **con la ricotta** kon la ree·ko·ta pasta served with ricotta, sheep's cheese & sometimes also parmesan

magro/a ⑩/① mag·ro/a thin • lean • meatless

maturo/a ⑩/① ma·too·ro/a ripe

maiale ⑩ ma·ya·le pork

mais ⑩ ma·eez maize

malfatti ⑩ pl mal·fa·tee dumplings with spinach, eggs & cheese

malloreddus ⑩ pl ma·lo·re·doos dumplings with saffron in a meat sauce

maltagliati ⑩ pl mal·ta·lya·tee odd shapes of pasta

mandorle ① pl man·dor·le almonds

manteca ① man·te·ka fresh cheese rolled in a ball and stuffed with butter

mantecato ⑩ man·te·ka·to any ingredients pounded to a paste

manzo ⑩ man·dzo beef

maraschino ⑩ ma·ras·kee·no cherry liqueur

marcetto ⑩ mar·che·to very spicy cheese paste

marille ① pl ma·ree·le crazily-shaped pasta designed to retain the maximum amount of sauce

marinara, alla ma·ree·na·ra, a·la dish containing seafood

maritozzi ⑩ pl ma·ree·to·tsee small, soft sweet cakes stuffed with pine nuts, sultanas, orange peel & fruit

marrone ⑩ ma·ro·ne large chestnut

marsala ① mar·sa·la fortified wine

marubini ⑩ pl ma·roo·bee·nee pasta stuffed with toasted bread, parmesan, marrow & eggs

mascarpone ⑩ mas·kar·po·ne very soft & creamy cheese

maturo/a ⑩/① ma·too·ro/a ripe

mazzafegato ① pl ma·tsa·fe·ga·to matured dry-cured pork sausage, made with minced liver, kidney, tripe & lung

mela ① me·la apple

melagrana ① me·la·gra·na pomegranate

melanzanata ① (di Lecce) me·lan·dza·na·ta (dee le·che) eggplant pasta sauce • baked eggplant, tomato, onion, basil & sheep's cheese

melanzane ① pl me·lan·dza·ne eggplants • aubergines
— **ripiene** ree·pye·ne baked eggplants stuffed with their pulp, eggs, cheese, herbs, spices & bread
— **violette** vee·o·le·te purple eggplant

meringa ① me·reen·ga meringue

merlano ⑩ mer·la·no whiting

merluzzo ⑩ mer·loo·tso cod

mesta ① e fasoj ⑩ pl mes·ta e fa·zoy polenta cooked with beans

miele ⑩ mye·le honey

migliaccio ⑩ 'e cigule ① pl mee·lya·cho e chee·goo·le baked polenta with pork, sausages, sheep's cheese & pepper

milanese, alla mee·la·ne·ze, a·la any sauce associated with Milan – normally includes butter

millecosedde ⑩ mee·le·ko·ze·de hearty soup with vegetables, legumes & short pasta

minestra ① mee·ne·stra general word for soup
— **alla pignata** a·la pee·nya·ta with beans, pork & vegetables
— **cò i cece** ko ee che·che with chickpeas & pasta

minestrone ⓜ mee·ne·stro·ne
  traditional soup usually including
  many vegetables & sometimes pasta
  or rice, bacon cubes & pork rinds
misticanza ⓕ mees·tee·kan·tsa salad
  with mixed greens
misto/a ⓜ/ⓕ mees·to/a mixed
mollusco ⓜ mo·loo·sko mollusc
montasio ⓜ mon·ta·zyo hard cheese
montato/a ⓜ/ⓕ mon·ta·to/a whipped
morbido/a ⓜ/ⓕ mor·bee·do soft
mortadella ⓕ **(di Bologna)**
  mor·ta·de·la (dee bo·lo·nya) salami
  made with minced pork, lard & black
  pepper
mostaccioli ⓜ pl mos·ta·cho·lee small,
  sweet, chocolate-coated biscuits
mozzetta ⓕ mot·tse·ta salami made
  with haunch of mountain-goat or
  chamois, salted & dried
mozzarella ⓕ mo·tsa·re·la soft, fresh
  white cheese made from cow's milk
  — di bufala dee boo·fa·la made from
  buffalo's milk
  — in carrozza een ka·ro·tsa on slices
  of bread, battered & fried
'mpanada ⓕ m·pa·na·da see impanada
'mpepata ⓕ **di cozze** m·pe·pa·ta dee
  ko·tse see impepata di cozze
muggine ⓜ moo·jee·ne mullet

N

napoletana, alla na·po·le·ta·na, a·la
  from or in the style of Naples –
  usually includes tomatoes & garlic
nasello ⓜ na·ze·lo hake
'ndugghia ⓕ n·doo·gya dry-cured
  pork & fennel-seed sausage
nero ⓜ **di seppia/calamaro** ne·ro dee
  se·pya/ka·la·ma·ro squid/calamari ink
nocciola ⓕ no·cho·la hazelnut
noce ⓜ no·che nut • walnut
  — di cocco dee ko·ko coconut
  — moscata mos·ka·ta nutmeg
norma, alla nor·ma, a·la pasta sauce
  with eggplant & tomato
nostrano ⓜ nos·tra·no hard cheese •
  local, home-made or domestic
  produce

O

oca ⓕ o·ka goose
offelle ⓕ pl o·fe·le sweet biscuits with
  mixed dried fruit
olio ⓜ o·lyo oil – almost always
  olive oil
ombrichelli ⓜ pl om·bree·ke·lee
  coarse home-made spaghetti
opinus ⓜ o·pee·noos pine-cone-
  shaped biscuits sprinkled with
  melted sugar & egg whites
orata ⓕ o·ra·ta bream • gilthead
orecchiette ⓕ pl o·re·kye·te shell-
  shaped, hand-made pasta, served
  with vegetables & olive oil or a rich
  meat sauce
orzo ⓜ or·dzo barley
  — e fagioli e fa·jo·lee thick barley &
  bean broth
ossi di morti ⓜ pl o·see dee mor·tee
  'bones of the dead' – very hard
  crunchy biscuits
ossobuco ⓜ o·so·boo·ko veal shanks
  — milanese mee·la·ne·ze cut into
  small pieces & cooked with spices
ostriche ⓕ pl os·tree·ke oysters

P

pagnottella ⓕ pa·nyo·te·la bread roll
palle ⓕ pl pa·le balls
  — del nonno del no·no 'grandpa's
  balls' – sweet fried ricotta balls •
  crinkly pork sausages
  — di riso dee ree·zo stuffed rice
  croquettes
palombo ⓜ pa·lom·bo dove • pigeon
  — alla todina a·la to·dee·na roasted
  pigeon
pan ⓜ **biscotto condito** pan bees·ko·to
  kon·dee·to toasted bread with oil,
  tomatoes, herbs
panadas ⓕ pl pa·na·das see pancotto
pancetta ⓕ pan·che·ta salt-cured bacon
pancotto ⓜ pan·ko·to soup made with
  boiled bread, cheese & eggs or fresh
  tomatoes

pane ⓜ *pa·ne* bread
— **all'olio** a·lo·lyo bread with oil
— **aromatico** a·ro·ma·tee·ko herb or vegetable bread
— **carasau** ka·ra·zow long-lasting bread eaten by shepherds
— **casereccio** ka·ze·re·cho firm, floury loaf
— **col mosto** kol mos·to bread with nuts, anise, almonds, raisins, sugar & must
— **di segale** dee se·ga·le rye bread
— **frattau** fra·tow slices of bread with sheep's cheese, tomato or meat sauce, boiling broth & eggs
— **fresa** fre·za flat, crispy bread
— **integrale** een·te·gra·le wholemeal bread
— **pugliese** poo·lye·ze large, crusty loaf
— **salato** sa·la·to salty bread
— **toscano** tos·ka·no crumbly, unsalted bread
— **unto** oon·to slices of bread toasted with garlic, olive oil, salt & pepper
panelle ⓕ pl pa·ne·le fried chickpea fritters
panforte ⓜ **(senese)** pan·for·te (se·ne·ze) hard cake made with almonds, fruit & spices
panino ⓜ pa·nee·no bread roll
paniscia ⓕ **novarese** pa·nee·sha no·va·re·ze rice-based dish with onion, sausage & soup
panna ⓕ pa·na cream
— **cotta** ko·ta thick creamy dessert
panpepato ⓜ pan·pe·pa·to sweet, ring-shaped cake
pan ⓜ **speziale** pan spe·cha·le bread with honey, nuts, raisins & fruit
panzanella ⓕ pan·tsa·ne·la Tuscan bread served with tomato sauce, onion, lettuce, anchovies, basil, olive oil, vinegar & salt
panzerotti ⓜ pl pan·tse·ro·tee filled pasta or pastries in a half-moon shape

paparot ⓜ pa·pa·rot spinach & corn soup
papassinas ⓜ pl pa·pa·see·nas small, sweet cone-shaped cakes
pappa ⓕ pa·pa baby food
— **col pomodoro** kol po·mo·do·ro soup made with thin slices of stale bread, tomatoes & spices
pappardelle ⓕ pl pa·par·de·le wide, flat pasta ribbons
— **alla lepre** a·la le·pre with stewed hare, red wine & tomato sauce
parmigiana, alla par·mee·ja·na, a·la any type of cheesy sauce
parmigiana ⓕ **di melanzane** par·mee·ja·na dee me·lan·dza·ne fried eggplant layered with eggs, basil, tomato sauce, onion & mozzarella
parmigiano ⓜ **(reggiano)** par·mee·ja·no (re·ja·no) parmesan cheese and often simply called **grana**
parrozzo ⓜ pa·ro·tso sweet bread, sometimes chocolate coated
passatelli ⓜ pl pa·sa·te·lee small dumplings made with eggs, parmesan, ox marrow & nutmeg
pasta ⓕ pas·ta general name for the numerous types of pasta shapes • dough • pastry
— **col bianchetto** kol byan·ke·to spaghetti with a whitebait, tomato, garlic & chilli sauce
— **cresciuta** kre·shoo·ta anchovy or courgette flower fritters
— **e fagioli** e fa·jo·lee bean soup with pasta
— **fresca** fres·ka general term for freshly made pasta
pastasciutta ⓕ pas·ta·shoo·ta dry pasta
pastissada/pastizzada ⓕ pas·tee·sa·da/pas·tee·tsa·da stew prepared with beef, ox or horse meat & vegetables
patate ⓕ pl pa·ta·te potatoes
pecorino ⓜ **(romano)** pe·ko·ree·no (ro·ma·no) hard & spicy cheese made from ewe's milk
penne ⓕ pl pe·ne short & tubular pasta

pepe ⓜ *pe·pe* pepper

peperonata ⓕ *pe·pe·ro·na·ta* capsicum, onion & tomato stew

peperoncini ⓜ pl *pe·pe·ron·chee·nee* hot chilli

peperoni ⓜ pl *pe·pe·ro·nee* peppers • capsicum
 — **ripieni** *ree·pye·nee* stuffed with various fillings

pere ⓕ pl *pe·ra* pears
 — **imbottite** *eem·bo·tee·te* baked stuffed pears

persico ⓜ *per·see·ko* perch

pesca ⓕ *pe·ska* peach

pesce ⓜ *pe·she* fish

pesto ⓜ *pes·to* sauce prepared with fresh basil, pine nuts, olive oil, garlic, cheese & salt

petto ⓜ *pe·to* breast

pettole ⓕ pl *pe·to·le* home-made, long thin, ribbons of pasta

piadina ⓕ *pya·dee·na* flat round bread

piccagge ⓕ pl *pee·ka·je* long ribbon pasta served with pesto or an artichoke & mushroom sauce

piccata ⓕ *pee·ka·ta* veal with a lemon & **Marsala** sauce

picchi pacchiu ⓜ *pee·kee pa·kyoo* pasta sauce with tomato & chilli

pici ⓜ pl *pee·chee* fresh pasta, like thick spaghetti

piccione ⓜ *pee·cho·ne* squab • pigeon

picula ⓕ **ad caval** *pee·koo·la ad ka·val* horse meat stew

pinoli ⓜ pl *pee·no·lee* pine nuts

pinza ⓕ **padovana** *peen·tsa pa·do·va·na* sweet pastry

pinzimonio ⓜ *peen·tsee·mo·nyo* seasoned virgin olive oil for dipping (see also **cazzimperio**)

piopparello ⓜ *pyo·pa·re·lo* common flat mushroom

pisarei ⓜ pl **e fasò** ⓜ pl *pee·za·ray e fa·zo* small dumplings flavoured with tomato sauce, bacon & boiled beans

piselli ⓜ pl *pee·ze·lee* green peas

pistum ⓜ *pees·toom* sweet & sour dumplings served with pork stock

pitta ⓕ *pee·ta* soft & flat loaf of bread

pitte ⓕ *pee·te* fring-shaped cake

pizza ⓕ *pee·tsa* there are more than 50 kinds of pizza, with varying bases and toppings
 — **a(l) taglio** *a(l) ta·lyo* slice of pizza
 — **dolce di Pasqua** *dol·che dee pas·kwa* sweet pizza dough with dried fruits
 — **Margherita** *mar·ge·ree·ta* topped with simple ingredients such as oil, tomato, **mozzarella**, basil & oregano
 — **rustica** *roos·tee·ka* topped with various combinations of ham, salami, sausage, egg or cheese

pizzaiola, alla *pee·tsa·yo·la, a·la* a tomato & oil sauce

pizzoccheri ⓜ pl *pee·tso·ke·ree* short, buckwheat pasta with cabbage & potatoes

polenta ⓕ *po·len·ta* corn meal porridge
 — **al ragù** *al ra·goo* served with a meat sauce
 — **concia** *kon·cha* flavoured with a variety of cheeses
 — **e osei** *e o·zay* served with sparrows, thrushes or larks • sponge cake with jam
 — **pasticciata** *pas·tee·cha·ta* baked with meat sauce, mushrooms & cheese
 — **sulla spianatoria** *soo·la spya·na·to·rya* with sausages, tomato & sheep's cheese served from a **spianatoria** (pastry board) placed in the middle of the table
 — **taragna** *ta·ra·nya* originally buckwheat polenta

polipo ⓜ *po·lee·po* octopus (see **polpi**)

pollo ⓜ *po·lo* chicken
 — **alla diavola** *a·la dya·vo·la* grilled with red pepper or chilli
 — **con peperoni e patate al coccio** *kon pe·pe·ro·nee e pa·ta·te al ko·cho* slowly cooked in a terracotta pot with sage, potatoes & capsicum

polpette ⓜ pol·pe·te *meatballs*

polpettine ⓕ pl pol·pe·tee·ne *small meatballs*

— **di carne con salsa di pomodoro** dee *kar*·ne kon *sal*·sa dee po·mo·*do*·ro *in tomato sauce*

polpettone ⓜ pol·pe·*to*·ne *meatloaf*

polpi ⓜ pl *pol*·pee *octopus (also called polipi)*

— **alla luciana** a·la loo·*cha*·na *sliced octopus with tomatoes, oil, garlic, parsley & lemon*

— **in purgatorio** een poor·ga·*to*·ryo *stewed with tomato, parsley, chilli & garlic*

pomodori ⓜ pl po·mo·*do*·ree *tomatoes*

— **secchi** se·kee *sun-dried tomatoes*

pomodorini ⓜ pl po·mo·do·*ree*·nee *tiny tomatoes • sun-dried tomatoes*

pompelmo ⓜ pom·*pel*·mo *grapefruit*

porchetta ⓕ por·*ke*·ta *stuffed suckling pig*

porcini ⓜ pl por·*chee*·nee *ceps (type of mushrooms)*

porco ⓜ *por*·ko *pig*

potizza ⓕ po·*tee*·tsa *soft cake prepared with leavened pastry*

prataiolo ⓜ pra·ta·*yo*·lo *popular button mushroom*

preboggion ⓜ pre·bo·*jon* *mixture of wild herbs*

prosciutto ⓜ pro·*shoo*·to *basic name for many types of thinly-sliced ham*

— **affumicato** a·foo·mee·*ka*·to *smoked salami*

— **San Daniele** san da·*nye*·le *sweet & delicate ham*

provola ⓕ *pro*·vo·la *semi-hard cheese made from buffalo & cow's milk*

provolone ⓜ pro·vo·*lo*·ne *rich medium hard cheese made from cow's milk*

prugna ⓕ *proo*·nya *plum*

puttanesca, alla poo·ta·*ne*·ska, *a*·la *'whore's style' – tomato, chilli, anchovies & black olive pasta sauce*

Q

quaglie ⓕ pl *kwa*·lye *quails*

quartirolo ⓜ kwar·tee·*ro*·lo *sweet & delicate soft cheese*

quattro formaggi *kwa*·tro for·*ma*·jee *pasta sauce with four different cheeses*

quattro stagioni *kwa*·tro sta·*jo*·nee *pizza with different toppings on each quarter*

R

rabarbaro ⓜ ra·*bar*·ba·ro *rhubarb*

radicchio ⓜ ra·*dee*·kyo *chicory*

— **rosso** *ro*·so *slightly bitter vegetable with long leaves*

rafano ⓜ **tedesco** ra·*fa*·no te·*des*·ko *horseradish*

ragù ⓜ ra·*goo* *generally a meat sauce but sometimes vegetarian*

— **alla bolognese** a·la bo·lo·*nye*·ze *sauce of minced veal & pork*

— **alla napoletana** a·la na·po·le·*ta*·na *sauce made with chunks of meat, vegetables & red wine*

rambasicci ⓜ pl ram·ba·*zee*·chee *stuffed cabbage leaves*

rapa ⓕ *ra*·pa *turnip*

ravioli ⓜ pl ra·vee·*o*·lee *pasta squares usually stuffed with meat, parmesan cheese & breadcrumbs*

— **liguri** *lee*·goo·ree *sometimes filled with ricotta & herbs*

raviolini ⓜ pl ra·vee·o·*lee*·nee *small ravioli*

ravioloni ⓜ pl ra·vee·o·*lo*·nee *large ravioli*

razza ⓕ *ra*·tsa *skate*

ri(so) ⓜ **in cagnon** *ree*(·zo) een ka·*nyon* *rice sauteed in garlic, butter, sage & sprinkled with parmesan*

ribes ⓜ **nero** *ree*·bes *ne*·ro *blackcurrant*

ribes ⓜ **rosso** *ree*·bes *ro*·so *redcurrant*

ribollita ⓕ ree·bo·*lee*·ta *reheated & thickened vegetable soup*

ricciarelli ⓜ pl ree·cha·*re*·lee *almond biscuits*

ricotta ① ree-ko-ta *fresh, moist, white cheese*
— **affumicata** a-foo-mee-ka-ta *smoked*
— **infornata** een-for-na-ta *oven baked*

rigaglie ① pl ree-ga-lye *giblets*

rigatoni ⓜ pl ree-ga-to-nee *short, fat tubes of pasta*
— **con la pagliata** kon la pa-lya-ta *served with small intestines of calves*

ripieno ⓜ ree-pye-no *stuffing*

risi ⓜ pl **e bisi** ⓜ pl ree-zee e bee-zee *thick rice-based soup with peas*

risi ⓜ pl **e bruscandoli** ⓜ pl ree-zee e broos-kan-do-lee *bitter hop sprouts cooked in a broth with rice*

riso ⓜ ree-zo *rice*
— **al salto** al sal-to *boiled rice sauteed with saffron*
— **comune** ko-moo-ne *lowest quality, usually used in soups*
— **fino** fee-no *good quality with large grains*
— **semifino** se-mee-fee-no *slightly better quality than comune, with larger grains*
— **superfino** soo-per-fee-no *best quality rice, used in risotto*

risotto ⓜ ree-zo-to *rice dish slowly cooked in broth to a creamy consistency*
— **alla milanese** a-la mee-la-ne-ze *with ox marrow, meat stock & saffron*
— **alla monzese** a-la mon-dze-ze *with sausage & saffron or red wine*
— **alla piemontese** a-la pye-mon-te-ze *with white wine & truffles (& sometimes tomato sauce)*
— **alla sbirraglia** a-la sbee-ra-lya *with chicken breasts*
— **alla trevisana** a-la tre-vee-za-na *with sausage or chicken livers*
— **allo zafferano** a-lo dza-fe-ra-no *see* **risotto alla milanese**
— **con filetti di pesce persico** kon fee-le-tee dee pe-she per-see-ko *with perch fillets*
— **con le rane** kon le ra-ne *with frog legs, frog broth & herbs*
— **nero** ne-ro *black risotto with chard, onion, cuttlefish & their ink*
— **polesano** po-le-za-no *with eel, grey mullet, bass, white wine & fish broth*

robiola ① ro-byo-la *soft cheese made mainly from cow's milk*

romana, alla ro-ma-na, a-la *sauce, usually tomato based*

rombo ⓜ rom-bo *turbot*

rosolata ① ro-zo-la-ta *saute*

rosbif ⓜ roz-beef *roast beef*

rospo ⓜ ros-po *angler fish*

rosumada ① ro-zoo-ma-da *egg-nog with red wine*

rotolo ⓜ ro-to-lo *folded sheet of pasta filled with spinach, ricotta or meat*

ruchetta ① roo-ke-ta *rocket*

rucola ① roo-ko-la *rocket*

rum-babà ⓜ room ba-ba *babà sprinkled with rum & sugar*

ruta ① roo-ta *rue (bitter herb)*

S

sa fregula ① sa fre-goo-la *soup with small balls of flour & saffron*

sagne chine ① sa-nye kee-ne *baked pasta with meatballs, eggs & cheese*

salama **da sugo ferrarese** sa-la-ma da soo-go fe-ra-re-ze *pork sausage*

salame ① **di Felino** sa-la-me dee fe-lee-no *dry-cured pork sausage*

salami ⓜ pl sa-la-mee *generally any type of (pork) sausage*

salamino ⓜ sa-la-mee-no *small salami*

salato/a ⓜ/① sa-la-to/a *salty*

sale ⓜ sa-le *salt*

salmì ⓜ sal-mee *marinade with spices & sometimes wine*

salmone ⓜ sal-mo-ne *salmon*

salsa ① sal-sa *sauce*
— **alfredo** al-fre-do *with butter, cream, parmesan & parsley*
— **alla checca** a-la ke-ka *cold sauce with tomatoes, olives, basil, capers & oregano*

— alla pizzaiola *a·la pee·tsa·yo·la* pizza-style sauce

— di cren *dee kren* with grated radish & apples, onion, broth & white wine

— di pomodoro al tonno e funghi *dee po·mo·do·ro al to·no e foon·gee* with tuna, mushroom & tomato

— di pomodoro alla siciliana *dee po·mo·do·ro a·la see·chee·lya·na* with eggplant, anchovies, olives, capers, tomato & garlic

— verde *ver·de* green sauce with herbs, capers, olives, nuts, anchovies, breadcrumbs, garlic & vinegar

saltimbocca ⓕ *sal·teem·bo·ka* 'jump into the mouth' – bite-sized

salume ⓜ *sa·loo·me* salami

sanguinaccio ⓜ *san·gwee·na·cho* black pudding made with pig's blood, olives & cocoa

saor, in *sowr, een* sweet & sour, vinegar-based marinade for fish

sarago ⓜ *sa·ra·go* white bream

sarde ⓕ pl *sar·de* sardines

— a scapece *a ska·pe·che* fried sardines

— alla marchigiana *a·la mar·kee·ja·na* baked, marinated sardines

sardele in saor ⓕ pl *sar·de·le een sowr* dish with fried, marinated pilchards

sartù 'e riso ⓜ *sar·too e ree·zo* savoury rice dish

sas melicheddas ⓜ pl *sas me·lee·ke·das* marzipan cakes sprinkled with sugar

sausa d'avie ⓕ *sow·sa da·vee·e* honey, nut & mustard sauce

savoiardi ⓜ pl *sa·vo·yar·dee* ladyfinger biscuits

sbrofadej *z·bro·fa·day* thin pasta

— in brodo *een bro·do* served in broth

scagliuozzoli ⓜ pl *ska·lyoo·o·tso·lee* fried polenta & provolone

scaloppine ⓕ pl *ska·lo·pee·ne* thin cutlets, usually veal, pork or turkey

— al marsala *al mar·sa·la* lean veal cutlet with marsala

scamorza ⓕ *ska·mor·tsa* soft, white cheese, similar to mozzarella & often smoked

scampi ⓜ pl *skam·pee* a small type of lobster

scapece ⓜ *ska·pe·che* vinegar-based marinade usually used for fish

— di Vasto *dee vas·to* dish prepared with sliced & fried fish, preserved in a marinade

scarole ⓕ *ska·ro·le* bitter leafy vegetable

schiaffettuni ⓜ pl *chini skya·fe·too·nee kee·nee* maccheroni with pork & eggs

schmorbraten *shmor·bra·ten* veal marinated & cooked in wine & tomato sauce

sciatt ⓜ *schat* soft, round fritters containing grappa

scimú'd ⓜ *shee·mood* salted & spicy skim milk cheese

sciroppo ⓜ *shee·ro·po* syrup

scivateddi ⓜ *shee·va·te·dee* thick spaghetti served with meat sauce & ricotta

scottiglia ⓕ *sko·tee·lya* rich stew with tomatoes & meat

sebadas ⓜ *se·ba·das* large, round & sweet ravioli with cheese & honey

seccia 'mbuttunata *se·cha m·boo·too·na·ta* stuffed cuttlefish stewed with tomato sauce

selvaggina ⓕ *sel·va·jee·na* game

semifreddo ⓜ *se·mee·fre·do* can refer to many cold, creamy desserts

— al torrone *al to·ro·ne* dessert with milk, vanilla, eggs & nougat

semola ⓕ *se·mo·la bran* – semolina

semolino ⓜ *se·mo·lee·no* semolina

senape ⓕ *se·na·pe* mustard

seno ⓜ *se·no* breast

seppia ⓕ *se·pya* cuttlefish

serpe ⓜ *ser·pe* cake with marzipan, almonds, icing sugar or chocolate

sfogliatelle ⓕ pl *sfo·lya·te·le* cake or pastry stuffed with ricotta, cinnamon, candied fruit & vanilla

sformato ⓜ sfor·ma·to *flan*
— **di spinaci con cibreo al vinsanto**
dee spee·na·chee kon chee·bre·o
al veen·san·to *flan with spinach &
served with liver*

sgombro ⓜ sgom·bro *mackerel*

sogliola ⓕ so·lyo·la *sole*

sopa ⓕ **còada** so·pa ko·a·da *soup of
meat stock, pigeon, cheese & bread*

soppressa ⓕ so·pre·sa *pork sausage*

soppressata ⓕ so·pre·sa·ta *matured
raw salami made with minced pig's
tongue, lean pork & spices • soft
salami made with pork & lard*
— **molisana** mo·lee·za·na *large pork
sausage*

sorbetto ⓜ sor·be·to *sorbet*

sott'aceti ⓜ pl so·ta·che·tee *pickles*

sott'olio ⓜ so·to·lyo *preserved in oil*

spaghetti ⓜ pl spa·ge·tee *ubiquitous
long thin strands of pasta*

spá'tzle ⓜ spa·tsle *little dumplings
that can be served in broth*

speck ⓜ spek *type of smoked ham*

spiedino/spiedo ⓜ spye·dee·no/
spye·do *skewer*

spezie ⓕ pl spe·tsye *spices*

spigola ⓕ spee·go·la *sea bass*

spinaci ⓜ pl spee·na·chee *spinach*

sponga(r)da ⓕ spon·ga(r)·da *sweet
pastry with vanilla, egg & sometimes
mixed dried fruits*

spugnola ⓕ spoo·nyo·la *morel
(sponge-like mushroom)*

stecchi ⓜ pl ste·kee *sticks • kebabs*
— **alla ligure** a·la lee·goo·re *with
veal, chicken, sweetbread, eggs,
mushrooms, artichokes & spices*

stiacciata ⓕ stya·cha·ta *sweet bun*

stinco ⓜ steen·ko *shank*

stoccafisso ⓜ sto·ka·fee·so *stockfish
(small air-dried cod)*
— **a brandacujun** a bran·da·koo·yoon
creamy dish of potatoes & stockfish
— **accomodato** a·ko·mo·da·to
*stockfish cooked in a casserole with
anchovies or mushrooms*

stracchino ⓜ stra·kee·no *soft &
delicate cheese*

stracciatella ⓕ stra·cha·te·la *broth with
whipped egg & parmesan*

stracotto ⓜ stra·ko·to *beef stew*

stracotto/a ⓜ/ⓕ stra·ko·to/a *cooked
for a long time • overcooked*

strangolapreti ⓜ pl stran·go·la·pre·tee
*'priest throttler' – cheese & egg
dumplings, varying from region to
region*

stravecchio ⓜ stra·ve·kyo *'very old' –
aged for a long time*

stringozzi ⓜ pl streen·go·tsee *short pasta
served with tomato or meat sauce*

strinù ⓜ stree·noo *tasty sausage,
usually grilled*

stroscia ⓕ **(di Pietrabruna)** stro·sha
(dee pye·tra·broo·na) *sweet cake*

strozzapreti ⓜ pl stro·tsa·pre·tee *long
strips of pasta • dumplings made
with spinach, chard & ricotta*

strudel ⓜ stroo·del *pastry with a
stuffing including apples*

stufatino ⓜ stoo·fa·tee·no *lean veal
stewed with tomatoes & spices*

supa ⓕ **barbetta** soo·pa bar·be·ta *rich
meat & vegetable stock*

suppa ⓕ soo·pa *soup*

supplì ⓜ soo·plee *fried rice balls
(similar to crocchettes)*

suricitti ⓜ pl soo·ree·chee·tee
flavoured polenta dumplings

susamelli ⓜ pl soo·za·me·lee *s-shaped
biscuits*

T

tacchino ⓜ ta·kee·no *turkey*
— **alla gosutta** a·la go·zoo·ta *turkey
casserole with fennel & broth*
— **con sugo di melagrana** kon soo·go
dee me·la·gra·na *with pomegranate
sauce*

tagliatelle ⓕ ta·lya·te·le *long, ribbon-
shaped pasta*
— **alla salsa di noci** a·la sal·sa dee
no·chee *with nuts, oil, butter, ricotta
& parmesan*

— con finocchio selvatico kon
fee·no·kyo sel·va·tee·ko *served with a
fennel, bacon & parsley sauce*

taglierini ⓜ pl ta·lye·ree·nee *thin strips
of pasta*

— al ragù al ra·goo *served with meat
sauce*

tagliolini (blò blò) ⓜ pl ta·lyo·lee·nee
(blo blo) *thin strips of pasta in broth,
with grated cheese*

tajarin ⓜ pl ta·ya·reen *thin pasta
usually served with meat sauce*

taleggio ⓜ ta·le·jo *sweet, soft & fatty
cheese with a soft rind*

taralli ⓜ pl ta·ra·lee *boiled & baked
pretzel-like biscuits*

tartufo ⓜ tar·too·fo *truffle (very
expensive kind of fungus)*

tè ⓜ te *tea*

tegamata ① di maiale te·ga·ma·ta
dee ma·ya·le *casserole of pork &
fennel seed*

tegame, in te·ga·me, een *fried • braised*

tegole ① pl d'Aosta te·go·le da·os·ta
almond biscuits

testaió ⓜ tes·ta·yo *squares of pasta
served with pesto & parmesan*

testaroli ⓜ pl tes·ta·ro·lee *discs of
pasta, like pancakes*

tiramisù ⓜ tee·ra·mee·soo *sponge
cake or* **savoiardi** *soaked in coffee &
arranged in layers with* mascarpone,
then sprinkled with cocoa

tòcco ⓜ di carne to·ko dee kar·ne
veal sauce

toma ① to·ma *firm cow or sheep's
cheese*

— piemontese pye·mon·te·ze *a
softer variety of toma*

tomaxelle ① pl to·ma·kse·le *veal
roulade in wine & broth*

tomino ⓜ to·mee·no *small fresh
cheese*

tonno ⓜ to·no *tuna*

torciarelli ⓜ pl al tartufo tor·cha·re·lee
al tar·too·fo *pasta served with a
sauce containing minced lean pork,
spices, mushrooms, truffles & cheese*

torcinelli ⓜ pl tor·chee·ne·lee *stewed
lamb or kid entrails*

torcolo ⓜ di San Costanzo tor·ko·lo
dee san kos·tan·dzo *ring-shaped cake*

torresani ⓜ pl to·re·za·nee *pigeon
kebabs*

torrone ⓜ to·ro·ne *nougat*

— al cioccolato al cho·ko·la·to *very
soft chocolate nougat*

torroni ⓜ pl di semi di sesamo
to·ro·nee dee se·mee dee se·za·mo
crunchy sweets with sesame seeds

torta ① tor·ta *cake • tart • pie*

tortelli ⓜ tor·te·lee *fat, stuffed pasta*

— di San Leo dee san le·o *with
spinach & cheeses*

— di zucca dee tsoo·ka *with
pumpkin*

tortellini ⓜ pl tor·te·lee·nee *pasta filled
with meat, parmesan & egg*

tortelloni ⓜ pl tor·te·lo·nee
large tortellini

tosella ① to·ze·la *fresh fried cheese*

totano ⓜ to·ta·no *type of squid*

tramezzino ⓜ tra·me·dzee·no
sandwich

Trebbiano ⓜ tre·bya·no *white grape
found throughout Italy*

trenette ① pl al pesto tre·ne·te al
pes·to *long, flat pasta with* pesto

trifola ① tree·fo·la *white truffle*

triglia ① tree·lya *red mullet*

trota ① tro·ta *trout*

tubetti ⓜ pl too·be·tee *short pasta tubes*

turcinelli ⓜ pl al arrostiti toor·chee·ne·lee
a·ro·stee·tee *lamb-offal stew*

U

uardi ⓜ pl e fasoi ⓜ pl war·dee e
fa·zoy *soup with beans, barley, ham
bone & spices*

umbrici ⓜ pl oom·bree·chee
hand-made, thick spaghetti

uova ⓜ pl wo·va *eggs*

uva ① pl oo·va *grapes*

— bianca byan·ka *green grapes*

— nera ne·ra *red grapes*

— passa pa·sa *raisins*

V

vapore, cotto/a a ⓜ/ⓕ va·po·re, ko·to/a a *steamed*

vecchio/a ⓜ/ⓕ ve·kyo/a *old • aged*

ventresca ⓕ **di tonno** ven·tres·ka dee to·no *tuna belly*

verdura/verdure ⓕ ver·doo·ra/ ver·doo·re *vegetable/vegetables*

verza ⓕ ver·dza *savoy cabbage*

vialone nano ⓜ vya·lo·ne na·no *short grain rice used for risotto*

vincisgrassi ⓜ pl veen·cheez·gra·see *rich, baked dish made of offal, cheese & sometimes, truffle*

viscidu ⓜ vee·shee·doo *dry, salty & sour cheese, sliced & pickled*

vitello ⓜ vee·te·lo *veal*
   — **tonnato** to·na·to *thin slices of veal covered with a tuna, capers & anchovy sauce*

vongole ⓕ pl von·go·le *clams*

Z

zabaglione ⓜ dza·ba·lyo·ne *mousse-like dessert made of beaten egg, marsala & sugar*

zampetto ⓜ dzam·pe·to *calf, lamb or pig trotter*

zenzero ⓜ dzen·dze·ro *ginger*

zeppule ⓕ pl **'e cicenielli** ⓜ pl dze·poo·le e chee·che·nye·lee *fritters with cheese & anchovies*

zeppule ⓕ pl **'e San Giuseppe** dze·poo·le e san joo·ze·pe *small, fried ring-shaped cakes*

zimin ⓜ pl dzee·meen *soup with beans, pork & chards • dish with calamari & chard*

ziti ⓜ pl dzee·tee *long fat hollow pasta*

zucca ⓕ tsoo·ka *pumpkin*
   — **gialla in agrodolce** ja·la een a·gro·dol·che *fried & served with spices & capers*

zucchero ⓜ tsoo·ke·ro *sugar*

zuccotto ⓕ **fiorentino** tsoo·ko·to fyo·ren·tee·no *sponge cake with liqueur, custard, chocolate & whipped cream*

zuppa ⓕ tsoo·pa *soup, usually thick*
   — **alla canavesana** a·la ka·na·ve·za·na *soup base of bread, cabbage, butter, lard, onions & garlic*
   — **di ceci** dee che·chee *rich chickpea soup*
   — **di pesce alla marinara** dee pe·she a·la ma·ree·na·ra *fish soup*
   — **'e zuffritto** e tsoo·free·to *sauce prepared with pig's offal, red wine & tomato sauce.*

emergencies

le emergenze

75A	Help!	*Aiuto!*	a·*yoo*·to
75B	Stop!	*Fermi!*	*fer*·mee
75C	Go away!	*Vai via!*	vai *vee*·a
75D	Thief!	*Ladro!*	*la*·dro
75E	Fire!	*Al fuoco!*	al *fwo*·ko
75F	Watch out!	*Attenzione!*	a·ten·*tsyo*·ne

76A It's an emergency!
È un'emergenza!   e oo·ne·mer·*jen*·tsa

76B Call the police!
Chiami la polizia!   kya·mee la po·lee·*tsee*·a

76C Call a doctor!
Chiami un medico!   kya·mee oon *me*·dee·ko

76D Call an ambulance!
Chiami un'ambulanza!   kya·mee o·nam·boo·*lan*·tsa

77A Could you help me, please?
Mi può aiutare,   mee pwo a·yoo·*ta*·re
per favore?   per fa·*vo*·re

77B I have to use the telephone.
Devo fare una   de·vo fa·re oo·na
telefonata.   te·le·fo·*na*·ta

signs

Carabinieri	ka·ra·bee·*nye*·ree	**Police (military)**
Polizia	po·lee·*tsee*·a	**Police (civilian)**
Posto di	*pos*·to dee	**Police Station**
Polizia	po·lee·*tsee*·a	
Pronto Soccorso	*pron*·to so·*kor*·so	**Casualty**
Questura	kwes·*too*·ra	**Police Headquarters (civilian)**

essentials

179

| **77C** I'm lost. | *Mi sono perso.* m | mee *so*·no *per*·so |
| **77D** I'm lost. | *Mi sono persa.* f | mee *so*·no *per*·sa |

77E Where are the toilets?
Dove sono i gabinetti?   do·ve *so*·no ee ga·bee·*ne*·tee

police

la polizia

78A Where's the police station?
Dov'è il posto di polizia?   do·ve eel *pos*·to dee po·lee·*tsee*·a

78B I want to report an offence.
Voglio fare una   *vo*·lyo *fa*·re *oo*·na
denuncia.   de·*noon*·cha

78C I have insurance.
Ho l'assicurazione.   o la·see·koo·ra·*tsyo*·ne

79C I've been robbed.
Sono stato derubato. m   *so*·no *sta*·to de·roo·*ba*·to

79D I've been robbed.
Sono stata derubata. f   *so*·no *sta*·ta de·roo·*ba*·ta

79A I've been raped.
Sono stato violentato. m   sono *sta*·to vyo·len·*ta*·to

79B I've been raped.
Sono stata violentata. f   sono *sta*·ta vyo·len·*ta*·ta

(My bag) was stolen.
Mi hanno rubato   mee *a*·no roo·*ba*·to
(la mia borsa).   (la *mee*·a *bor*·sa)

cop shops

In Italy, police tasks are handled by both the *polizia*, the civilian police, and the *carabinieri*, a police force administered by the Ministry of Defence. Both investigate crimes, but the *posto di polizia*, the regular civilian police station, or the *questura*, the police headquarters, is where you would go to report a theft. Nevertheless, if you happen to be closer to the *carabinieri*, they'll redirect you from their *caserma* (barracks) if necessary.

80A I've lost my bags.
Ho perso la mia borsa. o *per*·so la *mee*·a *bor*·sa

80B I've lost my money.
Ho perso il mio denaro. o *per*·so eel *mee*·o de·*na*·ro

80C I've lost my passport.
Ho perso il mio passaporto. o *per*·so eel *mee*·o pa·sa·*por*·to

He/She tried to ... me.	*Ha cercato di ...*	a cher·*ka*·to dee ...
assault	*aggredirmi*	a·gre·*deer*·mee
rape	*violentarmi*	vyo·len·*tar*·mee
rob	*derubarmi*	de·roo·*bar*·mee

81A I want to contact my consulate.
Vorrei contattare il mio consolato. vo·*ray* kon·ta·*ta*·re eel *mee*·o kon·so·*la*·to

81B I want to contact my embassy.
Vorrei contattare la mia ambasciata. vo·*ray* kon·ta·*ta*·re la *mee*·a am·ba·*sha*·ta

Can I call someone?
Posso chiamare qualcuno? *po*·so kya·*ma*·re kwal·*koo*·no

Can I call a lawyer?
Posso chiamare un avvocato? *po*·so kya·*ma*·re oo·na·vo·*ka*·to

Can I have a lawyer who speaks English?
Posso avere un avvocato che parli inglese? *po*·so a·*ve*·re oo·na·vo·*ka*·to ke *par*·lee een·*gle*·ze

Is there a fine we can pay to clear this?
C'è una multa che possiamo pagare per chiarire tutto questo? che *oo*·na *mool*·ta ke po·*sya*·mo pa·*ga*·re per kya·*ree*·re *too*·to *kwe*·sto

This drug is for personal use.
Questo medicinale è per uso personale. *kwe*·sto me·dee·chee·*na*·le e per *oo*·zo per·so·*na*·le

I have a prescription for this drug.
Ho una ricetta per questa medicina. o *oo*·na re·*che*·ta per *kwe*·sta me·dee·*chee*·na

I (don't) understand.
(Non) Capisco.   (non) ka·*pees*·ko

What am I accused of?
Di che cosa sono stato/a   dee ke *ko*·za *so*·no *sta*·to/a
accusato/a? m/f   a·koo·za·to/a

I'm sorry.
Mi scusi.   mee *skoo*·zee

I apologise.
Mi dispiace.   mee dees·*pya*·che

I didn't realise I was doing anything wrong.
Non sapevo che facessi   non sa·*pe*·vo ke fa·*che*·see
qualcosa di male.   kwal·*ko*·za dee *ma*·le

I didn't do it.
Non sono stato/a io. m/f   non *so*·no *sta*·to/a ee·o

I'm innocent.
Sono innocente.   *so*·no ee·no·*chen*·te

the police may say ...

You'll be charged with ...	*Sarai accusato/a di ...* m/f	sa·*rai* a·koo·za·to/a dee ...
He'll/She'll be charged with ...	*Lui/Lei sarà accusato/a di ...* m/f	*loo*·ee/*lay* sa·*ra* a·koo·za·to/a dee ...
assault	*aggressione*	a·gre·*syo*·ne
disturbing the peace	*disturbo della quiete pubblica*	dees·*toor*·bo de·la *kwye*·te *poo*·blee·ka
murder	*omicidio*	o·mee·*chee*·dyo
not having a visa	*non avere un visto*	no·na·*ve*·re oon *vee*·sto
possession (of illegal substances)	*possesso (di sostanze illecite)*	po·*se*·so (dee sos·*tan*·tse ee·*le*·chee·te)
rape	*stupro*	*stoo*·pro
shoplifting	*taccheggio*	ta·*ke*·jo
speeding	*eccesso di velocità*	e·*che*·so dee ve·lo·chee·*ta*
theft	*furto*	*foor*·to

doctor

il medico

82A Where's the nearest dentist?
Dov'è il dentista do·ve eel den·*tee*·sta
più vicino? m pyoo vee·*chee*·no

82B Where's the nearest dentist?
Dov'è la dentista do·ve la den·*tee*·sta
più vicina? f pyoo vee·*chee*·na

82C Where's the nearest doctor?
Dov'è il medico do·ve eel *me*·dee·ko
più vicino? pyoo vee·*chee*·no

82D Where's the nearest hospital?
Dov'è l'ospedale do·ve los·pe·*da*·le
più vicino? pyoo vee·*chee*·no

82E Where's the nearest (night) pharmacist?
Dov'è la farmacia (di do·ve la far·ma·*chee*·a (dee
turno) più vicina? toor·no) pyoo vee·*chee*·na

83A I need a doctor.
Ho bisogno di un medico. o bee·zo·nyo dee oon *me*·dee·ko

83B Could I see a female doctor?
Posso vedere una po·so ve·*de*·re oo·na
dottoressa? do·to·*re*·sa

Can the doctor come here?
Può venire qui il medico? pwo ve·*nee*·re kwee eel *me*·dee·ko

I've been vaccinated for ...	Sono stato/a vaccinato/a per ... m/f	so·no sta·to/a va·chee·na·to/a per ...
hepatitis A/B	l'epatite A/B	le·pa·tee·te a/bee
tetanus	il tetano	eel te·ta·no
typhoid	il tifo	eel tee·fo

I need ...	*Ho bisogno di ...*	o bee·zo·nyo dee ...
new glasses	*nuovi occhiali*	nwo·vee o·kya·lee
new contact lenses	*nuove lenti a contatto*	nwo·ve len·tee a kon·ta·to

83C **I've run out of my medication.**
Ho finito la mia medicina.
o fee·nee·to la mee·a me·dee·chee·na

Can I have a receipt for my insurance?
Potrebbe darmi una ricevuta per l'assicurazione?
po·tre·be dar·mee oo·na ree·che·voo·ta per la·see·koo·ra·tsyo·ne

the doctor may say ...

What's the problem?
Qual'è il problema?
kwa·le eel pro·ble·ma

Where does it hurt?
Dove Le fa male?
do·ve le fa ma·le

Do you have a temperature?
Ha la febbre?
a la fe·bre

How long have you been like this?
Da quanto (tempo) è che si sente così?
da kwan·to (tem·po) e ke see sen·te ko·zee

Have you had this before?
Si è mai sentito/a così prima? m/f
see e mai sen·tee·to/a ko·zee pree·ma

Are you sexually active?
È sessualmente attivo/a? m/f
e se·swal·men·te a·tee·vo/a

Have you had unprotected sex?
Ha avuto rapporti non protetti?
a a·voo·to ra·por·tee non pro·te·tee

the doctor may say ...

Are you allergic to anything?

| *È allergico/a* | e a·ler·jee·ko/a |
| *a qualcosa?* m/f | a kwal·ko·za |

Are you on medication?

| *Sta prendendo* | sta pren·den·do |
| *medicine?* | me·dee·chee·ne |

Are you pregnant?

| *È incinta?* | e een·cheen·ta |

How long are you travelling for?

| *Per quanto tempo* | per kwan·to tem·po |
| *viaggia?* | vee·a·ja |

Do you ...?

drink	*Beve?*	be·ve
smoke	*Fuma?*	foo·ma
take drugs	*Si droga?*	see dro·ga

You need to be admitted to hospital.

| *Deve essere ricoverato/a* | de·ve e·se·re ree·ko·ve·ra·to/a |
| *in ospedale.* m/f | ee·nos·pe·da·le |

You should have it checked when you go home.

Dovrebbe farlo	dov·re·be far·lo
controllare dal	kon·tro·la·re dal
medico quando	me·dee·ko kwan·do
ritorna a casa.	re·tor·na a ka·za

You should return home for treatment.

Dovrebbe tornare	do·vre·be tor·na·re
a casa per	a ka·za per
farsi curare.	far·see koo·ra·re

You're a hypochondriac.

| *È un ipocondriaco/a.* m/f | e oo·nee·po·kon·drya·ko/a |

Go and enjoy your holiday!

| *Vada a godersi* | va·da a go·der·see |
| *le vacanze!* | le va·kan·tse |

symptoms & conditions

84A I'm sick.
Mi sento male.   mee *sen*·to *ma*·le

My friend is sick.
Il mio amico è malato. m   eel *mee*·o a·*mee*·ko e ma·*la*·to
La mia amica è malata. f   la *mee*·a a·*mee*·ka e ma·*la*·ta

84B It hurts here.
Mi fa male qui.   mee fa *ma*·le kwee

I've been injured.
Sono stato/a ferito/a. m/f   *so*·no *sta*·to/a fe·*ree*·to/a

I've been vomiting.
Ho vomitato alcune volte.   o vo·mee·*ta*·to al·*koo*·ne *vol*·te

I can't sleep.
Non riesco a dormire.   non *ryes*·ko a dor·*mee*·re

Please use a new syringe.
Usi una siringa   oo·see *oo*·na see·*reen*·ga
nuova, per favore.   *nwo*·va per fa·*vo*·re

I have my own syringe.
Ho con me la mia siringa.   o kon me la *mee*·a see·*reen*·ga

I don't want a blood transfusion.
Non voglio una   non *vo*·lyo *oo*·na
trasfusione di sangue.   tras·foo·*syo*·ne dee *san*·gwe

I feel ...	*Ho ...*	o ...
dizzy	*il capogiro*	eel ka·po·*gee*·ro
hot and cold	*vampate di calore*	vam·*pa*·te dee ka·*lo*·re
nauseous	*la nausea*	la *now*·ze·a
shivery	*i brividi*	ee *bree*·vee·dee

I feel ...	Mi sento ...	mee sen·to ...
better	meglio	me·lyo
strange	strano/a m/f	stra·no/a
weak	debole	de·bo·le
worse	peggio	pe·jo

I feel ...	Sono ...	so·no ...
anxious	ansioso/a m/f	an·syo·zo/a
depressed	depresso/a m/f	de·pre·so/a

I have a ...	Ho ...	o ...
cold	un raffreddore	oon ra·fre·do·re
cough	la tosse	la to·se
fever	la febbre	la fe·bre
headache	mal di testa	mal dee tes·ta
heart	un problema	oon pro·ble·ma
condition	cardiaco	kar·dee·a·ko
migraine	un'emicrania	oo·ne·mee·kra·nya

I'm ...	Sono ...	so·no ...
asthmatic	asmatico/a m/f	az·ma·tee·ko/a
diabetic	diabetico/a m/f	dee·a·be·tee·ko/a
epileptic	epilettico/a m/f	e·pee·le·tee·ko/a

I've (recently) had ...
Ho avuto ... (di recente).   o a·voo·to ... (dee re·chen·te)

He's/She's (recently) had ...
Ha avuto ... (di recente).   a a·voo·to ... (dee re·chen·te)

I'm on medication for ...
Prendo la medicina per ...   pren·do la me·dee·chee·na per ...

He's/She's on medication for ...
Prende la medicina per ...   pren·de la me·dee·chee·na per ...

For more symptoms and conditions, see the **dictionary**.

women's health

I think I'm pregnant.
   Penso di essere incinta.   pen·so dee e·se·re een·*cheen*·ta

I'm pregnant.
   Sono incinta.   so·no een·*cheen*·ta

I'm on the Pill.
   Prendo la pillola.   pren·do la pee·lo·la

I haven't had my period for (two) weeks.
   Sono (due) settimane   so·no (doo·e) se·tee·*ma*·ne
   che non mi vengono le   ke non mee *ven*·go·no le
   mestruazioni.   mes·troo·a·*tsyo*·nee

I've noticed a lump/swelling here.
   Ho notato un nodulo/   o no·*ta*·to oon *no*·doo·lo/
   gonfiore qui.   gon·*fyo*·re kwee

the doctor may say ...

Are you using contraception?
   Prende contraccettivi?   pren·de kon·tra·che·*tee*·vee

Are you menstruating?
   Ha le mestruazioni?   a le mes·troo·a·*tsyo*·nee

Are you pregnant?
   È incinta?   e een·*cheen*·ta

When did you last have your period?
   Quand'è l'ultima volta   kwan·*de* lool·tee·ma vol·ta
   che Le sono venute le   ke le so·no ve·*noo*·te le
   mestruazioni?   mes·troo·a·*tsyo*·nee

You're pregnant.
   È incinta.   e een·*cheen*·ta

I need ...	*Ho bisogno ...*	o bee·zo·nyo ...
contraception	*di contraccettivi*	dee kon·tra·che·*tee*·vee
the morning-after pill	*della pillola del mattino dopo*	de·la *pee*·lo·la del ma·*tee*·no *do*·po
a pregnancy test	*di un test di gravidanza*	dee oon test dee gra·vee·*dan*·tsa

For more terms relating to women's health, see the **dictionary**.

allergies

le allergie

85A **I'm allergic to antibiotics.**
Sono allergico/a agli antibiotici. m/f
so·no a·*ler*·jee·ko/a *a*·lyee an·tee·bee·o·tee·chee

85B **I'm allergic to anti-inflammatories.**
Sono allergico/a agli antinfiammatori. m/f
so·no a·*ler*·jee·ko/a *a*·lyee an·teen·fya·ma·*to*·ree

85C **I'm allergic to aspirin.**
Sono allergico/a all'aspirina. m/f
so·no a·*ler*·jee·ko/a a·las·pee·*ree*·na

85D **I'm allergic to bees.**
Sono allergico/a alle api. m/f
so·no a·*ler*·jee·ko/a *a*·le *a*·pee

85E **I'm allergic to codeine.**
Sono allergico/a alla codeina. m/f
so·no a·*ler*·jee·ko/a a·la ko·de·ee·na

85F **I'm allergic to penicillin.**
Sono allergico/a alla penicillina. m/f
so·no a·*ler*·jee·ko/a a·la pe·nee·chee·*lee*·na

I have a skin allergy.
Ho un'allergia alla pelle.
o oo·na·ler·*jee*·a *a*·la *pe*·le

For other allergies, see **vegetarian & special meals**, page 159.

parts of the body

My (stomach) hurts.
Mi fa male (lo stomaco).   mee fa *ma*·le (lo *sto*·ma·ko)

I can't move (my ankle).
Non riesco a muovere   non *ryes*·ko a *mwo*·ve·re
(la caviglia).   (la ka·*vee*·lya)

I have a cramp (in my foot).
Ho crampi (al piede).   o *kram*·pee (al *pye*·de)

(My throat) is swollen.
(La gola) è gonfia.   (la *go*·la) e *gon*·fya

For more parts of the body, see the **dictionary**.

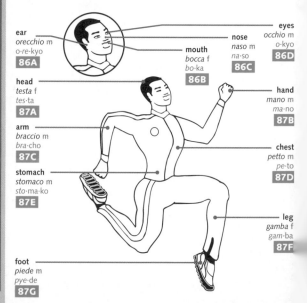

ear
orecchio m
o·re·kyo
86A

mouth
bocca f
bo·ka
86B

nose
naso m
na·so
86C

eyes
occhio m
o·kyo
86D

head
testa f
tes·ta
87A

hand
mano m
ma·no
87B

arm
braccio m
bra·cho
87C

chest
petto m
pe·to
87D

stomach
stomaco m
sto·ma·ko
87E

leg
gamba f
gam·ba
87F

foot
piede m
pye·de
87G

chemist

la farmacia

I need something for (diarrhoea).
Ho bisogno di o bee·zo·nyo dee
qualcosa per (la diarrea). kwal·ko·za per (la dee·a·re·a)

Do I need a prescription for (antihistamines)?
C'è bisogno di una che bee·zo·nyo dee oo·na
ricetta per (gli re·che·ta per (lyee
antistaminici)? an·tee·sta·mee·nee·chee)

How many times a day?
Quante volte al giorno? kwan·te vol·te al jor·no

Will it make me drowsy?
Mi farà dormire? mee fa·ra dor·mee·re

For more chemist items, see the **dictionary**.

listen for ...

de·ve kom·ple·*ta*·re eel *cheek*·lo
Deve completare il **You must complete the**
ciclo. **course.**

doo·e *vol*·te al *jor*·no (kon ee *pas*·tee)
Due volte al giorno **Twice a day**
(con i pasti). **(with food).**

kwe·sto la mai *pre*·so
Questo l'ha mai preso? **Have you taken this before?**

sa·ra *pron*·to fra (*ven*·tee mee·*noo*·tee)
Sarà pronto fra **It'll be ready to pick up in**
(venti minuti). **(twenty minutes).**

dentist

dentista

I have a ...	Ho ...	o ...
broken tooth	*un dente rotto*	oon *den*·te *ro*·to
cavity	*una cavità*	oo·na ka·vee·*ta*
toothache	*mal di denti*	mal dee *den*·tee

I need a/an ...	*Ho bisogno di ...*	o bee·zo·nyo dee ...
anaesthetic	*un anestetico*	oo·na·nes·*te*·tee·ko
filling	*un'otturazione*	oo·no·too·ra·*tsyo*·ne
crown	*una corona*	*oo*·na ko·*ro*·na

I've lost a filling.
Ho perso un'otturazione.   o *per*·so oo·no·too·ra·*tsyo*·ne

My dentures are broken.
La mia dentiera è rotta.   la *mee*·a den·*tye*·ra e *ro*·ta

My gums hurt.
Mi fanno male le gengive.   mee *fa*·no *ma*·le le jen·*jee*·ve

I don't want it extracted.
Non voglio che mi venga   non *vo*·lyo ke mee *ven*·ga
tolto.   *tol*·to

Ouch!
Ahi!   *a*·ee

listen for ...

a·pra *be*·ne la *bo*·ka	**Open wide.**
Apra bene la bocca.	
non le fa·*ra* ma·le per *nyen*·te	**This won't hurt a bit.**
Non Le farà male per niente.	
for·se le fa·*ra* oon po *ma*·le	**This might hurt a little.**
Forse Le farà un po' male.	
mor·da *kwe*·sto	**Bite down on this.**
Morda questo.	
sha·kwee	**Rinse!**
Sciacqui!	
tor·nee kwee ke non o fee·*nee*·to	**Come back, I haven't**
Torni qui che non	**finished.**
ho finito.	

As the climate change debate heats up, the matter of sustainability becomes an important part of the travel vernacular. In practical terms, this means assessing our impact on the environment and local cultures and economies – and acting to make that impact as positive as possible. Here are some basic phrases to get you on your way …

communication & cultural differences

I'd like to learn some of your local dialects.

Vorrei imparare qualche   vo·ray eem·pa·ra·re kwal·ke
dialetto regionale.   dee·a·le·to re·jo·na·le

Would you like me to teach you some English?

Vuole che le insegni   vwo·le ke le een·se·nyee
un po' d'inglese?   oon po deen·gle·ze

Is this a local or national custom?

Questa è un'usanza   kwe·sta e oon oo·san·tsa
locale o nazionale?   lo·ka·le o na·tsyo·na·le

I respect your customs.

Rispetto le vostre usanze.   rees·pe·to le vos·tre oo·san·tse

community benefit & involvement

What sorts of issues is this community facing?

Quali problemi ci sono   kwa·lee prob·le·mee chee so·no
da queste parti?   da kwe·ste par·tee

climate change	*cambiamento del clima* m	kam·bya·men·to del klee·ma
organised crime	*criminalità organizzata* f	kree·mee·na·lee·ta or·ga·nee·dza·ta

racism	*razzismo* m	ra·*tsees*·mo
relations between church and state	*rapporti fra Chiesa e Stato* m	ra·*por*·tee fra *kye*·za e *sta*·to
unemployment	*disoccupazione* f	dees·o·ku·pa·*tsyo*·ne

I'd like to volunteer my skills.

Vorrei offrirvi la mia competenza.

vo·*ray* o·*freer*·vee la *mee*·a kom·pe·*ten*·tsa

Are there any volunteer programs available in the area?

Ci sono programmi di volontariato da queste parti?

chee *so*·no pro·*gra*·mee dee vo·lon·ta·*rya*·to da *kwe*·ste *par*·tee

environment

Where can I recycle this?

Dove lo posso riciclare?

do·ve lo *po*·so ree·chee·*kla*·re

transport

Can we get there by public transport?

Possiamo arrivarci con i mezzi pubblici?

po·*sya*·mo a·ree·*var*·chee kon ee *me*·dze *poo*·blee·chee

Can we get there by bike?

Possiamo arrivarci in bicicletta?

po·*sya*·mo a·ree·*var*·chee een bee·chee·*kle*·ta

I'd prefer to walk there.

Preferisco andarci a piedi.

pre·fe·*rees*·ko an·*dar*·chee a *pye*·dee

accommodation

I'd like to stay at a locally-run hotel.

Vorrei stare in un albergo a gestione locale.

vo·*ray* *sta*·re een oon al·*ber*·go a jes·*tyo*·ne lo·*ka*·le

Can I turn the air conditioning off and open the window?
Posso spegnere l'aria   po·so spe·nye·re la·ree·a
condizionata e aprire   kon·dee·tsyo·na·ta e a·pree·re
la finestra?   la fee·nes·tra

There's no need to change my sheets.
Non c'è bisogno di   non che bee·zo·nyo dee
cambiare le lenzuola.   kam·bya·re le len·tswo·la

shopping

Where can I buy locally produced goods/souvenirs?
Dove posso comprare   do·ve po·so kom·pra·re
oggetti/souvenirs di   o·je·tee/soov·neer dee
produzione locale?   pro·doo·tsyo·ne lo·ka·le

Do you sell Fair Trade products?
Vendete prodotti del   ven·de·te pro·do·tee del
Commercio Equo e Solidale?   ko·mer·cho e·kwo e so·lee·da·le

food

Do you sell ...?	*Vendete ...?*	ven·de·te ...
locally produced	*prodotti*	pro·do·tee
food	*alimentari*	a·lee·men·ta·ree
	locali	lo·ka·lee
organic	*prodotti*	pro·do·tee
produce	*biologici*	bee·o·lo·jee·chee

Can you tell me which traditional foods I should try?
Mi può dire quali piatti   mee pwo dee·re kwa·lee pya·tee
tradizionali dovrei   tra·dee·tsyo·na·lee do·vray
provare?   pro·va·re

sightseeing

Are cultural tours available?
Si possono fare   see po·so·no fa·re
gite culturali?   jee·te kool·too·ra·lee

Does your company ...?	La vostra agenzia ...?	la vos·tra a·jen·tsee·a ...
donate money to charity	fa offerte a organizzazioni umanitarie	fa o·fer·te a or·ga·nee·tsa·tsyo·nee oo·ma·nee·ta·rye
hire local guides	assume guide del posto	as·soo·me gwee·de del pos·to
visit local businesses	visita imprese locali	vee·see·ta eem·pre·se lo·ka·lee

Does the guide speak ...?	La guida parla ...?	la gwee·da par·la ...
Abruzzese	Abruzzese	a·broo·tse·ze
Apulian	Pugliese	poo·lee·e·ze
Calabrian	Calabrese	ka·la·bre·ze
Emiliano-Romagnolo	Emiliano-Romagnolo	e·mee·lee·a·no ro·ma·nyo·lo
Friulian	Friulano	free·oo·la·no
Laziale	Laziale	la·tsee·a·le
Ligurian	Ligure	lee·goo·re
Lombard	Lombardo	lom·bar·do
Marchigiano	Marchigiano	mar·kee·ja·no
Neapolitan	Napoletano	na·po·le·ta·no
Piemontese	Piemontese	pee·e·mon·te·ze
Romanesque	Romanesco	ro·ma·nes·ko
Sardinian	Sardo	sar·do
Sicilian	Siciliano	see·chee·lee·a·no
Tuscan	Toscano	tos·ka·no
Umbrian	Umbro	oom·bro
Venetian	Veneto	ve·ne·to

Nouns in this dictionary, and adjectives affected by gender, have their gender indicated by ⓜ and/or ⓕ. If it's a plural noun, you'll also see pl. Where a word that could be either a noun or a verb has no gender indicated, it's a verb.

A

aboard *a bordo* a·bor·do
abortion *aborto* ⓜ a·bor·to
above *sopra* so·pra
abroad *all'estero* a·les·te·ro
accident *incidente* ⓜ een·chee·den·te
accommodation *alloggio* ⓜ a·lo·jo
acupuncture *agopuntura* ⓕ
  a·go·poon·too·ra
adaptor *spina* ⓕ *multipla* spee·na
  mool·tee·pla
addicted *dipendente* ⓜ/ⓕ
  dee·pen·den·te
address *indirizzo* ⓜ een·dee·ree·tso
administration *amministrazione* ⓕ
  a·mee·nee·stra·tsyo·ne
admission price *prezzo* ⓜ *d'ingresso*
  pre·tso deen·gre·so
admit (let in) *far entrare* far en·tra·re
adult *adulto/a* ⓜ/ⓕ a·dool·to/a
adventure *avventura* ⓕ a·ven·too·ra
advertisement *annuncio* ⓜ a·noon·cho
aerobics *aerobica* ⓕ a·e·ro·bee·ka
Africa *Africa* ⓕ a·free·ka
after *dopo* do·po
afternoon *pomeriggio* ⓜ po·me·ree·jo
aftershave *dopobarba* ⓜ do·po·bar·ba
again *di nuovo* dee nwo·vo
age *età* ⓕ e·ta
aggressive *aggressivo/a* ⓜ/ⓕ
  a·gre·see·vo/a
agree *essere d'accordo* e·se·re da·kor·do
agriculture *agricoltura* ⓕ
  a·gree·kol·too·ra
AIDS *AIDS* ⓜ a·eedz
air *aria* ⓕ a·rya

airmail *via* ⓕ *aerea* vee·a a·e·re·a
air-conditioned *ad aria condizionata*
  ad a·rya kon·dee·tsyo·na·ta
airline *linea* ⓕ *aerea* lee·ne·a a·e·re·a
airport *aeroporto* ⓜ a·e·ro·por·to
airport tax *tassa* ⓕ *aeroportuale* ta·sa
  a·e·ro·por·twa·le
aisle (plane, train) *corridoio* ⓜ
  ko·ree·do·yo
alarm clock *sveglia* ⓕ sve·lya
alcohol *alcol* ⓜ al·kol
all (singular) *tutto/a* ⓜ/ⓕ too·to/a
all (plural) *tutti/e* ⓜ/ⓕ too·tee/too·te
allergy *allergia* ⓕ a·ler·jee·a
almond *mandorla* ⓕ man·dor·la
alone *da solo/a* ⓜ/ⓕ da so·lo/a
already *già* ja
also *anche* an·ke
altar *altare* ⓜ al·ta·re
altitude *quota* ⓕ kwo·ta
always *sempre* sem·pre
ambassador *ambasciatore/*
  ambasciatrice ⓜ/ⓕ am·ba·sha·to·re/
  am·ba·sha·tree·che
ambulance *ambulanza* ⓕ
  am·boo·lan·tsa
America *America* ⓕ a·me·ree·ka
amount *quantità* ⓕ kwan·tee·ta
ancient *antico/a* ⓜ/ⓕ an·tee·ko/a
and *e* e
angry *arrabbiato/a* ⓜ/ⓕ a·ra·bya·to/a
animal *animale* ⓜ a·nee·ma·le
ankle *caviglia* ⓕ ka·vee·lya
annual *annuale* a·noo·a·le
answer *risposta* ⓕ rees·pos·ta
ant *formica* ⓕ for·mee·ka
antibiotics *antibiotici* ⓜ pl
  an·tee·bee·o·tee·che

antihistamines *antistaminici* ⓜ pl
an·tee·sta·*mee*·nee·chee
antinuclear *antinucleare*
an·tee·noo·kle·a·re
antique *pezzo* ⓜ *di antiquariato* pe·tso
dee an·tee·kwa·rya·to
antiseptic *antisettico* ⓜ an·tee·se·tee·ko
appendix *appendice* ⓕ a·pen·*dee*·che
apple *mela* ⓕ *me*·la
appointment *appuntamento* ⓜ
a·poon·ta·*men*·to
apricot *albicocca* ⓕ al·bee·*ko*·ka
archaeological *archeologico/a* ⓜ/ⓕ
ar·ke·o·lo·jee·ko/a
architect *architetto* ⓜ ar·kee·*te*·to
architecture *architettura* ⓕ
ar·kee·te·*too*·ra
argue *litigare* lee·tee·*ga*·re
arm *braccio* ⓜ *bra*·cho
arrest *arrestare* a·res·*ta*·re
arrivals *arrivi* ⓜ pl a·*ree*·vee
arrive *arrivare* a·ree·*va*·re
art *arte* ⓕ *ar*·te
art gallery *galleria* ⓕ *d'arte* ga·le·*ree*·a
dar·te
artist *artista* ⓜ&ⓕ ar·*tee*·sta
ashtray *portacenere* ⓜ por·ta·*che*·ne·re
Asia *Asia* ⓕ a·zya
ask (a question) *domandare*
do·man·*da*·re
ask (for something) *richiedere*
ree·*kye*·de·re
asparagus *asparagi* ⓜ pl as·*pa*·ra·jee
aspirin *aspirina* ⓕ as·pee·*ree*·na
asthma *asma* ⓕ *az*·ma
athletics *atletica* ⓕ at·*le*·tee·ka
aubergine *melanzana* ⓕ me·lan·*dza*·na
aunt *zia* ⓕ *tsee*·a
Australia *Australia* ⓕ ow·*stra*·lya
automatic *automatico/a* ⓜ/ⓕ
ow·to·ma·tee·ko/a
automatic teller machine (ATM)
Bancomat ⓜ *ban*·ko·mat
autumn *autunno* ⓜ ow·*too*·no
avenue *viale* ⓜ vee·*a*·le
avocado *avocado* ⓜ a·vo·*ka*·do
awful *orrendo/a* ⓜ/ⓕ o·ren·do/a

B

B&W (film) *in bianco e nero* een
byan·ko e *ne*·ro
baby *bimbo/a* ⓜ/ⓕ *beem*·bo/a
baby food *cibo* ⓜ *da bebè* *chee*·bo
da be·*be*
baby powder *borotalco* ⓜ bo·ro·*tal*·ko
babysitter *baby-sitter* ⓜ&ⓕ
be·bee·*see*·ter
back (body) *schiena* ⓕ *skye*·na
backpack *zaino* ⓜ *dzai*·no
bacon *pancetta* ⓕ pan·*che*·ta
bad *cattivo/a* ⓜ/ⓕ ka·*tee*·vo/a
bag (general) *borsa* ⓕ *bor*·sa
bag (shopping) *sacchetto* ⓜ sa·*ke*·to
baggage *bagaglio* ⓜ ba·*ga*·lyo
baggage allowance *bagaglio* ⓜ
consentito ba·*ga*·lyo kon·sen·*tee*·to
baggage claim *ritiro* ⓜ *bagagli*
ree·*tee*·ro ba·*ga*·lyee
bakery *panetteria* ⓕ pa·ne·te·*ree*·a
balance (account) *saldo* ⓜ *sal*·do
balcony *balcone* ⓜ bal·*ko*·ne
ball (dancing) *ballo* ⓜ *ba*·lo
ball (inflated) *pallone* ⓜ pa·*lo*·ne
ball (sports) *palla* ⓕ *pa*·la
ballet *balletto* ⓜ ba·*le*·to
band (music) *gruppo* ⓜ *groo*·po
bandage *fascia* ⓕ *fa*·sha
Band-aids *cerotti* ⓜ pl che·*ro*·tee
bank (money) *banca* ⓕ *ban*·ka
bank account *conto* ⓜ *in banca* *con*·to
een *ban*·ka
banknote *banconota* ⓕ ban·ko·*no*·ta
baptism *battesimo* ⓜ ba·*te*·zee·mo
bar *locale* ⓜ lo·*ka*·le
bar fridge *frigobar* ⓜ *free*·go·bar
barber *barbiere* ⓜ bar·*bye*·re
baseball *baseball* ⓜ *bays*·bol
basket *cestino* ⓜ ches·*tee*·no
basketball *pallacanestro* ⓕ
pa·la·ka·*ne*·stro
bath *bagno* ⓜ *ba*·nyo
bathing suit *costume* ⓜ *da bagno*
kos·*too*·me da *ba*·nyo
bathroom *bagno* ⓜ *ba*·nyo

battery (for car) *batteria* ① ba·te·ree·a
battery (general) *pila* ① pee·la
be *essere* e·se·re
beach *spiaggia* ① spya·ja
beans *fagioli* ⑩ pl fa·jo·lee
beansprouts *germogli* ⑩ pl *(di soia)*
  jer·mo·lyee (dee so·ya)
beautician *estetista* ⑩&① es·te·tee·sta
beautiful *bello/a* ⑩/① be·lo/a
beauty salon *parrucchiere* ⑩
  pa·roo·kye·re
because *perché* per·ke
bed *letto* ⑩ le·to
bedding *coperte* ① pl e *lenzuola* ① pl
  ko·per·te e len·zwo·la
bedroom *camera* ① *da letto* ka·me·ra
  da le·to
bee *ape* ① a·pe
beef *manzo* ⑩ man·dzo
beer *birra* ① bee·ra
beetroot *barbabietola* ① bar·ba·bye·to·la
before *prima* pree·ma
beggar *mendicante* ⑩&①
  men·dee·kan·te
begin *cominciare* ko·meen·cha·re
behind *dietro* dye·tro
below *sotto* so·to
best *migliore* mee·lyo·re
bet *scommessa* ① sko·me·sa
better *migliore* mee·lyo·re
between *fra* fra
bible *bibbia* ① bee·bya
bicycle *bicicletta* ① bee·chee·kle·ta
big *grande* gran·de
bike chain *catena* ① *di bicicletta*
  ka·te·na dee bee·chee·kle·ta
bike lock *lucchetto* ⑩ loo·ke·to
bike path *ciclopista* ① chee·klo·pee·sta
bill (account) *conto* ⑩ kon·to
binoculars *binocolo* ⑩ bee·no·ko·lo
bird *uccello* ⑩ oo·che·lo
birthday *compleanno* ⑩ kom·ple·a·no
biscuit *biscotto* ⑩ bees·ko·to
bite (dog) *morso* ⑩ mor·so
bite (insect) *puntura* ① poon·too·ra
black *nero/a* ⑩/① ne·ro/a
blanket *coperta* ① ko·per·ta
blind *cieco/a* ⑩/① chye·ko/a

blister *vescica* ① ve·shee·ka
blocked *bloccato/a* ⑩/① blo·ka·to/a
blonde *biondo/a* ⑩/① byon·do/a
blood *sangue* ⑩ san·gwe
blood group *gruppo* ⑩ *sanguigno*
  groo·po san·gwee·nyo
blood pressure *pressione* ① *del sangue*
  pre·syo·ne del san·gwe
blood test *analisi* ① *del sangue*
  a·na·lee·zee del san·gwe
blue (dark) *blu* bloo
blue (light) *azzurro/a* ⑩/① a·dzoo·ro/a
board (a plane, ship) *salire su*
  sa·lee·re su
boarding house *pensione* ① pen·syo·ne
boarding pass *carta* ① *d'imbarco* kar·ta
  deem·bar·ko
boat *barca* ① bar·ka
body *corpo* ⑩ kor·po
bone *osso* ⑩ o·so
book *libro* ⑩ lee·bro
book (make a booking) *prenotare*
  pre·no·ta·re
booked out *completo/a* ⑩/①
  kom·ple·to/a
bookshop *libreria* ① lee·bre·ree·a
boots *stivali* ⑩ pl stee·va·lee
boots (ski) *scarponi* ⑩ pl *(da sci)*
  skar·po·nee (da shee)
boots (soccer) *scarpette* ① pl skar·pe·te
border *confine* ⑩ kon·fee·ne
bored *annoiato/a* ⑩/① a·no·ya·to/a
boring *noioso/a* ⑩/① no·yo·zo/a
borrow *prendere in prestito* pren·de·re
  een pres·tee·to
bottle *bottiglia* ① bo·tee·lya
bottle opener *apribottiglie* ⑩
  a·pree·bo·tee·lye
(at the) bottom *(in) fondo* ⑩ (een)
  fon·do
bowl *piatto* ⑩ *fondo* pya·to fon·do
box *scatola* ① ska·to·la
boxing *pugilato* ⑩ poo·jee·la·to
boy *bambino* ⑩ bam·bee·no
boy(friend) *ragazzo* ⑩ ra·ga·tso
bra *reggiseno* ⑩ re·jee·se·no
Braille *braille* ⑩ bray
brake *freno* ⑩ fre·no

DICTIONARY

200

brave *coraggioso/a* ⓜ/ⓕ ko·ra·jo·zo/a
bread *pane* ⓜ pa·ne
  rye bread *pane* ⓜ *di segala* pa·ne dee
  se·ga·la
  sourdough bread *pane* ⓜ *a pasta*
  acida pa·ne a pas·ta a·chee·da
  wholemeal bread *pane* ⓜ *integrale*
  pa·ne een·te·gra·le
break *rompere* rom·pe·re
break down *guastarsi* gwas·tar·see
breakfast *(prima) colazione* ⓕ *(pree*·ma)
  ko·la·tsyo·ne
breast *seno* ⓜ se·no
breathe *respirare* res·pee·ra·re
bribe *corrompere* ko·rom·pe·re
bridge *ponte* ⓜ pon·te
briefcase *valigetta* ⓕ va·lee·je·ta
brilliant *brillante* ⓜ/ⓕ bree·lan·te
bring *portare* por·ta·re
broken *rotto/a* ⓜ/ⓕ ro·to/a
broken down *guastato/a* ⓜ/ⓕ
  gwas·ta·to/a
bronchitis *bronchite* ⓕ bron·kee·te
brother *fratello* ⓜ fra·te·lo
brown *marrone* ⓜ/ⓕ ma·ro·ne
bruise *livido* ⓜ lee·vee·do
brussels sprouts *cavoletti* ⓜ pl *di*
  Bruxelles ka·vo·le·tee dee brook·sel
bucket *secchio* ⓜ se·kyo
Buddhist *buddista* ⓜ&ⓕ boo·dee·sta
budget *bilancio* ⓜ bee·lan·cho
buffet (meal) *pasto* ⓜ *freddo* pas·to
  fre·do
bug *insetto* ⓜ een·se·to
build *costruire* kos·troo·ee·re
builder *costruttore/costruttrice* ⓜ/ⓕ
  kos·troo·to·re/kos·troo·tree·che
building *edificio* ⓜ e·dee·fee·cho
burn *bruciare* broo·cha·re
bus (city) *autobus* ⓜ ow·to·boos
bus (coach) *pullman* ⓜ pool·man
bus station *stazione* ⓕ *d'autobus*
  sta·tsyo·ne dow·to·boos
bus stop *fermata* ⓕ *d'autobus* fer·ma·ta
  dow·to·boos
business *affari* ⓜ pl a·fa·ree
business class *classe* ⓕ *business* kla·se
  beez·nes

business person *uomo/donna d'affari*
  ⓜ/ⓕ wo·mo/do·na da·fa·ree
business studies *commercio* ⓜ
  ko·mer·cho
business trip *viaggio* ⓜ *d'affari* vee·a·jo
  da·fa·ree
busker *musicista* ⓜ&ⓕ *di strada*
  moo·zee·chee·sta dee stra·da
but *ma* ma
butcher's shop *macelleria* ⓕ
  ma·che·le·ree·a
butter *burro* ⓜ boo·ro
butterfly *farfalla* ⓕ far·fa·la
button *bottone* ⓜ bo·to·ne
buy *comprare* kom·pra·re

C

cabbage *cavolo* ⓜ ka·vo·lo
cable car *funivia* ⓕ foo·nee·*vee*·a
cafe *bar* ⓜ bar
cake *torta* ⓕ tor·ta
cake shop *pasticceria* ⓕ
  pa·stee·che·ree·a
calculator *calcolatrice* ⓕ
  kal·ko·la·tree·che
calendar *calendario* ⓜ ka·len·da·ryo
camera *macchina* ⓕ *fotografica*
  ma·kee·na fo·to·gra·fee·ka
camera shop *fotografo* ⓜ fo·to·gra·fo
camp *campeggiare* kam·pe·ja·re
camp site *campeggio* ⓜ kam·pe·jo
camping store *negozio* ⓜ *da campeggio*
  ne·go·tsyo da kam·pe·jo
can (tin) *scatola* ⓕ ska·to·la
can *potere* po·te·re
can opener *apriscatole* ⓜ
  a·pree·ska·to·le
Canada *Canada* ⓜ ka·na·da
cancel *cancellare* kan·che·la·re
cancer *cancro* ⓜ kan·kro
candle *candela* ⓕ kan·de·la
candy *dolciumi* ⓜ pl dol·choo·mee
cantaloupe *melone* ⓜ me·lo·ne
capsicum *peperone* ⓜ pe·pe·ro·ne
car *macchina* ⓕ ma·kee·na
car hire *autonoleggio* ⓜ ow·to·no·le·jo

car owner's title *libretto* ⑩ *di circolazione* lee·*bre*·to dee cheer·ko·la·*tsyo*·ne

car park *parcheggio* ⑩ par·*ke*·jo

car racing *automobilismo* ⑩ ow·to·mo·bee·*leez*·mo

car registration *bollo* ⑩ *di circolazione* *bo*·lo dee cheer·ko·la·*tsyo*·ne

caravan *roulotte* ① roo·*lot*

cards *carte* ① pl *kar*·te

carpenter *carpentiere* ⑩ kar·pen·*tye*·re

carrot *carota* ① ka·*ro*·ta

carry *portare* por·*ta*·re

carry-on luggage *bagaglio* ⑩ *a mano* ba·*ga*·lyo a *ma*·no

carton *scatola* ① *ska*·to·la

cash *soldi* ⑩ pl *sol*·dee

cash a cheque *riscuotere un assegno* ree·*skwo*·te·re oon a·*se*·nyo

cash register *cassa* ① *ka*·sa

cashew *noce* ① *(di acagiù)* *no*·che (dee a·ka·*joo*)

cashier *cassiere/a* ⑩/① ka·*sye*·re/a

casino *casinò* ⑩ ka·zee·*no*

cassette *cassetta* ① ka·*se*·ta

castle *castello* ⑩ kas·*te*·lo

cat *gatto* ⑩ *ga*·to

cathedral *duomo* ⑩ *dwo*·mo

Catholic *cattolico/a* ⑩/① ka·to·*lee*·ko/a

cauliflower *cavolfiore* ⑩ ka·vol·*fyo*·re

cave *grotta* ① *gro*·ta

caviar *caviale* ⑩ ka·*vya*·le

CD *cidì* ⑩ chee·*dee*

celebration *celebrazione* ① che·le·bra·*tsyo*·ne

cell phone *(telefono) cellulare* ⑩ (te·*le*·fo·no) che·loo·*la*·re

cent *centesimo* ⑩ chen·*te*·zee·mo

centimetre *centimetro* ⑩ chen·*tee*·me·tro

central heating *riscaldamento* ⑩ *centrale* rees·kal·da·*men*·to chen·*tra*·le

centre *centro* ⑩ *chen*·tro

cereal *cereali* ⑩ pl che·re·*a*·lee

certificate *certificato* ⑩ cher·tee·fee·*ka*·to

chain *catena* ① ka·*te*·na

chair *sedia* ① *se*·dya

chairlift (skiing) *seggiovia* ① se·jo·*vee*·a

championships *campionato* ⑩ kam·pyo·*na*·to

chance *fortuna* ① for·*too*·na

change (coins) *spiccioli* ⑩ pl *spee*·cho·lee

change (money) *resto* ⑩ *res*·to

change *cambiare* kam·*bya*·re

change room (sport) *spogliatoio* ⑩ spo·lya·*to*·yo

charming *affascinante* a·fa·shee·*nan*·te

chat up *agganciare* a·gan·*cha*·re

cheap *economico/a* ⑩/① e·ko·no·*mee*·ko/a

cheat *imbrogliare* eem·bro·*lya*·re

check (bill) *conto* ⑩ *kon*·to

check *controllare* kon·tro·*la*·re

check-in (airport) *accetazione* ① a·che·ta·*tsyo*·ne

check-in (hotel) *registrazione* ① re·jee·stra·*tsyo*·ne

cheese *formaggio* ⑩ for·*ma*·jo

chef *cuoco/a* ⑩/① *kwo*·ko/a

chemist *farmacista* ⑩&① far·ma·*chee*·sta

cheque *assegno* ⑩ a·*se*·nyo

chess *scacchi* ⑩ pl *ska*·kee

chest *petto* ⑩ *pe*·to

chicken *pollo* ⑩ *po*·lo

chickpeas *ceci* ⑩ pl *che*·chee

child *bambino/a* ⑩/① bam·*bee*·no/a

child seat *seggiolino* ⑩ se·jo·*lee*·no

child minding (group) *asilo nido* ⑩ a·*zee*·lo *nee*·do

child minding (private) *baby-sitter* ⑩&① be·bee·*see*·ter

chilli *peperoncino* ⑩ pe·pe·ron·*chee*·no

chilli sauce *salsa* ① *di peperoncino rosso* *sal*·sa dee pe·pe·ron·*chee*·no *ro*·so

chocolate *cioccolato* ⑩ cho·ko·*la*·to

Christian *cristiano/a* ⑩/① krees·*tya*·no/a

Christmas *Natale* ⑩ na·*ta*·le

church *chiesa* ① *kye*·za

cider *sidro* ⑩ *see*·dro

cigar *sigaro* ⑩ *see*·ga·ro

cigarette *sigaretta* ① see·ga·*re*·ta

cigarette lighter *accendino* ⑩ a·chen·*dee*·no

cinema *cinema* ⓜ *chee·ne·ma*

circus *circo* ⓜ *cheer·ko*

citizenship *cittadinanza* ⓕ
chee·ta·dee·nan·tsa

city *città* ⓕ *chee·ta*

class *classe* ⓕ *kla·se*

classical *classico/a* ⓜ/ⓕ *kla·see·ko/a*

clean *pulito/a* ⓜ/ⓕ *poo·lee·to/a*

cleaning *pulizia* ⓕ *poo·lee·tsee·a*

client *cliente* ⓜ&ⓕ *klee·en·te*

cliff *scogliera* ⓕ *sko·lye·ra*

climb *scalare* *ska·la·re*

cloakroom *guardaroba* ⓜ *gwar·da·ro·ba*

clock *orologio* ⓜ *o·ro·lo·jo*

close (nearby) *vicino/a* ⓜ/ⓕ
vee·chee·no/a

close (shut) *chiudere* *kyoo·de·re*

closed *chiuso/a* ⓜ/ⓕ *kyoo·zo/a*

clothes line *corda* ⓕ *del bucato* *kor·da*
del boo·ka·to

clothing *abbigliamento* ⓜ
a·bee·lya·men·to

clothing store *negozio* ⓜ *di*
abbigliamento *ne·go·tsyo dee*
a·bee·lya·men·to

cloud *nuvola* ⓕ *noo·vo·la*

cloudy *nuvoloso/a* ⓜ/ⓕ *noo·vo·lo·zo/a*

clutch *frizione* ⓕ *free·tsyo·ne*

coach (bus) *pullman* ⓜ *pool·man*

coast *costa* ⓕ *kos·ta*

coat *cappotto* ⓜ *ka·po·to*

cocaine *cocaina* ⓕ *ko·ka·ee·na*

cockroach *scarafaggio* ⓜ *ska·ra·fa·jo*

cocoa *cacao* ⓜ *ka·ka·o*

coffee *caffè* ⓜ *ka·fe*

coins *monete* ⓕ pl *mo·ne·te*

cold *freddo/a* ⓜ/ⓕ *fre·do/a*

have a cold *essere raffreddato/a* ⓜ/ⓕ
e·se·re ra·fre·da·to/a

colleague *collega* ⓜ&ⓕ *ko·le·ga*

collect call *chiamata* ⓕ *a carico del*
destinatario *kya·ma·ta a ka·ree·ko del*
des·tee·na·ta·ryo

college *collegio* ⓜ *universitario* *ko·le·jo*
oo·nee·ver·see·ta·ryo

colour *colore* ⓜ *ko·lo·re*

comb *pettine* ⓜ *pe·tee·ne*

come *venire* *ve·nee·re*

comedy *commedia* ⓕ *comica* *ko·me·dya*
ko·mee·ka

comfortable *comodo/a* ⓜ/ⓕ *ko·mo·do/a*

commission *commissione* ⓕ
ko·mee·syo·ne

communion *comunione* ⓕ
ko·moo·nyo·ne

communist *comunista* ⓜ&ⓕ
ko·moo·nee·sta

companion *compagno/a* ⓜ/ⓕ
kom·pa·nyo/a

company (firm) *ditta* ⓕ *dee·ta*

compass *bussola* ⓕ *boo·so·la*

complain *lamentarsi* *la·men·tar·see*

complimentary (free) *gratuito/a* ⓜ/ⓕ
gra·too·ee·to/a

computer *computer* ⓜ *kom·pyoo·ter*

computer game *gioco* ⓜ *elettronico*
jo·ko e·le·tro·nee·ko

concert *concerto* ⓜ *kon·cher·to*

conditioner *balsamo* ⓜ *per i capelli*
bal·sa·mo per ee ka·pe·lee

condom *preservativo* ⓜ *pre·zer·va·tee·vo*

confession (religious) *confessione* ⓕ
kon·fe·syo·ne

confirm (a booking) *confermare*
kon·fer·ma·re

connection (transport) *coincidenza* ⓕ
ko·een·chee·den·tsa

conservative *conservatore/*
conservatrice ⓜ/ⓕ *kon·ser·va·to·re/*
kon·ser·va·tree·che

constipation *stitichezza* ⓕ *stee·tee·ke·tsa*

consulate *consolato* ⓜ *kon·so·la·to*

contact lenses *lenti* ⓕ pl *a contatto*
len·tee a kon·ta·to

contraceptive *contraccettivo* ⓜ/ⓕ
kon·tra·che·tee·vo

contract *contratto* ⓜ *kon·tra·to*

convenience store *alimentari* ⓜ
a·lee·men·ta·ree

convent *convento* ⓜ *kon·ven·to*

cook *cuoco/a* ⓜ/ⓕ *kwo·ko/a*

cook *cucinare* *koo·chee·na·re*

cookie *biscotto* ⓜ *bees·ko·to*

corn flakes *fiocchi* ⓜ pl *di mais* *fyo·kee*
dee ma·ees

corner *angolo* ⓜ an·go·lo
correct *giusto/a* ⓜ/ⓕ joo·sto/a
corrupt *corrotto/a* ⓜ/ⓕ ko·ro·to/a
cost *costare* kos·ta·re
cot *culla* ⓕ koo·la
cotton *cotone* ⓜ ko·to·ne
cotton balls *batuffoli* ⓜ pl *di cotone* ba·too·fo·lee dee ko·to·ne
cough *tossire* to·see·re
cough medicine *sciroppo* ⓜ *per la tosse* shee·ro·po per la to·se
count *contare* kon·ta·re
counter (at bar) *bancone* ⓜ ban·ko·ne
country (nation) *paese* ⓜ pa·e·ze
countryside *campagna* ⓕ kam·pa·nya
courgette *zucchini* ⓜ pl tsoo·kee·nee
court (legal) *corte* ⓕ kor·te
court (tennis) *campo* ⓜ *da tennis* kam·po da te·nees
cover charge (restaurant) *coperto* ⓜ ko·per·to
cover charge (venue) *ingresso* ⓜ een·gre·so
cow *mucca* ⓕ moo·ka
craft (product) *pezzo* ⓜ *d'artigianato* pe·tso dar·tee·ja·na·to
craft (trade) *mestiere* ⓜ mes·tye·re
crash (accident) *incidente* ⓜ een·chee·den·te
crazy *pazzo/a* ⓜ/ⓕ pa·tso/a
cream (food) *panna* ⓕ pa·na
cream cheese *formaggio* ⓜ *fresco* for·ma·jo fres·ko
creche *asilo* ⓜ *nido* a·zee·lo nee·do
credit card *carta* ⓕ *di credito* kar·ta dee kre·dee·to
cricket *cricket* ⓜ kree·ket
crime (infringment) *delitto* ⓜ de·lee·to
crime (issue) *criminalità* ⓕ kree·mee·na·lee·ta
Croatia *Croazia* ⓕ kro·a·tsya
cross (religious) *croce* ⓕ kro·che
crowded *affollato/a* ⓜ/ⓕ a·fo·la·to/a
cucumber *cetriolo* ⓜ che·tree·o·lo
cup *tazza* ⓕ ta·tsa
currency exchange *cambio* ⓜ *valuta* kam·byo va·loo·ta

current (electricity) *corrente* ⓕ ko·ren·te
current affairs *attualità* ⓕ a·too·a·lee·ta
curry *curry* ⓜ koo·ree
curry powder *polvere* ⓕ *da curry* pol·ve·re da koo·ree
customs *dogana* ⓕ do·ga·na
cut *tagliare* ta·lya·re
cutlery *posate* ⓕ pl po·za·te
CV *curriculum vitae* ⓜ koo·ree·koo·loom vee·te
cycle *andare in bicicletta* an·da·re een bee·chee·kle·ta
cycling *ciclismo* ⓜ chee·kleez·mo
cyclist *ciclista* ⓜ&ⓕ chee·klee·sta
cystitis *cistite* ⓕ chees·tee·te

D

dad *papà* ⓜ pa·pa
damage *danno* ⓜ da·no
dance *ballare* ba·la·re
dancing *ballo* ⓜ ba·lo
dangerous *pericoloso/a* ⓜ/ⓕ pe·ree·ko·lo·zo/a
dark *scuro/a* ⓜ/ⓕ skoo·ro/a
date (appointment) *appuntamento* ⓜ a·poon·ta·men·to
date (day) *data* ⓕ da·ta
date (go out with) *uscire con* oo·shee·re kon
date of birth *data* ⓕ *di nascita* da·ta dee na·shee·ta
daughter *figlia* ⓕ fee·lya
day *giorno* ⓜ jor·no
day after tomorrow *dopodomani* do·po·do·ma·nee
day before yesterday *altro ieri* ⓜ al·tro ye·ree
dead *morto/a* ⓜ/ⓕ mor·to/a
deaf *sordo/a* ⓜ/ⓕ sor·do/a
deep *profondo/a* ⓜ/ⓕ pro·fon·do/a
delay *ritardo* ⓜ ree·tar·do
delicatessen *salumeria* ⓕ sa·loo·me·ree·a
democracy *democrazia* ⓕ de·mo·kra·tsee·a
demonstration (protest) *manifestazione* ⓕ ma·nee·fes·ta·tsyo·ne

dental floss *filo* ⓜ *dentario* fee·lo
den·ta·ree·o
dentist *dentista* ⓜ&ⓕ den·tee·sta
deodorant *deodorante* ⓜ de·o·do·ran·te
depart *partire* par·tee·re
department store *grande magazzino* ⓜ
gran·de ma·ga·dzee·no
departure *partenza* ⓕ par·ten·tsa
deposit (bank) *deposito* ⓜ de·po·zee·to
deposit (refundable) *caparra* ⓕ ka·pa·ra
derailleur *deragliatore* ⓜ de·ra·lya·to·re
dessert *dolce* ⓜ dol·che
destination *destinazione* ⓕ
des·tee·na·tsyo·ne
diabetes *diabete* ⓜ dee·a·be·te
dial tone *segnale* ⓜ *(acustico)* se·nya·le
(a·koos·tee·ko)
diaper *pannolino* ⓜ pa·no·lee·no
diaphragm *diaframma* ⓜ dee·a·fra·ma
diarrhoea *diarrea* ⓕ dee·a·re·a
diary *agenda* ⓕ a·jen·da
dictionary *vocabolario* ⓜ vo·ka·bo·la·ryo
die *morire* mo·ree·re
diesel *diesel* ⓜ dee·zel
diet *dieta* ⓕ dye·ta
different *diverso/a* dee·ver·so/a
different (from) *differente (da)*
dee·fe·ren·te (da)
difficult *difficile* dee·fee·chee·le
digital *digitale* dee·jee·ta·le
dining car *carrozza* ⓕ *ristorante* ka·ro·tsa
rees·to·ran·te
dinner *cena* ⓕ che·na
direct *diretto/a* ⓜ/ⓕ dee·re·to/a
direct-dial *telefono* ⓜ *diretto* te·le·fo·no
dee·re·to
direction *direzione* ⓕ dee·re·tsyo·ne
director (films) *regista* ⓜ&ⓕ re·jee·sta
dirty *sporco/a* ⓜ/ⓕ spor·ko/a
disabled *disabile* dee·za·bee·le
discount *sconto* ⓜ skon·to
discrimination *discriminazione* ⓕ
dees·kree·mee·na·tsyo·ne
disease *malattia* ⓕ ma·la·tee·a
disinfectant *disinfettante* ⓜ
deez·een·fe·tan·te
disk (computer) *dischetto* ⓜ dees·ke·to

disposable *usa e getta* oo·za e je·ta
dive *tuffarsi* ⓜ too·far·see
diving (sea) *immersioni* ⓕ pl
ee·mer·syo·nee
divorced *divorziato/a* ⓜ/ⓕ
dee·vor·tsya·to/a
dizzy *stordito/a* ⓜ/ⓕ stor·dee·to/a
do *fare* fa·re
doctor *medico* ⓜ me·dee·ko
dog *cane* ⓜ ka·ne
dole *sussidio* ⓜ *di disoccupazione*
soo·see·dyo dee dee·zo·koo·pa·tsyo·ne
doll *bambola* ⓕ bam·bo·la
dollar *dollaro* ⓜ do·la·ro
door *porta* ⓕ por·ta
dope (drugs) *roba* ⓕ ro·ba
double *doppio/a* ⓜ/ⓕ do·pyo/a
double bed *letto* ⓜ *matrimoniale* le·to
ma·tree·mo·nya·le
double room *camera* ⓕ *doppia* ka·mer·a
do·pya
down *giù* joo
dozen *dozzina* ⓕ do·dzee·na
drag queen *travestito* ⓜ tra·ves·tee·to
drama *dramma* ⓜ dra·ma
dream *sogno* ⓜ so·nyo
dream *sognare* so·nya·re
dress *abito* ⓜ a·bee·to
drink *bevanda* ⓕ be·van·da
drink *bere* be·re
drinkable *potabile* po·ta·bee·le
drive *guidare* gwee·da·re
drivers licence *patente* ⓕ *(di guida)*
pa·ten·te (dee gwee·da)
drug (medicinal) *medicina* ⓕ
me·dee·chee·na
drug addiction *tossicodipendenza* ⓕ
to·see·ko·dee·pen·den·tsa
drug dealer *spacciatore/spacciatrice*
ⓜ/ⓕ spa·cha·to·re/spa·cha·tree·che
drugs (illegal) *droga* ⓕ sg dro·ga
drums *batteria* ⓕ ba·te·ree·a
drunk *ubriaco/a* ⓜ/ⓕ oo·bree·a·ko/a
dry *secco/a* ⓜ/ⓕ se·ko/a
dry *asciugare* a·shoo·ga·re
dry cleaning *lavaggio* ⓜ *a secco* la·va·jo
a se·ko

duck *anatra* ① a·na·tra
dummy (pacifier) *ciuccotto* ⓜ choo·cho·to
during *durante* doo·ran·te

E

each *ciascuno/a* ⓜ/① chas·koo·no/a
ear *orecchio* ⓜ o·re·kyo
early *presto* ⓜ/① pres·to
earplugs *tappi* ⓜ pl *per le orecchie* ta·pee per le o·re·kye
earrings *orecchini* ⓜ pl o·re·kee·nee
Earth *Terra* ① te·ra
earthquake *terremoto* ⓜ te·re·mo·to
east *est* ⓜ est
Easter *Pasqua* ① pas·kwa
easy *facile* fa·chee·le
eat *mangiare* man·ja·re
economy class *classe* ① *turistica* kla·se too·ree·stee·ka
eczema *eczema* ⓜ ek·dze·ma
education *istruzione* ① ees·troo·tsyo·ne
egg *uovo* ⓜ wo·vo
eggplant *melanzana* ① me·lan·dza·na
elections *elezioni* ① pl e·le·tsyo·nee
electrician *elettricista* ⓜ&① e·le·tree·chee·sta
electricity *elettricità* ① e·le·tree·chee·ta
elevator *ascensore* ⓜ a·shen·so·re
email *email* ⓜ e·mayl
embarrassed *imbarazzato/a* ⓜ/① eem·ba·ra·tsa·to/a
embassy *ambasciata* ① am·ba·sha·ta
emergency *emergenza* ① e·mer·jen·tsa
emotional *emotivo/a* ⓜ/① e·mo·tee·vo/a
employee *impiegato/a* ⓜ/① eem·pye·ga·to/a
employer *datore/datrice* ⓜ/① *di lavoro* da·to·re/da·tree·ce dee la·vo·ro
empty *vuoto/a* ⓜ/① vwo·to/a
end *fine* ① fee·ne
end *finire* fee·nee·re
endangered species *specie* ① *in via di estinzione* spe·che een vee·a dee es·teen·tsyo·ne
engagement (couple) *fidanzamento* ⓜ fee·dan·tsa·men·to

engine *motore* ⓜ mo·to·re
engineer *ingegnere* ⓜ&① een·je·nye·re
England *Inghilterra* ① een·geel·te·ra
English *inglese* een·gle·ze
enjoy (oneself) *divertirsi* dee·ver·teer·see
enough *abbastanza* a·bas·tan·tsa
enter *entrare* en·tra·re
entertainment guide *guida* ① *agli spettacoli* gwee·da a·lyee spe·ta·ko·lee
entry *entrata* ① en·tra·ta
(padded) envelope *busta* ① *(imbottita)* boo·sta eem·bo·tee·ta
environment *ambiente* ⓜ am·byen·te
epilepsy *epilessia* ① e·pee·le·see·a
equipment *attrezzatura* ① a·tre·tsa·too·ra
escalator *scala* ① *mobile* ska·la mo·bee·le
euro *euro* ⓜ e·oo·ro
Europe *Europa* ① e·oo·ro·pa
European *europeo/a* ⓜ/① e·oo·ro·pe·o/a
euthanasia *eutanasia* ① e·oo·ta·na·zee·a
evening *sera* ① se·ra
everything *tutto* ⓜ too·to
example *esempio* ⓜ e·zem·pyo
excellent *ottimo/a* ⓜ/① o·tee·mo/a
excess bagage *bagaglio* ⓜ *in eccedenza* ba·ga·lyo een e·che·den·tsa
exchange *cambio* ⓜ kam·byo
exchange *cambiare* kam·bya·re
exchange rate *tasso* ① *di cambio* ta·so dee kam·byo
excluded *escluso/a* ⓜ/① es·kloo·zo/a
exhaust (car) *tubo* ⓜ *di scappamento* too·bo dee ska·pa·men·to
exhibition *esposizione* ① es·po·zee·tsyo·ne
exit *uscita* ① oo·shee·ta
expensive *caro/a* ⓜ/① ka·ro/a
experience *esperienza* ① es·pe·ryen·tsa
exploitation *sfruttamento* ⓜ sfroo·ta·men·to
express *espresso/a* ⓜ/① es·pre·so/a
express mail *posta* ① *prioritaria* pos·ta pree·o·ree·ta·rya
extension (visa) *proroga* ① pro·ro·ga
eye *occhio* ⓜ o·kyo
eye drops *collirio* ⓜ ko·lee·ryo

F

fabric *stoffa* ① sto·fa
face *faccia* ① fa·cha
factory *fabbrica* ① fa·bree·ka
factory worker *operaio/a* ⓜ/① o·pe·ra·yo/a
fall (autumn) *autunno* ⓜ ow·too·no
family *famiglia* ① fa·mee·lya
family name *cognome* ⓜ ko·nyo·me
famous *famoso/a* ⓜ/① fa·mo·zo/a
fan (person) *tifoso/a* ⓜ/① tee·fo·zo/a
fan (machine) *ventilatore* ⓜ ven·tee·la·to·re
fan belt *cinghia* ① *della ventola* cheen·gya de·la ven·to·la
far *lontano/a* ⓜ/① lon·ta·no/a
farm *fattoria* ① fa·to·ree·a
farmer *agricoltore/agricoltrice* ⓜ/① a·gree·kol·to·re/a·gree·kol·tree·che
fashion *moda* ① mo·da
fast *veloce* ve·lo·che
fat *grasso/a* ⓜ/① gra·so/a
father *padre* ⓜ pa·dre
father-in-law *suocero* ⓜ swo·che·ro
faucet *rubinetto* ① roo·bee·ne·to
fault (someone's) *colpa* ① kol·pa
faulty *difettoso/a* ⓜ/① dee·fe·to·zo/a
favourite *preferito/a* ⓜ/① pre·fe·ree·to/a
fax *fax* ⓜ faks
fee *compenso* ⓜ kom·pen·so
feel *sentire* sen·tee·re
feelings *sentimenti* ⓜ pl sen·tee·men·tee
fence *recinto* ① re·cheen·to
fencing (sport) *scherma* ① sker·ma
ferry *traghetto* ⓜ tra·ge·to
festival *festa* ① fes·ta
fever *febbre* ① fe·bre
few *pochi/e* ⓜ/① po·kee/po·ke
fiance(e) *fidanzato/a* ⓜ/① fee·dan·tsa·to/a
fiction *narrativa* ① na·ra·tee·va
fig *fico* ⓜ fee·ko
fight *lite* ① lee·te
film (cinema) *film* ⓜ feelm
film (roll for camera) *rullino* ⓜ roo·lee·no
film speed *ASA* a·za

find *trovare* tro·va·re
fine (payment) *multa* ① mool·ta
finger *dito* ① dee·to
finish *finire* fee·nee·re
fire *fuoco* ⓜ fwo·ko
firewood *legna* ① *da ardere* le·nya da ar·de·re
first *primo/a* ⓜ/① pree·mo/a
first class *prima classe* ① pree·ma kla·se
first-aid kit *valigetta* ① *del pronto soccorso* va·lee·je·ta del pron·to so·kor·so
fish *pesce* ⓜ pe·she
fish shop *pescheria* ① pe·ske·ree·a
fishing *pesca* ① pe·ska
flag *bandiera* ① ban·dye·ra
flash (camera) *flash* ⓜ flesh
flashlight (torch) *torcia* ① *elettrica* tor·cha e·le·tree·ka
flat *appartamento* ⓜ a·par·ta·men·to
flat *piatto/a* ⓜ/① pya·to/a
flea *pulce* ① pool·che
flight *volo* ⓜ vo·lo
flood *inondazione* ① ee·non·da·tzyo·nee
floor (ground) *pavimento* ⓜ pa·vee·men·to
floor (storey) *piano* ⓜ pya·no
florist *fioraio* ⓜ&① fyo·ra·yo
flour *farina* ① fa·ree·na
flower *fiore* ⓜ fyo·re
flu *influenza* ① een·floo·en·tsa
fly *mosca* ① mos·ka
fly *volare* vo·la·re
foggy *nebbioso/a* ⓜ/① ne·byo·zo/a
follow *seguire* se·gwee·re
food *cibo* ⓜ chee·bo
food poisoning *intossicazione* ① *alimentare* een·to·see·ka·tsyo·ne a·lee·men·ta·re
food supplies *provviste* ⓜ pl *alimentari* pro·vee·ste a·lee·men·ta·ree
foot *piede* ⓜ pye·de
football (soccer) *calcio* ⓜ kal·cho
footpath *marciapiede* ⓜ mar·cha·pye·de
foreign *straniero/a* ⓜ/① stra·nye·ro/a
forest *foresta* ① fo·res·ta
forever *per sempre* per sem·pre

forget *dimenticare* dee·men·tee·ka·re
forgive *perdonare* per·do·na·re
fork *forchetta* ① for·ke·ta
form (paper) *modulo* ⑩ mo·doo·lo
fortnight *quindici giorni* ⑩ pl
kween·dee·chee jor·nee
foyer *atrio* ⑩ a·tryo
fragile *fragile* fra·jee·le
France *Francia* ① fran·cha
free (gratis) *gratuito/a* ⑩/①
gra·too·ee·to/a
free (not bound) *libero/a* ⑩/①
lee·be·ro/a
freeze *congelare* kon·je·la·re
fresh *fresco/a* ⑩/① fres·ko/a
fridge *frigorifero* ⑩ free·go·ree·fe·ro
friend *amico/a* ⑩/① a·mee·ko/a
frozen *congelato/a* ⑩/① kon·je·la·to/a
frozen foods *surgelati* ⑩ pl soor·je·la·tee
fruit *frutta* ① froo·ta
fruit juice (bottled) *succo* ⑩ *di frutta*
soo·ko dee froo·ta
fruit juice (fresh) *spremuta* ①
spre·moo·ta
fry *friggere* free·je·re
frying pan *padella* ① pa·de·la
full *pieno/a* ⑩/① pye·no/a
full-time *a tempo pieno* a tem·po pye·no
fun *divertimento* ⑩ dee·ver·tee·men·to
have fun *divertirsi* dee·ver·teer·see
funeral *funerale* ⑩ foo·ne·ra·le
funny *divertente* dee·ver·ten·te
furniture *mobili* ⑩ pl mo·bee·lee
future *futuro* ⑩ foo·too·ro

G

game (play) *gioco* ⑩ jo·ko
game (sport) *partita* ① par·tee·ta
garage *garage* ⑩ ga·raj
garbage *spazzatura* ① pl spa·tsa·too·ra
garden *giardino* ⑩ jar·dee·no
gardening *giardinaggio* ⑩ jar·dee·na·jo
garlic *aglio* ⑩ a·lyo
gas (for cooking) *gas* ⑩ gaz
gas (petrol) *benzina* ① ben·dzee·na

gas cartridge *cartuccia* ① *di ricambio*
del gas kar·too·cha dee ree·kam·byo
del gaz
gastroenteritis *gastroenterite* ①
gas·tro·en·te·ree·te
gate *cancello* ⑩ kan·che·lo
gay *gay* gei
gears (bicycle) *cambio* ⑩ kam·byo
general *generale* je·ne·ra·le
Germany *Germania* ① jer·ma·nya
gift *regalo* ⑩ re·ga·lo
ginger *zenzero* ⑩ dzen·dze·ro
girl(friend) *ragazza* ① ra·ga·tsa
give *dare* da·re
glandular fever *mononucleosi* ⑩
mo·no·noo·kle·o·zee
glass (material) *vetro* ⑩ ve·tro
glass (drinking) *bicchiere* ⑩ bee·kye·re
glasses (spectacles) *occhiali* ⑩ pl
o·kya·lee
gloves *guanti* ⑩ pl gwan·tee
go *andare* an·da·re
go out with *uscire con* oo·shee·re kon
goat *capra* ① ka·pra
god (general) *dio/dea* ⑩/① dee·o/de·a
goggles (skiing) *occhiali* ⑩ pl *(da sci)*
o·kya·lee (da shee)
gold *oro* ⑩ o·ro
golf ball *palla* ① *da golf* pa·la da golf
golf course *campo* ⑩ *da golf* kam·po
da golf
good *buono/a* ⑩/① bwo·no/a
government *governo* ⑩ go·ver·no
grams *grammi* ⑩ pl gra·mee
grandchild *nipote* ⑩&① nee·po·te
grandfather *nonno* ⑩ no·no
grandmother *nonna* ① no·na
grapefruit *pompelmo* ⑩ pom·pel·mo
grapes *uva* ① pl oo·va
grass *erba* ① er·ba
grave (tomb) *tomba* ① tom·ba
great *ottimo/a* ⑩/① o·tee·mo/a
green *verde* ver·de
greengrocer *fruttivendolo/a* ⑩/①
froo·tee·ven·do·lo/a
grey *grigio/a* ⑩/① gree·jo/a
grocery *drogheria* ① dro·ge·ree·a
groundnut *arachide* ① a·ra·kee·de

grow *crescere* kre·she·re
guesthouse *pensione* ⑤ pen·syo·ne
guide (audio) *guida* ⑤ *audio* gwee·da ow·dyo
guide (person) *guida* ⑤ gwee·da
guide dog *cane* ⑩ *guida* ka·ne gwee·da
guidebook *guida* ⑤ *(turistica)* gwee·da (too·ree·stee·ka)
guided tour *visita* ⑤ *guidata* vee·zee·ta gwee·da·ta
guilty *colpevole* kol·pe·vo·le
guitar *chitarra* ⑤ kee·ta·ra
gum (mouth) *gengiva* ⑤ jen·jee·va
gum (chewing) *gomma* ⑤ *da masticare* go·ma da ma·stee·ka·re
gym *palestra* ⑤ pa·le·stra
gymnastics *ginnastica* ⑤ jee·nas·tee·ka
gynaecologist *ginecologo/a* ⑩/⑤ jee·ne·ko·lo·go/a

H

hail *grandine* ⑤ gran·dee·ne
hailstorm *grandinata* ⑤ gran·dee·na·ta
haircut *taglio* ⑩ *di capelli* ta·lyo dee ka·pe·lee
hairdresser *parrucchiere/a* ⑩/⑤ pa·roo·kye·re/a
halal *halal* a·lal
half *mezzo* ⑩ me·dzo
hallucinate *allucinare* a·loo·chee·na·re
ham (boiled) *prosciutto* ⑩ *(cotto)* pro·shoo·to (ko·to)
hammer *martello* ⑩ mar·te·lo
hammock *amaca* ⑤ a·ma·ka
hand *mano* ⑤ ma·no
handbag *borsetta* ⑤ bor·se·ta
handball *pallamuro* ⑤ pa·la·moo·ro
handicrafts *oggetti* ⑩ pl *d'artigianato* o·je·tee dar·tee·ja·na·to
handkerchief *fazzoletto* ⑩ fa·tso·le·to
handlebars *manubrio* ⑤ ma·noo·bryo
handmade *fatto/a* ⑩/⑤ *a mano* fa·to/a a ma·no
handsome *bello/a* ⑩/⑤ be·lo/a
happy *felice* ⑩/⑤ fe·lee·che
harassment *molestia* ⑤ mo·les·tya
harbour *porto* ⑩ por·to

hard (not easy) *difficile* dee·fee·chee·le
hard (not soft) *duro/a* ⑩/⑤ doo·ro/a
hardware store *ferramenta* ⑤ fe·ra·men·ta
hash *hashish* ⑩ a·sheesh
hat *cappello* ⑩ ka·pe·lo
have *avere* a·ve·re
hay fever *febbre* ⑤ *da fieno* fe·bre da fye·no
he *lui* loo·ee
head *testa* ⑤ tes·ta
headache *mal* ⑩ *di testa* mal dee tes·ta
headlights *fari* ⑩ pl fa·ree
health *salute* ⑤ sa·loo·te
hear *sentire* sen·tee·re
hearing aid *apparecchio* ⑩ *acustico* a·pa·re·kyo a·koos·tee·ko
heart *cuore* ⑩ kwo·re
heart condition *problema* ⑩ *cardiaco* pro·ble·ma kar·dee·a·ko
heat *caldo* ⑩ kal·do
heater *stufa* ⑤ stoo·fa
heating *riscaldamento* ⑩ rees·kal·da·men·to
heavy *pesante* pe·zan·te
height *altezza* ⑤ al·te·tsa
helmet *casco* ⑩ kas·ko
help *aiutare* a·yoo·ta·re
hepatitis *epatite* ⑤ e·pa·tee·te
herbalist *erborista* ⑩&⑤ er·bo·ree·sta
herbs *erbe* ⑤ pl er·be
here *qui* kwee
heroin *eroina* ⑤ e·ro·ee·na
herring *aringa* ⑤ a·reen·ga
high *alto/a* ⑩/⑤ al·to/a
high school *scuola* ⑤ *superiore* skwo·la soo·pe·ryo·re
hike *escursione* ⑤ *a piedi* es·koor·syo·ne a pye·de
hiking *escursionismo* ⑩ *a piedi* es·koor·syo·neez·mo a pye·de
hiking boots *scarponi* ⑩ pl skar·po·nee
hiking route *itinerario* ⑩ *escursionistico* e·tee·ne·ra·ryo es·koor·syo·nee·stee·ko
hill *collina* ⑤ ko·lee·na
Hindu *indù* ⑩&⑤ een·doo
hire *noleggiare* no·le·ja·re
historical *storico/a* ⑩/⑤ sto·ree·ko/a

history storia ⓕ *sto*·rya
hitchhike fare l'autostop fa·re
  low-to-stop
HIV positive sieropositivo/a ⓜ/ⓕ
  sye·ro·po·*zee*·tee·vo/a
hobby passatempo ⓜ pa·sa·*tem*·po
hockey hockey ⓜ *o*·kee
holidays vacanze ⓕ pl va·*kan*·tse
Holy Week settimana ⓕ santa
  se·tee·*ma*·na *san*·ta
home casa ⓕ *ka*·za
homeless senzatetto ⓜ&ⓕ sen·tsa·*te*·to
homemaker casalingo/a ⓕ
  ka·za·*leen*·go/a
homeopathy omeopatia ⓕ
  o·me·o·pa·*tee*·a
homosexual omosessuale ⓜ&ⓕ
  o·mo·se·*swa*·le
honey miele ⓜ *mye*·le
honeymoon luna ⓕ di miele *loo*·na
  dee *mye*·le
horse cavallo ⓜ ka·*va*·lo
horse riding andare a cavallo
  an·*da*·re a ka·*va*·lo
horseradish rafano ⓜ *ra*·fa·no
hospital ospedale ⓜ os·pe·*da*·le
hospitality ospitalità ⓕ os·pee·ta·lee·*ta*
hot caldo/a ⓜ/ⓕ *kal*·do/a
hot water acqua ⓕ calda *a*·kwa *kal*·da
hotel albergo ⓜ al·*ber*·go
hour ora ⓕ *o*·ra
house casa ⓕ *ka*·za
how come *ko*·me
how much quanto/a ⓜ/ⓕ *kwan*·to/a
hug abbracciare a·bra·*cha*·re
huge enorme e·*nor*·me
human rights diritti ⓜ pl umani
  dee·*ree*·tee oo·*ma*·nee
(to be) hungry avere fame ⓕ
  a·*ve*·re *fa*·me
hunting caccia ⓕ *ka*·cha
(to be) in a hurry avere fretta ⓕ
  a·*ve*·re *fre*·ta
hurt fare male fa·re *ma*·le
husband marito ⓜ ma·*ree*·to
hydrating fluid fluido ⓜ idratante
  floo·ee·do ee·dra·*tan*·te

I

I io ee·o
ice ghiaccio ⓜ *gya*·cho
ice axe piccozza ⓕ pee·*ko*·tsa
ice cream gelato ⓜ je·*la*·to
ice-cream parlour gelateria ⓕ
  je·la·te·*ree*·a
ice hockey hockey ⓜ su ghiaccio
  o·kee soo *gya*·cho
identification documento ⓜ d'identità
  do·koo·*men*·to dee·den·tee·*ta*
identification card (ID) carta ⓕ
  d'identità *kar*·ta dee·den·tee·*ta*
idiot idiota ⓜ&ⓕ ee·*dyo*·ta
if se se
ill malato/a ⓜ/ⓕ ma·*la*·to/a
illegal illegale ee·le·*ga*·le
immigration immigrazione ⓕ
  ee·mee·gra·*tsyo*·ne
important importante eem·por·*tan*·te
impossible impossibile eem·po·*see*·bee·le
included compreso/a ⓜ/ⓕ kom·*pre*·zo/a
indicator (car) freccia ⓕ *fre*·cha
indigestion indigestione ⓕ
  een·dee·je·*styo*·ne
industry industria ⓕ een·*doos*·trya
infection infezione ⓕ een·fe·*tsyo*·ne
inflammation infiammazione ⓕ
  een·fya·ma·*tsyo*·ne
influenza influenza ⓕ een·floo·*en*·tsa
information informazioni ⓕ pl
  een·for·ma·*tsyo*·nee
ingredient ingrediente ⓜ
  een·gre·*dyen*·te
inhaler inalatore ⓜ ee·na·la·*to*·re
injection iniezione ⓕ ee·nye·*tsyo*·ne
injured ferito/a ⓜ/ⓕ fe·*ree*·to/a
injury ferita ⓕ fe·*ree*·ta
innocent innocente ee·no·*chen*·te
insect insetto ⓜ een·*se*·to
inside dentro *den*·tro
instructor (general) istruttore/istruttrice
  ⓜ/ⓕ ee·stroo·*to*·re/ee·stroo·*tree*·che
instructor (skiing) maestro/a ⓜ/ⓕ
  ma·*es*·tro/a
insurance assicurazione ⓕ
  a·see·koo·ra·*tsyo*·ne

interesting *interessante* een·te·re·*san*·te
intermission *intervallo* ⓜ een·ter·*va*·lo
international *internazionale*
  een·ter·na·tsyo·*na*·le
Internet (cafe) *Internet (point)* ⓜ
  een·ter·net (poynt)
interpreter *interprete* ⓜ/ⓕ een·*ter*·pre·te
intersection *incrocio* ⓜ een·*kro*·cho
interview *colloquio* ⓜ *(selettivo)*
  ko·*lo*·kwyo (se·le·*tee*·vo)
invite *invitare* een·vee·*ta*·re
Ireland *Irlanda* ⓕ eer·*lan*·da
iron (for clothes) *ferro* ⓜ *da stiro*
  fe·ro da *stee*·ro
island *isola* ⓕ *ee*·zo·la
IT *informatica* ⓕ een·for·*ma*·tee·ka
Italian *italiano/a* ⓜ/ⓕ ee·ta·*lya*·no/a
Italy *Italia* ⓕ ee·*ta*·lya
itch *prurito* ⓜ proo·*ree*·to
itinerary *itinerario* ⓜ ee·tee·ne·*ra*·ryo
IUD *spirale* ⓕ spee·*ra*·le

J

jacket *giacca* ⓕ *ja*·ka
jail *prigione* ⓕ pree·*jo*·ne
jam *marmellata* ⓕ mar·me·*la*·ta
Japan *Giappone* ⓕ ja·*po*·ne
jar *barattolo* ⓜ ba·*ra*·to·lo
jealous *geloso/a* ⓜ/ⓕ je·*lo*·zo/a
jeans *jeans* ⓜ pl jeens
jet lag *disturbi* ⓜ pl *da fuso orario*
  dees·*toor*·bee da *foo*·zo o·ra·ryo
jewellery *gioielli* ⓜ pl jo·*ye*·lee
Jewish *ebreo/a* ⓜ/ⓕ e·*bre*·o/a
job *lavoro* ⓜ la·*vo*·ro
jockey *fantino* ⓜ fan·*tee*·no
jogging *footing* ⓜ *foo*·teeng
joke *scherzo* ⓜ *sker*·tso
journalist *giornalista* ⓜ&ⓕ jor·na·*lee*·sta
judge *giudice* ⓜ joo·*dee*·che
judo *giudò* ⓜ joo·do
juice *succo* ⓜ *soo*·ko
jump *saltare* sal·*ta*·re
jumper *maglione* ⓜ ma·*lyo*·ne
jumper leads *cavi* ⓜ pl *con morsetti*
  ka·vee kon mor·*se*·tee

K

key *chiave* ⓕ *kya*·ve
keyboard *tastiera* ⓕ tas·*tye*·ra
kick *dare un calcio* da·re oon *kal*·cho
kill *ammazzare* a·ma·*tsa*·re
kilogram *chilo* ⓜ *kee*·lo
kilometre *chilometro* ⓜ kee·*lo*·me·tro
kind *gentile* jen·*tee*·le
kindergarten *asilo* ⓜ a·*zee*·lo
king *re* ⓜ re
kiss *bacio* ⓜ *ba*·cho
kiss *baciare* ba·*cha*·re
kitchen *cucina* ⓕ koo·*chee*·na
kitten *gattino* ⓜ ga·*tee*·no
kiwifruit *kiwi* ⓜ *kee*·wee
knapsack *zaino* ⓜ *dzai*·no
knee *ginocchio* ⓜ jee·*no*·kyo
knife *coltello* ⓜ kol·*te*·lo
know (a person) *conoscere* ko·no·*she*·re
know (how to) *sapere* sa·*pe*·re
kosher *kasher* ka·sher

L

labourer *lavoratore/lavoratrice* ⓜ/ⓕ
  la·vo·ra·*to*·re/la·vo·ra·*tree*·che
lace *merletto* ⓜ mer·*le*·to
lager *birra* ⓕ *chiara* bee·ra *kya*·ra
lake *lago* ⓜ *la*·go
lamb *agnello* ⓜ a·*nye*·lo
land *terra* ⓕ *te*·ra
lane *vicolo* vee·ko·lo
landlady *padrona* ⓕ *di casa* pa·*dro*·na
  dee *ka*·za
landlord *padrone* ⓜ *di casa* pa·*dro*·ne
  dee *ka*·za
language *lingua* ⓕ *leen*·gwa
laptop (computer) *portatile* ⓜ
  (kom·*pyoo*·ter) por·ta·*tee*·le
lard *lardo* ⓜ *lar*·do
large *grande* *gran*·de
last *ultimo/a* ⓜ/ⓕ *ool*·tee·mo/a
late *in ritardo* een ree·*tar*·do
laugh *ridere* *ree*·de·re
laundrette *lavanderia* ⓕ *a gettone*
  la·van·de·*ree*·a je·*to*·ne
laundry *lavanderia* ⓕ la·van·de·*ree*·a

law legge ① le·je
lawyer avvocato/a ⑩/① a·vo·ka·to/a
laxatives lassativi ⑩ pl la·sa·tee·vee
lazy pigro/a ⑩/① pee·gro/a
leader capo ⑩ ka·po
leaf foglia ① fo·lya
learn imparare eem·pa·ra·re
leather cuoio ⑩ kwo·yo
leave partire par·tee·re
leek porro ⑩ po·ro
left (direction) sinistra ① see·nee·stra
left luggage (office) deposito ⑩ bagagli de·po·zee·to ba·ga·lyee
left wing (di) sinistra (dee) see·nee·stra
leg (body part) gamba ① gam·ba
leg (in race) tappa ① ta·pa
legal legale le·ga·le
legume legume ⑩ le·goo·me
lemon limone ⑩ lee·mo·ne
lemonade limonata ① lee·mo·na·ta
lens obiettivo ⑩ o·bye·tee·vo
Lent quaresima ① kwa·re·zee·ma
lentil lenticchia ① len·tee·kya
lesbian lesbica ① lez·bee·ka
less (di) meno (dee) me·no
letter lettera ① le·te·ra
lettuce lattuga ① la·too·ga
level (tier) livello ⑩ lee·ve·lo
liar bugiardo/a ⑩/① boo·jar·do/a
library biblioteca ① bee·blyo·te·ka
lice pidocchi ⑩ pl pee·do·kee
licence plate number numero ⑩ di targa noo·me·ro dee tar·ga
lie (not stand) stendersi sten·der·see
life vita ① vee·ta
life jacket giubbotto ⑩ di salvataggio joo·bo·to dee sal·va·ta·jo
lift (elevator) ascensore ⑩ a·shen·so·re
light luce ① loo·che
light (colour) chiaro/a ⑩/① kya·ro/a
light (not heavy) leggero/a ⑩/① le·je·ro/a
light bulb lampadina ① lam·pa·dee·na
light meter esposimetro ⑩ es·po·zee·me·tro
lighter accendino ⑩ a·chen·dee·no
lights (on car) fari ⑩ pl fa·ree
like piacere pya·che·re
lime limetta ① lee·me·ta

line linea ① lee·ne·a
lip balm burro ⑩ per le labbra boo·ro per le la·bra
lips labbra ① pl la·bra
lipstick rossetto ⑩ ro·se·to
liquor store bottiglieria ① bo·tee·lye·ree·a
list elenco ⑩ e·len·ko
listen ascoltare as·kol·ta·re
litre litro ⑩ lee·tro
(a) little un po' oon po
live vivere vee·ve·re
liver fegato ⑩ fe·ga·to
lizard lucertola ① loo·cher·to·la
local locale lo·ka·le
lock (door) serratura ① se·ra·too·ra
locked chiuso/a ⑩/① (a chiave) kyoo·zo/a (a kya·ve)
locker armadietto ⑩ ar·ma·dye·to
lollies caramelle ① pl ka·ra·me·le
long lungo/a ⑩/① loon·go/a
long-distance (bus) interurbano/a ⑩/① een·ter·oor·ba·no/a
look guardare gwar·da·re
look after curare koo·ra·re
look for cercare cher·ka·re
lookout veduta ① ve·doo·ta
loose change spiccioli ⑩ pl spee·cho·lee
lose perdere per·de·re
lost perso/a ⑩/① per·so/a
lost-property office ufficio ⑩ oggetti smarriti oo·fee·cho o·je·tee sma·ree·tee
a lot (of) molto/a ⑩/① mol·to/a
loud forte ⑩/① for·te
love amare a·ma·re
lover amante ⑩ a·man·te
low basso/a ⑩/① ba·so/a
lubricant lubrificante ⑩ loo·bree·fee·kan·te
luck fortuna ① for·too·na
lucky fortunato/a ⑩/① for·too·na·to/a
luggage bagaglio ⑩ ba·ga·lyo
luggage lockers armadietti ⑩ pl per i bagagli ar·ma·dye·tee per ee ba·ga·lyee
luggage tag etichetta ① e·tee·ke·ta
lump nodulo ⑩ no·doo·lo
lunch pranzo ⑩ pran·dzo
lungs polmoni ⑩ pl pol·mo·nee
luxurious di lusso dee loo·so

M

machine *macchina* ① *ma*·kee·na
made of (cotton) *fatto/a* ⓜ/① *di*
(*cotone*) *fa*·to/a dee (ko·*to*·ne)
magazine *rivista* ① ree·vee·sta
mail *posta* ① pos·ta
mail box *buca* ① *delle lettere* boo·ka
de·le *le*·te·re
main *principale* preen·chee·*pa*·le
make *fare* fa·re
make-up *trucco* ⓜ *troo*·ko
mallet *mazzuolo* ⓜ ma·*tswo*·lo
mammogram *mammografia* ①
ma·mo·gra·*fee*·a
man *uomo* ⓜ *wo*·mo
manager *manager* ⓜ *me*·nee·je
mandarin *mandarino* ⓜ man·da·*ree*·no
mango *mango* ⓜ *man*·go
manual *manuale* ma·noo·*a*·le
manual worker *manovale* ⓜ&①
ma·no·*va*·le
many *molti/e* ⓜ/① pl *mol*·tee/*mol*·te
map *pianta* ① *pyan*·ta
marble *marmo* ⓜ *mar*·mo
margarine *margarina* ① mar·ga·*ree*·na
marijuana *marijuana* ① ma·ree·*wa*·na
marital status *stato* ⓜ *civile* sta·to
chee·vee·le
market *mercato* ⓜ mer·*ka*·to
marmalade *marmellata* ① mar·me·*la*·ta
marriage *matrimonio* ⓜ ma·tree·mo·nyo
married *sposato/a* ⓜ/① spo·*za*·to/a
marry *sposare* spo·*za*·re
martial arts *arti* ① pl *marziali* ar·tee
mar·*tsya*·lee
mass (Catholic) *messa* ① *me*·sa
massage *massaggio* ⓜ ma·*sa*·jo
mat *tappeto* ⓜ ta·*pe*·to
match (sport) *partita* ① par·*tee*·ta
matches *fiammiferi* ⓜ pl fya·*mee*·fe·ree
mattress *materasso* ⓜ ma·te·*ra*·so
maybe *forse* *for*·se
mayonnaise *maionese* ① ma·yo·*ne*·ze
mayor *sindaco* ⓜ *seen*·da·ko
measles *morbillo* ⓜ mor·*bee*·lo
meat *carne* ① *kar*·ne

mechanic *meccanico* ⓜ&①
me·*ka*·nee·ko
media *mezzi* ⓜ pl *di comunicazione*
me·tsee dee ko·moo·nee·ka·*tsyo*·ne
medicine *medicina* ① me·dee·*chee*·na
meditation *meditazione* ①
me·dee·ta·*tsyo*·ne
meet *incontrare* een·kon·*tra*·re
melon *melone* ⓜ me·*lo*·ne
member *socio/a* ⓜ/① *so*·cho/a
menstruation *mestruazione* ①
me·stroo·a·*tsyo*·ne
menu *menu* ⓜ me·noo
message *messaggio* ⓜ me·*sa*·jo
metal *metallo* ⓜ me·*ta*·lo
metre (distance) *metro* ⓜ *me*·tro
metro station *stazione* ① *della*
metropolitana sta·*tsyo*·ne de·la
me·tro·po·lee·*ta*·na
microwave oven *forno* ⓜ *a microonde*
for·no a mee·kro·on·de
midnight *mezzanotte* ① me·dza *no*·te
migraine *emicrania* ① e·mee·*kra*·nya
military *le forze* ① pl *armate* le *for*·tse
ar·*ma*·te
military service *servizio* ⓜ *militare*
ser·*vee*·tsyo mee·lee·*ta*·re
milk *latte* ⓜ *la*·te
millimetre *millimetro* ⓜ mee·*lee*·me·tro
mince *carne* ① *tritata* kar·ne tree·*ta*·ta
mineral water *acqua* ① *minerale* a·kwa
mee·ne·*ra*·le
mini-bar *frigobar* ⓜ *free*·go·bar
mints *caramelle* ① pl *alla menta*
ka·ra·*me*·le a·la *men*·ta
minute *minuto* ⓜ mee·*noo*·to
mirror *specchio* ⓜ *spe*·kyo
miscarriage *aborto* ⓜ *spontaneo*
a·*bor*·to spon·*ta*·ne·o
miss (feel absence of) *mancare*
man·*ka*·re
mistake *sbaglio* ⓜ *sba*·lyo
mix *mescolare* mes·ko·*la*·re
mobile phone *(telefono) cellulare* ⓜ
(te·*le*·fo·no) che·loo·*la*·re
modem *modem* ⓜ *mo*·dem
modern *moderno/a* ⓜ/① mo·*der*·no/a
moisturiser *idratante* ⓜ ee·dra·*tan*·te

monastery *monastero* ⓜ mon·as·te·ro
money *denaro* ⓜ de·na·ro
month *mese* ⓜ me·ze
monument *monumento* ⓜ
mo·noo·men·to
(full) moon *luna* ① *(piena)* loo·na
(pye·na)
more *(di) più* (dee) pyoo
morning *mattina* ① ma·tee·na
morning after pill *la pillola* ① *del
mattino dopo* la pee·lo·la del
ma·tee·no do·po
morning sickness *nausea* ① *mattutina*
now·ze·a ma·too·tee·na
mosque *moschea* ① mos·ke·a
mosquito *zanzara* ① tsan·tsa·ra
mother *madre* ① ma·dre
mother-in-law *suocera* ① swo·che·ra
motorboat *motoscafo* ⓜ mo·to·ska·fo
motorbike *moto* ① mo·to
motorway (tollway) *autostrada* ①
ow·to·stra·da
mountain *montagna* ① mon·ta·nya
mountain bike *mountain bike* ⓜ
mown·tayn baik
mountain path *sentiero* ① *di montagna*
sen·tye·ro dee mon·ta·nya
mountain range *catena* ① *di montagne*
ka·te·na dee mon·ta·nye
mountaineering *alpinismo* ⓜ
al·pee·neez·mo
mouse (computer) *mouse* ⓜ mows
mouse (rodent) *topo* ⓜ to·po
mouth *bocca* ① bo·ka
movie *film* ⓜ feelm
mud *fango* ⓜ fan·go
muesli *muesli* ⓜ moos·lee
mum *mamma* ① ma·ma
muscle *muscolo* ⓜ moo·sko·lo
museum *museo* ⓜ moo·ze·o
mushroom *fungo* ⓜ foon·go
music *musica* ① moo·zee·ka
musician *musicista* ⓜ&①
moo·zee·chee·sta
Muslim *musulmano/a* ⓜ/①
moo·sool·ma·no/a
mussels *cozze* ① pl ko·tse
mustard *senape* ① se·na·pe
mute *muto/a* ⓜ/① moo·to/a

N

nail clippers *tagliaunghie* ⓜ
ta·lya·oon·gye
name *nome* ⓜ no·me
napkin *tovagliolo* ⓜ to·va·lyo·lo
nappy *pannolino* ⓜ pa·no·lee·no
nappy rash *sfogo* ⓜ *da pannolino* sfo·go
da pa·no·lee·no
national *nazionale* na·tsyo·na·le
national park *parco* ⓜ *nazionale* par·ko
na·tsyo·na·le
nationality *nazionalità* ①
na·tsyo·na·lee·ta
nature *natura* ① na·too·ra
nausea *nausea* ① now·ze·a
near (to) *vicino (a)* vee·chee·no (a)
nearby *vicino/a* ⓜ/① vee·chee·no/a
necessary *necessario/a* ⓜ/①
ne·che·sa·ryo/a
neck *collo* ⓜ ko·lo
need *avere bisogno di*
a·ve·re bee·zo·nyo dee
needle (sewing) *ago* ⓜ a·go
needle (syringe) *ago* ⓜ *da siringa*
a·go da see·reen·ga
neither *nessuno/a dei due* ⓜ/①
ne·soo·no/a day doo·e
net *rete* ① re·te
Netherlands *Paesi Bassi* ⓜ pl
pa·e·zee ba·see
never *mai* mai
new *nuovo/a* ⓜ/① nwo·vo/a
New Year's Day *Capodanno* ⓜ
ka·po da·no
New Year's Eve *san Silvestro* ⓜ
san seel·ves·tro
New Zealand *Nuova Zelanda* ①
nwo·va dze·lan·da
news *notizie* ① pl no·tee·tsye
newsagency *edicola* ① e·dee·ko·la
newspaper *giornale* ⓜ jor·na·le
next *prossimo/a* ⓜ/① pro·see·mo/a
next to *accanto a* a·kan·to a
nice (meal) *buono/a* ⓜ/① bwo·no/a
nice (person) *gentile* jen·tee·le
nice (weather) *bello/a* ⓜ/① be·lo/a
nickname *soprannome* ⓜ so·pra·no·me
night *notte* ① no·te

no *no* no
noisy *rumoroso/a* ⓜ/ⓕ roo·mo·ro·zo/a
non-direct *non-diretto/a* ⓜ/ⓕ
non·dee·re·to/a
none *niente* nyen·te
non-smoking *non fumatore* non
foo·ma·to·re
noodles *pasta* ⓕ pas·ta
noon *mezzogiorno* ⓜ me·dzo jor·no
north *nord* ⓜ nord
nose *naso* ⓜ na·zo
notebook *quaderno* ⓜ kwa·der·no
nothing *niente* nyen·te
novel *romanzo* ⓜ ro·man·dzo
now *adesso* a·de·so
nuclear energy *energia* ⓕ *nucleare*
en·er·jee·a noo·kle·a·re
nuclear testing *esperimenti* ⓜ pl
nucleari es·pe·ree·men·tee
noo·kle·a·ree
nuclear waste *scorie* ⓕ pl *radioattive*
sko·rye ra·dyo·a·tee·ve
number *numero* ⓜ noo·me·ro
number plate *targa* ⓕ tar·ga
nun *suora* ⓕ swo·ra
nurse *infermiere/a* ⓜ/ⓕ een·fer·mye·re/a
nut *noce* ⓕ no·che

O

oats *avena* ⓕ a·ve·na
occupation (work) *mestiere* ⓜ
mes·tye·re
ocean *oceano* ⓜ o·che·a·no
off (spoiled) *guasto/a* ⓜ/ⓕ gwa·sto/a
office *ufficio* ⓜ oo·fee·cho
office worker *impiegato/a* ⓜ/ⓕ
eem·pye·ga·to/a
often *spesso* spe·so
oil *olio* ⓜ o·lyo
old *vecchio/a* ⓜ/ⓕ ve·kyo/a
old city *centro* ⓜ *storico* chen·tro
sto·ree·ko
olive *oliva* ⓕ o·lee·va
olive oil *olio* ⓜ *d'oliva* o·lyo do·lee·va
on *su* soo
once *una volta* ⓕ oo·na vol·ta
one-way (ticket) *(un biglietto di) solo
andata* (oon bee·lye·to dee) so·lo
an·da·ta

onion *cipolla* ⓕ chee·po·la
only *solo* so·lo
open *aperto/a* ⓜ/ⓕ a·per·to/a
open *aprire* a·pree·re
opening hours *orario* ⓜ *di apertura*
o·ra·ryo dee a·per·too·ra
opera *opera* ⓕ *lirica* o·pe·ra lee·ree·ka
opera house *teatro* ⓜ *dell'opera* te·a·tro
del·o·pe·ra
operation (medical) *intervento* ⓜ
een·ter·ven·to
operator *operatore/operatrice* ⓜ/ⓕ
o·pe·ra·to·re/o·pe·ra·tree·che
opinion *opinione* ⓕ o·pee·nyo·ne
opposite *di fronte a* dee fron·te a
or *o* o
orange (colour) *arancione* a·ran·cho·ne
orange (fruit) *arancia* ⓕ a·ran·cha
orange juice (bottled) *succo* ⓜ *d'arancia*
soo·ko da·ran·cha
orange juice (fresh) *spremuta* ⓜ
d'arancia spre·moo·ta da·ran·cha
orchestra *orchestra* ⓕ or·kes·tra
order *ordine* ⓜ or·dee·ne
order *ordinare* or·dee·na·re
ordinary *ordinario/a* ⓜ/ⓕ
or·dee·na·ryo/a
original *originale* ⓜ/ⓕ o·ree·jee·na·le
other *altro/a* ⓜ/ⓕ al·tro/a
outside *fuori* fwo·ree
ovarian cyst *cisti* ⓕ *ovarica* chee·stee
o·va·ree·ka
oven *forno* ⓜ for·no
over (above) *sopra* so·pra
overdose *dose* ⓕ *eccessiva* do·ze
e·che·see·va
owner *proprietario/a* ⓜ/ⓕ
pro·prye·ta·ryo/a
oxygen *ossigeno* ⓜ o·see·je·no
oyster *ostrica* ⓕ o·stree·ka
ozone layer *strato* ⓜ *d'ozono*
stra·to do·dzo·no

P

pacemaker *pacemaker* ⓜ pays·may·ke
pacifier *ciucciotto* ⓜ choo·cho·to
package *pacchetto* ⓜ pa·ke·to
packet (general) *pacchetto* ⓜ pa·ke·to

padded envelope *busta* ① *imbottita*
boos·ta eem·bo·tee·ta

padlock *lucchetto* ⓜ loo·ke·to

page *pagina* ① pa·jee·na

pain *dolore* ⓜ do·lo·re

painful *doloroso/a* ⓜ/① do·lo·ro·zo/a

painkillers *analgesico* ⓜ an·al·je·zee·ko

paint *dipingere* dee·peen·je·re

painter *pittore/pittrice* ⓜ/① pee·to·re/
pee·tree·che

painting (the art) *pittura* ① pee·too·ra

painting (canvas) *quadro* ⓜ kwa·dro

pair *paio* ① pa·yo

palace *palazzo* ⓜ pa·la·tso

pan *pentola* ① pen·to·la

pants *pantaloni* ⓜ pl pan·ta·lo·nee

panty liners *salva slip* ⓜ pl sal·va sleep

pantyhose *collant* ① pl ko·lant

pap smear *pap test* ⓜ pap test

paper *carta* ① kar·ta

papers *documenti* ⓜ pl do·koo·men·tee

paperwork *moduli* ⓜ pl mo·doo·lee

parcel *pacchetto* ⓜ pa·ke·to

parents *genitori* ⓜ pl je·nee·to·ree

park *parco* ⓜ par·ko

parliament *parlamento* ⓜ par·la·men·to

part *parte* ① par·te

part-time *ad orario ridotto* ad o·ra·ryo
ree·do·to

partner (intimate) *compagno/a* ⓜ/①
kom·pa·nyo/a

party (celebration) *festa* ① fes·ta

party (politics) *partito* ⓜ par·tee·to

pass (document) *tessera* ① te·se·ra

pass (mountain) *passo* ⓜ pa·so

pass (sport) *passaggio* ⓜ pa·sa·jo

passenger *passeggero/a* ⓜ/①
pa·se·je·ro/a

passport *passaporto* ⓜ pa·sa·por·to

past *passato* ⓜ pa·sa·to

pate (food) *paté* ⓜ pa·te

path *sentiero* ⓜ sen·tye·ro

pay *pagare* pa·ga·re

payment *pagamento* ⓜ pa·ga·men·to

pea *pisello* ⓜ pee·ze·lo

peace *pace* ① pa·che

peach *pesca* ① pe·ska

peak *cima* ① chee·ma

peanuts *arachidi* ① pl a·ra·kee·dee

pear *pera* ① pe·ra

pedal *pedale* ⓜ pe·da·le

pedestrian *pedone* ⓜ/① pe·do·ne

pegs (tent) *picchetti* ⓜ pl pee·ke·tee

pen (ballpoint) *penna* ① *(a sfera)*
pe·na (a sfe·ra)

pencil *matita* ① ma·tee·ta

penis *pene* ⓜ pe·ne

penicillin *penicillina* ①
pe·nee·chee·lee·na

penknife *temperino* ⓜ tem·pe·ree·no

pensioner *pensionato/a* ⓜ/①
pen·syo·na·to/a

people *gente* ① jen·te

pepper *pepe* ⓜ pe·pe

per (day) *al (giorno)* al *(jor·no)*

per cent *per cento* ① per·chen·to

performance *spettacolo* ① spe·ta·ko·lo

perfume *profumo* ⓜ pro·foo·mo

period pain *dolori* ⓜ pl *mestruali*
do·lo·ree me·stroo·a·lee

permanent *permanente* ⓜ/①
per·ma·nen·te

permission *permesso* ⓜ per·me·so

permit *permesso* ⓜ per·me·so

person *persona* ① per·so·na

personal *personale* ⓜ per·so·na·le

petition *petizione* ① pe·tee·tsyo·ne

petrol *benzina* ① ben·dzee·na

petrol station *distributore* ⓜ
dee·stree·boo·to·re

pharmacy *farmacia* ① far·ma·chee·a

phone book *elenco* ⓜ *telefonico*
e·len·ko te·le·fo·nee·ko

phone box *cabina* ① *telefonica*
ka·bee·na te·le·fo·nee·ka

phone call *chiamata* ① kya·ma·ta

phonecard *scheda* ① *telefonica* ske·da
te·le·fo·nee·ka

photo *foto* ① fo·to

photographer *fotografo* ⓜ fo·to·gra·fo

photography *fotografia* ① fo·to·gra·fee·a

phrasebook *vocabolarietto* ⓜ
vo·ka·bo·la·rye·to

pick (up) *raccogliere* ra·ko·lye·re

pickaxe *piccone* ⓜ pee·ko·ne

pickles *sottoaceti* ⓜ pl so·to·a·che·tee

picnic picnic ⓜ peek·neek
pie torta ① tor·ta
piece pezzo ⓜ pe·tso
pig maiale ⓜ ma·ya·le
pill pillola ① pee·lo·la
the Pill la pillola ① (anticoncezionale) la
  pee·lo·la (an·tee·kon·che·tsyo·na·le)
pillow cuscino ⓜ koo·shee·no
pillowcase federa ① fe·de·ra
pineapple ananas ⓜ a·na·nas
pink rosa ⓜ/① ro·za
pistachio pistacchio ⓜ pee·sta·kyo
place (location) luogo ⓜ lwo·go
place (seat) posto ⓜ pos·to
place of birth luogo ⓜ di nascita lwo·go
  dee na·shee·ta
plane aereo ⓜ a·e·re·o
planet pianeta ⓜ pya·ne·ta
plant pianta ① pyan·ta
plastic plastica ① pla·stee·ka
plate piatto ⓜ pya·to
plateau altopiano ⓜ al·to·pya·no
platform binario ⓜ bee·na·ryo
play (a game) giocare a jo·ka·re
play (guitar) suonare (la chitarra)
  swo·na·re (la kee·ta·ra)
play (soccer) giocare (a calcio) jo·ka·re
  (a kal·cho)
play (sport) praticare pra·tee·ka·re
play (theatre) commedia ① ko·me·dya
playground parco ⓜ giochi par·ko jo·kee
plug (bath) tappo ⓜ ta·po
plug (electricity) spina ① spee·na
plum prugna ① proo·nya
pocket tasca ① tas·ka
poetry poesia ① po·e·zee·a
point punto ⓜ poon·to
point indicare een·dee·ka·re
poisonous velenoso/a ⓜ/① ve·le·no·zo/a
police (civilian) polizia ① po·lee·tsee·a
police (military) carabinieri ⓜ pl
  ka·ra·bee·nye·ree
police station posto ⓜ di polizia pos·to
  dee po·lee·tsee·a
politician politico ⓜ po·lee·tee·ko
politics politica ① po·lee·tee·ka
pollen polline ⓜ po·lee·ne
polls elezioni ① pl e·le·tsyo·nee

pollution inquinamento ⓜ
  een·kwee·na·men·to
pony cavallino ⓜ ka·va·lee·no
pool (game) biliardo ① beel·yar·do
pool (swimming) piscina ① pee·shee·na
poor povero/a ⓜ/① po·ve·ro/a
popular popolare po·po·la·re
pork maiale ⓜ ma·ya·le
port porto ⓜ por·to
possible possibile po·see·bee·le
post code codice ⓜ postale ko·dee·che
  pos·ta·le
poste restante fermo ⓜ posta fer·mo
  pos·ta
post office ufficio ⓜ postale oo·fee·cho
  pos·ta·le
postage tariffa ① postale ta·ree·fa
  pos·ta·le
postcard cartolina ① kar·to·lee·na
pot (ceramics) pignatta ① pee·nya·ta
pot (dope) erba ① er·ba
pot (cooking) pentola ① pen·to·la
potato patata ① pa·ta·ta
pottery oggetti ⓜ pl in ceramica o·je·tee
  een che·ra·mee·ka
pound (money) sterlina ① ster·lee·na
poverty povertà ① po·ver·ta
power potere ⓜ po·te·re
prawn gambero ⓜ gam·be·ro
prayer preghiera ① pre·gye·ra
prefer preferire pre·fe·ree·re
pregnancy test kit test ⓜ di gravidanza
  test dee gra·vee·dan·tsa
pregnant incinta een·cheen·ta
premenstrual tension tensione ①
  premestruale ten·syo·ne
  pre·me·stroo·a·le
prepare preparare pre·pa·ra·re
prescription ricetta ① ree·che·ta
present (gift) regalo ⓜ re·ga·lo
president presidente ⓜ/① pre·zee·den·te
pressure pressione ① pre·syo·ne
pretty carino/a ⓜ/① ka·ree·no/a
previous precedente pre·che·den·te
price prezzo ⓜ pre·tso
priest prete ⓜ pre·te
prime minister primo ministro ⓜ/①
  pree·mo mee·nee·stro

printer (computer) *stampante* ① stam·*pan*·te
prison *prigione* ① pree·*jo*·ne
prisoner *prigioniero/a* ⓜ/① pree·jo·*nye*·ro/a
private *privato/a* ⓜ/① pree·va·*to*/a
produce *produrre* pro·*doo*·re
profit *profitto* ⓜ pro·*fee*·to
program *programma* ⓜ pro·*gra*·ma
projector *proiettore* ⓜ pro·ye·*to*·re
promise *promessa* ① pro·*me*·sa
protect *proteggere* pro·*te*·je·re
protected (species) *(specie)* ① *protetta* (*spe*·che) pro·*te*·ta
protest *manifestazione* ① ma·nee·fes·ta·*tsyo*·ne
protest *protestare* pro·tes·*ta*·re
provisions *provviste* ① pl pro·*vee*·ste
prune *prugna* ① *proo*·nya
pub *pub* poob
public holiday *festa* ① *fes*·ta
public telephone *telefono* ⓜ *pubblico* te·*le*·fo·no *poo*·blee·ko
public toilet *gabinetto* ⓜ *pubblico* ga·bee·*ne*·to *poo*·blee·ko
pull *tirare* tee·*ra*·re
pump *pompa* ① *pom*·pa
pumpkin *zucca* ① *tsoo*·ka
puncture *bucatura* ① boo·ka·*too*·ra
puppy *cucciolo* ⓜ koo·*cho*·lo
pure *puro/a* ⓜ/① *poo*·ro/a
purple *viola* vee·*o*·la
push *spingere* *speen*·je·re
put *mettere* *me*·te·re

Q

qualifications *titoli* ⓜ pl *di studio* *tee*·to·lee dee *stoo*·dee·o
quality *qualità* ① kwa·lee·*ta*
quantity *quantità* ① kwan·tee·*ta*
quarantine *quarantena* ① kwa·ran·*te*·na
quarrel *bisticcio* ⓜ bees·*tee*·cho
quarter *quarto* ⓜ *kwar*·to
queen *regina* ① re·*jee*·na
question *domanda* ① do·*man*·da
queue *coda* ① *ko*·da
quick *rapido/a* ⓜ/① *ra*·pee·do/a
quiet *tranquillo/a* ⓜ/① tran·*kwee*·lo/a

R

rabbit *coniglio* ⓜ ko·*nee*·lyo
race (sport) *gara* ① *ga*·ra
racetrack *pista* ① *pee*·sta
racing bike *bici* ① *da corsa* *bee*·chee da *kor*·sa
racism *razzismo* ⓜ ra·*tseez*·mo
racquet *racchetta* ① ra·*ke*·ta
radiator *radiatore* ⓜ ra·dya·*to*·re
radish *ravanello* ⓜ ra·va·*ne*·lo
(railway) station *stazione* ① *(ferroviaria)* sta·*tsyo*·ne fe·ro·vee·a·re·a
rain *pioggia* ⓜ *pyo*·ja
raincoat *impermeabile* ⓜ eem·per·me·a·*bee*·le
raisin *uva* ① *passa* *oo*·va *pa*·sa
rape *stupro* ⓜ *stoo*·pro
rare *raro/a* ⓜ/① *ra*·ro/a
rash *sfogo* ⓜ *sfo*·go
raspberry *lampone* ⓜ lam·*po*·ne
rat *topo* ⓜ *to*·po
raw *crudo/a* ⓜ/① *kroo*·do/a
razor *rasoio* ⓜ *(elettrico)* ra·*zo*·yo (e·*le*·tree·ko)
razor blades *lamette* ① pl *(da barba)* la·*me*·te (da *bar*·ba)
read *leggere* *le*·je·re
ready *pronto/a* ⓜ/① *pron*·to/a
realistic *realistico/a* ⓜ/① re·a·*lee*·stee·ko/a
reason *ragione* ① ra·*jo*·ne
receipt *ricevuta* ① ree·che·*voo*·ta
receive *ricevere* ree·*che*·ve·re
recently *di recente* dee re·*chen*·te
recommend *raccomandare* ra·ko·man·*da*·re
recyclable *riciclabile* ree·chee·*kla*·bee·le
recycle *riciclare* ree·chee·*kla*·re
red *rosso/a* ⓜ/① *ro*·so/a
referee *arbitro* ⓜ *ar*·bee·tro
refrigerator *frigo* ⓜ *free*·go
refugee *rifugiato/a* ⓜ/① re·foo·*gya*·to/a
refund *rimborso* ⓜ reem·*bor*·so
refuse *rifiutare* ree·fyoo·*ta*·re
region *regione* ① re·*jo*·ne
registered mail *(posta) raccomandata* ① *(pos*·ta) ra·ko·man·*da*·ta

regular *normale* nor·ma·le
relationship *rapporto* ⓜ ra·por·to
relax *rilassarsi* ree·la·sar·see
relic *reliquia* ⓕ re·lee·kwee·a
religion *religione* ⓕ re·lee·jo·ne
religious *religioso/a* ⓜ/ⓕ re·lee·jo·zo/a
remote *remoto/a* ⓜ/ⓕ re·mo·to/a
remote control *telecomando* ⓜ
te·le·ko·man·do
rent *affitto* ⓜ a·fee·to
rent *prendere in affitto* pren·de·re
een a·fee·to
repair *riparare* ree·pa·ra·re
reservation *prenotazione* ⓕ
pre·no·ta·tsyo·ne
rest *riposare* ree·po·za·re
restaurant *ristorante* ⓜ rees·to·ran·te
resume *curriculum vitae* ⓜ
koo·ree·koo·loom vee·tay
retired *pensionato/a* ⓜ/ⓕ
pen·syo·na·to/a
return *ritornare* ree·tor·na·re
return (ticket) *(biglietto) di andata e
ritorno* (bee·lye·to) dee an·da·ta e
ree·tor·no
reverse-charges call *chiamata* ⓕ *a
carico del destinatario* kya·ma·ta a
ka·ree·ko del des·tee·na·ta·ryo
rhythm *ritmo* ⓜ reet·mo
rice *riso* ⓜ ree·zo
brown rice *riso* ⓜ *integrale* ree·zo
een·te·gra·le
rich (wealthy) *ricco/a* ⓜ/ⓕ ree·ko/a
ride *corsa* ⓕ kor·sa
ride (a bike) *andare in bicicletta* an·da·re
een bee·chee·kle·ta
ride (a horse) *cavalcare* ka·val·ka·re
right (correct) *giusto/a* ⓜ/ⓕ joo·sto/a
right (direction) *a destra* a de·stra
right-wing *(di) destra* (dee) de·stra
ring (on finger) *anello* ⓜ a·ne·lo
ring (by phone) *telefonare* te·le·fo·na·re
rip-off *bidone* ⓜ bee·do·ne
risk *rischio* ⓜ rees·kyo
river *fiume* ⓜ fyoo·me
road *strada* ⓕ stra·da
rob *derubare* de·roo·ba·re
rock *roccia* ⓕ ro·cha

rock (music) *(musica)* ⓕ *rock*
(moo·zee·ka) rok
rock climbing *(andare su) roccia* ⓕ
(an·da·re soo) ro·cha
rock group *gruppo* ⓜ *rock*
groo·po rok
roll (bread) *panino* ⓜ pa·nee·no
romantic *romantico/a* ⓜ/ⓕ
ro·man·tee·ko/a
room *camera* ⓕ ka·me·ra
rope *corda* ⓕ kor·da
round *rotondo/a* ⓜ/ⓕ ro·ton·do/a
roundabout *rotonda* ⓕ ro·ton·da
route *itinerario* ⓜ ee·tee·ne·ra·ryo
rowing *canottaggio* ⓜ ka·no·ta·jo
rubbish *spazzatura* ⓕ spa·tsa·too·ra
rug *tappeto* ⓜ ta·pe·to
rugby *rugby* ⓜ roog·bee
ruins *rovine* ⓕ pl ro·vee·ne
rules *regole* ⓕ pl re·go·le
run *correre* ko·re·re
running (sport) *footing* ⓜ foo·teeng

S

Sabbath *sabato* ⓜ sa·ba·to
sad *triste* tree·ste
saddle *sella* ⓕ se·la
safe *cassaforte* ⓕ ka·sa·for·te
safe *sicuro/a* ⓜ/ⓕ see·koo·ro/a
safe sex *rapporti* ⓜ pl *protetti* ra·por·tee
pro·te·tee
safety gear *corredo* ⓜ *antinfortunistico*
ko·re·do an·teen·for·too·nee·stee·ko
saint *santo/a* ⓜ/ⓕ san·to/a
salad *insalata* ⓕ een·sa·la·ta
salami *salame* ⓜ sa·la·me
salary *stipendio* ⓜ stee·pen·dyo
(on) sale *in vendita* een ven·dee·ta
sales tax *IVA* ⓕ ee·va
salmon *salmone* ⓜ sal·mo·ne
salt *sale* ⓜ sa·le
same *stesso/a* ⓜ/ⓕ ste·so/a
sand *sabbia* ⓕ sa·bya
sandals *sandali* ⓜ pl san·da·lee
sandwich *tramezzino* ⓜ tra·me·dzee·no
sanitary napkins *assorbenti* ⓜ pl *igienici*
as·or·ben·tee ee·je·nee·chee

sardines *sardine* ① pl sar·dee·ne
sauce *sugo* ⑩ soo·go
sauna *sauna* ① sow·na
sausage *salsiccia* ① sal·see·cha
say *dire* dee·re
scanner *scanner* ⑩ ska·ner
scarf *sciarpa* ① shar·pa
school *scuola* ① skwo·la
science *scienza* ① shen·tsa
scissors *forbici* ① pl for·bee·chee
score *punteggio* ⑩ poon·te·jo
score *segnare* se·nya·re
scoreboard *tabellone* ⑩ *segnapunti*
ta·be·lo·ne se·nya·poon·tee
Scotland *Scozia* ① sko·tsya
sculpture *scultura* ① skool·too·ra
sea *mare* ⑩ ma·re
seasickness *mal* ⑩ *di mare* mal dee
ma·re
seaside *al mare* al ma·re
season *stagione* ① sta·jo·ne
seat (chair) *sedile* ⑩ se·dee·le
seat (place) *posto* ⑩ pos·to
seatbelt *cintura* ① *di sicurezza*
cheen·too·ra dee see·koo·re·tsa
second *secondo* ⑩ se·kon·do
second *secondo/a* ⑩/① se·kon·do/a
second class *seconda classe* ①
se·kon·da kla·se
second-hand *di seconda mano* ⑩/①
dee se·kon·da ma·no
secretary *segretario/a* ⑩/①
se·gre·ta·ryo/a
see *vedere* ve·de·re
(to be) self-employed *lavorare in
proprio* la·vo·ra·re een pro·pryo
selfish *egoista* ⑩/① e·go·ee·sta
self-service *self-service* self·ser·vees
sell *vendere* ven·de·re
send *mandare* man·da·re
sensual *sensuale* ⑩/① sen·soo·a·le
separate *separato/a* ⑩/① se·pa·ra·to/a
(TV) series *serie* ① *(televisiva)* se·ree·e
(te·le·vee·see·va)
serious *serio/a* ⑩/① se·ryo/a
service *servizio* ⑩ ser·vee·tsyo
service charge *servizio* ⑩ ser·vee·tsyo

service station *stazione* ① *di servizio*
sta·tsyo·ne dee ser·vee·tsyo
several *diversi/e* ⑩/① pl dee·ver·see/
dee·ver·se
sew *cucire* koo·chee·re
sex *sesso* ⑩ se·so
sexism *sessismo* ⑩ se·seez·mo
sexy *erotico/a* ⑩/① e·ro·tee·ko/a
shade *ombra* ① om·bra
shadow *ombra* ① om·bra
shampoo *shampoo* ⑩ sham·poo
shape *forma* ① for·ma
share (with) *condividere*
kon·dee·vee·de·re
sharp *affilato/a* ⑩/① a·fee·la·to/a
shave *rasatura* ① ra·za·too·ra
shave *fare la barba* fa·re la bar·ba
shaving cream *crema* ① *da barba*
kre·ma da bar·ba
she *lei* lay
sheep *pecora* ① pe·ko·ra
sheet (bed) *lenzuolo* ⑩ len·tswo·lo
ship *nave* ① na·ve
shirt *camicia* ① ka·mee·cha
shoe shop *negozio* ⑩ *di scarpe*
ne·go·tsyo dee skar·pe
shoes *scarpe* ① pl skar·pe
shop *negozio* ⑩ ne·go·tsyo
shopping centre *centro* ⑩ *commerciale*
chen·tro ko·mer·cha·le
short (height) *basso/a* ⑩/① ba·so/a
short (length) *corto/a* ⑩/① kor·to/a
shorts *pantaloncini* ⑩ pl
pan·ta·lon·chee·nee
shoulder *spalla* ① spa·la
shout *urlare* oor·la·re
show *spettacolo* ⑩ spe·ta·ko·lo
show *mostrare* mos·tra·re
shower *doccia* ① do·cha
shrine *santuario* ⑩ san·too·a·ryo
shut *chiuso/a* ⑩/① kyoo·zo/a
shy *timido/a* ⑩/① tee·mee·do/a
sick *malato/a* ⑩/① ma·la·to/a
side *lato* ⑩ la·to
sign *segno* ⑩ se·nyo
signature *firma* ① feer·ma
silk *seta* ① se·ta

silver *argento* ⓜ ar·*jen*·to
similar *simile* ⓜ/ⓕ *see*·mee·le
simple *semplice* ⓜ/ⓕ *sem*·plee·che
since (time) *da* da
sing *cantare* kan·*ta*·re
singer *cantante* ⓜ/ⓕ kan·*tan*·te
single (man) *celibe* ⓜ *che*·lee·be
single (woman) *nubile* ⓕ *noo*·bee·le
single room *camera* ⓕ *singola* ka·me·ra
　seen·go·la
singlet *canottiera* ⓕ ka·no·*tye*·ra
sister *sorella* ⓕ so·*re*·la
sit *sedere* se·*de*·re
size (clothes) *taglia* ⓕ *ta*·lya
size (general) *dimensioni* ⓕ pl
　dee·men·*syo*·nee
ski *sciare* shee·*a*·re
ski lift *sciovia* ⓕ shee·o·*vee*·a
skiing *sci* ⓜ shee
ski(s) *sci* ⓜ sg&pl shee
skimmed milk *latte* ⓜ *scremato* la·te
　skre·*ma*·to
skin *pelle* ⓕ *pe*·le
skirt *gonna* ⓕ *go*·na
sky *cielo* ⓜ *che*·lo
sleep *dormire* dor·*mee*·re
sleeping bag *sacco* ⓜ *a pelo*
　sa·ko a *pe*·lo
sleeping car *vagone* ⓜ *letto*
　va·*go*·ne *le*·to
sleeping pills *sonniferi* ⓜ pl
　so·nee·*fe*·ree
(to be) sleepy *avere sonno* ⓜ
　a·*ve*·re *so*·no
slice *fetta* ⓕ *fe*·ta
slide (film) *diapositiva* ⓕ
　dee·a·po·zee·*tee*·va
slope *pista* ⓕ *pee*·sta
Slovenia *Slovenia* ⓕ slo·*ve*·nya
slow *lento/a* ⓜ/ⓕ *len*·to/a
slowly *lentamente* len·ta·*men*·te
small *piccolo/a* ⓜ/ⓕ *pee*·ko·lo/a
smell *odore* ⓜ o·*do*·re
smile *sorridere* so·ree·*de*·re
smoke *fumare* foo·*ma*·re
snack *spuntino* ⓜ spoon·*tee*·no
snail *lumaca* ⓕ loo·*ma*·ka

snake *serpente* ⓜ ser·*pen*·te
snorkel *boccaglio* ⓜ bo·*ka*·lyo
snorkelling *snorkelling* snor·ke·*leeng*
snow *neve* ⓕ *ne*·ve
snow boarding *surf* ⓜ *da neve*
　soorf da *ne*·ve
snow chains *catene* ⓕ pl *da neve*
　ka·*te*·ne da *ne*·ve
soap *sapone* ⓜ sa·*po*·ne
soap opera *telenovela* ⓕ te·le·no·*ve*·la
soccer *calcio* ⓜ *kal*·cho
social welfare *assistenza* ⓕ *sociale*
　a·sees·*ten*·tsa so·*cha*·le
socialist *socialista* ⓜ&ⓕ so·cha·*lee*·sta
socks *calzini* ⓜ pl cal·*tsee*·nee
soft *morbido/a* ⓜ/ⓕ mor·*bee*·do/a
soft drink *bibita* ⓕ *bee*·bee·ta
soldier *soldato* ⓜ sol·*da*·to
some *alcuni/e* ⓜ/ⓕ pl al·*koo*·nee/
　al·*koo*·ne
someone *qualcuno/a* ⓜ/ⓕ
　kwal·*koo*·no/a
something *qualcosa* kwal·*ko*·za
sometimes *a volte* a *vol*·te
son *figlio* ⓜ *fee*·lyo
song *canzone* ⓕ kan·*tso*·ne
soon *fra poco* fra *po*·ko
sore *doloroso/a* ⓜ/ⓕ do·lo·*ro*·zo/a
soup *minestra* ⓕ mee·*nes*·tra
sour cream *panna* ⓕ *acida* pa·na
　a·chee·da
south *sud* ⓜ sood
souvenir *ricordino* ⓜ ree·kor·*dee*·no
souvenir shop *negozio* ⓜ *di souvenir*
　ne·*go*·tsyo dee soo·ve·*neer*
soy milk *latte* ⓜ *di soia* la·te dee *so*·ya
soy sauce *salsa* ⓕ *di soia* sal·sa dee
　so·ya
space *spazio* ⓜ *spa*·tsyo
spade *vanga* ⓕ *van*·ga
Spain *Spagna* ⓕ *spa*·nya
speak *parlare* par·*la*·re
special *speciale* spe·*cha*·le
specialist *specialista* ⓜ&ⓕ
　spe·cha·*lee*·sta
speed *velocità* ⓕ ve·lo·chee·*ta*

speed limit *limite* ⓜ *di velocità*
lee·mee·te dee ve·lo·chee·ta

speedometer *tachimetro* ⓜ
ta·kee·me·tro

spermicide *spermicida* ①
sper·mee·chee·da

spider *ragno* ⓜ ra·nyo

spinach *spinaci* ⓜ pl spee·na·chee

spoke(s) *raggio/raggi* ⓜ ra·jo/ra·jee

spoon *cucchiaio* ⓜ koo·kya·yo

sport *sport* ⓜ sport

sports store *negozio* ⓜ *di articoli
sportivi* ne·go·tsyo dee ar·tee·ko·lee
spor·tee·vee

sportsperson *sportivo/a* ⓜ/①
spor·tee·vo/a

sprain *storta* ① stor·ta

spring (season) *primavera* ①
pree·ma·ve·ra

square (town) *piazza* ① pya·tsa

stadium *stadio* ⓜ sta·dyo

stage (theatre) *palcoscenico* ⓜ
pal·ko·she·nee·ko

stage (in race) *tappa* ① ta·pa

stairway *scale* ① pl ska·le

stamp *francobollo* ⓜ fran·ko·bo·lo

standby (ticket) *(in lista) d'attesa* (een
lee·sta) da·te·za

(four-)star *(a quattro) stelle* (a kwa·tro)
ste·le

stars *stelle* ① pl ste·le

start *inizio* ⓜ ee·nee·tsyo

start *cominciare* ko·meen·cha·re

station *stazione* ① sta·tsyo·ne

stationer *cartolaio* ⓜ kar·to·la·yo

statue *statua* ① sta·too·a

stay (at a hotel) *fermarsi* fer·mar·see

steak (beef) *bistecca* ① bees·te·ka

steal *rubare* roo·ba·re

steep *ripido/a* ⓜ/① ree·pee·do/a

stingy *avaro/a* ⓜ/① a·va·ro/a

stockings *calze* ① pl kal·tse

stolen *rubato/a* ⓜ/① roo·ba·to/a

stomach *stomaco* ⓜ sto·ma·ko

stomachache *mal* ⓜ *di pancia* mal dee
pan·cha

stone *pietra* ① pye·tra

stoned (drugged) *fumato/a* ⓜ/①
foo·ma·to/a

stop *fermata* ① fer·ma·ta

stop *fermare* fer·ma·re

storm *temporale* ⓜ tem·po·ra·le

story *racconto* ⓜ ra·kon·to

stove *stufa* ① *(a gas)* stoo·fa a gaz

straight *diritto/a* ⓜ/① dee·ree·to/a

strange *strano/a* ⓜ/① stra·no/a

stranger *sconosciuto/a* ⓜ/①
sko·no·shoo·to/a

strawberry *fragola* ① fra·go·la

stream *ruscello* ⓜ roo·she·lo

street *strada* ① stra·da

(on) strike *(in) sciopero* ⓜ een sho·pe·ro

string *spago* ⓜ spa·go

strong *forte* ⓜ/① for·te

student *studente/studentessa* ⓜ/①
stoo·den·te/stoo·den·te·sa

stupid *stupido/a* ⓜ/① stoo·pee·do/a

style *stile* ⓜ stee·le

subtitles *sottotitoli* ⓜ pl so·to·tee·to·lee

suburb *quartiere* ⓜ kwar·tye·re

subway *metropolitana* ①
me·tro·po·lee·ta·na

sugar *zucchero* ⓜ tsoo·ke·ro

suitcase *valigia* ① va·lee·ja

summer *estate* ⓜ es·ta·te

sun *sole* ⓜ so·le

sunblock *crema* ① *solare* kre·ma so·la·re

sunburn *scottatura* ① sko·ta·too·ra

sunglasses *occhiali* ⓜ pl *da sole*
o·kya·lee da so·le

sunny *soleggiato/a* ⓜ/① so·le·ja·to/a

sunrise *alba* ① al·ba

sunscreen *crema* ① *solare* kre·ma so·la·re

sunset *tramonto* ⓜ tra·mon·to

supermarket *supermercato* ⓜ
soo·per·mer·ka·to

superstition *superstizione* ①
soo·per·stee·tsyo·ne

supplies *provviste* ⓜ pl pro·vee·ste

support (cheer on) *fare il tifo* fa·re eel
tee·fo

supporters *tifosi* ⓜ pl tee·fo·zee

surf *praticare il surf* pra·tee·ka·re eel soorf

surface mail *posta* ① *ordinaria* pos·ta
or·dee·na·rya

surfboard *tavola da surf* ta·vo·la da soorf
surname *cognome* ⓜ ko·nyo·me
surprise *sorpresa* ⓕ sor·pre·sa
sweater *maglione* ⓜ ma·lyo·ne
sweet *dolce* dol·che
swelling *gonfiore* ⓕ gon·fyo·re
swim *nuotare* nwo·ta·re
swimming *nuoto* ⓜ nwo·to
swimming pool *piscina* ⓕ pee·shee·na
swimsuit *costume* ⓜ *da bagno*
ko·stoo·me da ba·nyo
Switzerland *Svizzera* ⓕ svee·tse·ra
synagogue *sinagoga* ⓕ see·na·go·ga
synthetic *sintetico/a* ⓜ/ⓕ
seen·te·tee·ko/a
syringe *siringa* ⓕ see·reen·ga

T

table *tavola* ⓕ ta·vo·la
table tennis *ping-pong* ⓜ peeng·pong
tablecloth *tovaglia* ⓕ to·va·lya
tailor *sarto* ⓜ sar·to
take *prendere* pren·de·re
take (photo) *fare* fa·re
talk *parlare* par·la·re
tall *alto/a* ⓜ/ⓕ al·to/a
tampons *tamponi* ⓜ pl tam·po·nee
tanning lotion *lozione* ⓕ *abbronzante*
lo·tsyo·ne a·bron·dzan·te
tap (faucet) *rubinetto* ⓜ roo·bee·ne·to
tasty *gustoso/a* ⓜ/ⓕ goo·sto·zo/a
tax *tassa* ⓕ ta·sa
taxi *tassì* ⓜ ta·see
taxi stand *posteggio* ⓜ *di tassì* po·ste·jo
dee ta·see
tea *tè* ⓜ te
teacher (general) *insegnante* ⓜ&ⓕ
een·sen·yan·te
teacher (primary) *maestro/a* ⓜ/ⓕ
ma·es·tro/a
teacher (secondary) *professore/*
professoressa ⓜ/ⓕ pro·fe·so·re/
pro·fe·so·re·sa
team *squadra* ⓕ skwa·dra
teaspoon *cucchiaino* ⓜ koo·kya·ee·no
teeth *denti* ⓜ pl den·tee

telegram *telegramma* ⓜ te·le·gra·ma
telephone *telefono* ⓜ te·le·fo·no
telephone *telefonare* te·le·fo·na·re
telephone centre *centro* ⓜ *telefonico*
chen·tro te·le·fo·nee·ko
telephoto lens *teleobiettivo* ⓜ
te·le·o·bye·tee·vo
television *televisione* ⓕ te·le·vee·zyo·ne
tell *raccontare* ra·kon·ta·re
temperature (fever) *febbre* ⓕ fe·bre
temperature (weather) *temperatura* ⓕ
tem·pe·ra·too·ra
temple *tempio* ⓜ tem·pyo
tennis *tennis* ⓜ te·nees
tennis court *campo* ⓜ *da tennis*
kam·po da te·nees
tent *tenda* ⓕ ten·da
tent pegs *picchetti* ⓜ pl *(per la tenda)*
pee·ke·tee (per la ten·da)
terrible *terribile* ⓜ/ⓕ te·ree·bee·le
test *esame* ⓜ e·za·me
thank *ringraziare* reen·gra·tsya·re
theatre *teatro* ⓜ te·a·tro
there *là* la
they *loro* lo·ro
thick *spesso/a* ⓜ/ⓕ spe·so/a
thief *ladro/a* ⓜ/ⓕ la·dro/a
thin *magro/a* ⓜ/ⓕ ma·gro/a
think *pensare* pen·sa·re
third *terzo/a* ⓜ/ⓕ ter·tso/a
(to be) thirsty *avere sete* ⓕ a·ve·re se·te
this (one) *questo/a* ⓜ/ⓕ kwe·sto/a
thread (sewing) *filo* ⓜ fee·lo
throat *gola* ⓕ go·la
thrush (medical) *mughetto* ⓜ moo·ge·to
ticket *biglietto* ⓜ bee·lye·to
ticket collector *controllore* ⓜ
kon·tro·lo·re
ticket machine *distributore* ⓜ
automatico di biglietti
dee·stree·boo·to·re ow·to·ma·tee·ko
dee bee·lye·tee
ticket office *biglietteria* ⓕ
bee·lye·te·ree·a
tide *marea* ⓕ ma·re·a
tight *stretto/a* ⓜ/ⓕ stre·to/a
time *tempo* ⓜ tem·po

time difference *differenza* ① *di fuso orario* dee·fe·ren·tsa dee foo·zo o·ra·ryo

timetable *orario* ⓜ o·ra·ryo

tin (can) *scatoletta* ① ska·to·le·ta

tin opener *apriscatole* ⓜ a·pree·ska·to·le

tiny *minuscolo/a* ⓜ/① mee·noos·ko·lo/a

tip (gratuity) *mancia* ① man·cha

tired *stanco/a* ⓜ/① stan·ko/a

tissues *fazzolettini* ⓜ pl *di carta* fa·tso·le·tee·nee dee kar·ta

toast *pane* ⓜ *tostato* pa·ne tos·ta·to

toaster *tostapane* ⓜ tos·ta·pa·ne

tobacco *tabacco* ⓜ ta·ba·ko

tobacconist *tabaccheria* ① ta·ba·ke·ree·a

toboganing *andare in slitta* an·da·re een slee·ta

today *oggi* o·jee

toe *dito* ⓜ *del piede* dee·to del pye·de

tofu *tofu* ⓜ to·foo

together *insieme* een·sye·me

toilet *gabinetto* ⓜ ga·bee·ne·to

toilet paper *carta* ① *igienica* kar·ta ee·je·nee·ka

toilets *servizi* ⓜ pl *igienici* ser·vee·tse ee·je·nee·chee

token *gettone* ⓜ je·to·ne

tomato *pomodoro* ⓜ po·mo·do·ro

tomato sauce *salsa* ① *di pomodoro* sal·sa dee po·mo·do·ro

tomorrow *domani* do·ma·nee

tonight *stasera* sta·se·ra

too (expensive) *troppo (caro/a)* tro·po (ka·ro/a)

too many *troppi/e* ⓜ/① pl tro·pee/ tro·pe

too much *troppo/a* ⓜ/① sg tro·po/a

tooth (front) *dente* ⓜ den·te

toothache *mal* ⓜ *di denti* mal dee den·tee

toothbrush *spazzolino* ⓜ *da denti* spa·tso·lee·no da den·tee

toothpaste *dentifricio* ⓜ den·tee·free·cho

toothpick *stuzzicadenti* ⓜ stoo·tsee·ka·den·tee

torch (flashlight) *torcia* ① *elettrica* tor·cha e·le·tree·ka

touch *toccare* to·ka·re

tour *gita* ① jee·ta

tourist *turista* ⓜ&① too·ree·sta

tourist office *ufficio* ⓜ *del turismo* oo·fee·cho del too·reez·mo

towel *asciugamano* ⓜ a·shoo·ga·ma·no

tower *torre* ① to·re

toxic waste *rifiuti* ⓜ pl *tossici* ree·fyoo·tee to·see·chee

toyshop *negozio* ⓜ *di giocattoli* ne·go·tsyo dee jo·ka·to·lee

track (path) *sentiero* ⓜ sen·tye·ro

track (sports) *pista* ① pee·sta

trade *commercio* ⓜ ko·mer·cho

traffic *traffico* ⓜ tra·fee·ko

traffic jam *ingorgo* ⓜ een·gor·go

traffic lights *semaforo* ⓜ se·ma·fo·ro

trail *pista* ⓜ pee·sta

train *treno* ⓜ tre·no

train station *stazione* ① *(ferroviaria)* sta·tsyo·ne (fe·ro·vyar·ya)

tram *tram* ⓜ tram

transit lounge *sala* ① *di transito* sa·la dee tran·zee·to

translate *tradurre* tra·doo·re

transport *trasporto* ⓜ tras·por·to

travel *viaggiare* vee·a·ja·re

travel agency *agenzia* ① *di viaggio* a·jen·tsee·a dee vee·a·jo

travel sickness (air) *mal* ⓜ *di aereo* mal dee a·e·re·o

travel sickness (car) *mal* ⓜ *di macchina* mal dee ma·kee·na

travel sickness (sea) *mal* ⓜ *di mare* mal dee ma·re

travellers cheque *assegno* ⓜ *di viaggio* a·se·nyo dee vee·a·jo

tree *albero* ⓜ al·be·ro

trip *gita* ① jee·ta

trolley (luggage) *carrello* ⓜ ka·re·lo

trousers *pantaloni* ⓜ pl pan·ta·lo·nee

truck *camion* ⓜ ka·myon

true *vero/a* ⓜ/① ve·ro/a

try (attempt) *provare* pro·va·re

T-shirt *maglietta* ① ma·lye·ta

tube (tyre) *camera* ① *d'aria* ka·me·ra da·rya

tuna *tonno* ⓜ to·no
tune *melodia* ① me·lo·dee·a
turkey *tacchino* ⓜ ta·kee·no
turn *girare* jee·ra·re
TV *TV* ① tee·voo
tweezers *pinzette* ① pl peen·tse·te
twice *due volte* doo·e vol·te
twin beds *due letti* doo·e le·tee
twins *gemelli/e* ⓜ/① pl je·me·lee/
je·me·le
type *tipo* ⓜ tee·po
typical *tipico/a* ⓜ/① tee·pee·ko·la
tyre *gomma* ① go·ma

U

ugly *brutto/a* ⓜ/① broo·to·a
ultrasound *ecografia* ① e·ko·gra·fee·a
umbrella *ombrello* ⓜ om·bre·lo
uncomfortable *scomodo/a* ⓜ/①
sko·mo·do·a
understand *capire* ka·pee·re
underwear *biancheria* ① intima
byan·ke·ree·a een·tee·ma
unemployed *disoccupato/a* ⓜ/①
dee·zo·koo·pa·to·a
uniform *divisa* ① dee·vee·za
universe *universo* ⓜ oo·nee·ver·so
university *università* ① oo·nee·ver·see·ta
unleaded *senza piombo* sen·tsa pyom·bo
unsafe *pericoloso/a* ⓜ/①
pe·ree·ko·lo·zo·a
until *fino a* fee·no a
unusual *insolito/a* ⓜ/① een·so·lee·to/a
up *su* soo
uphill *in salita* een sa·lee·ta
urgent *urgente* ⓜ/① oor·jen·te
USA *Stati* ⓜ pl *Uniti d'America*
sta·tee oo·nee·tee da·me·ree·ka
useful *utile* oo·tee·le

V

vacant *libero/a* ⓜ/① lee·be·ro·a
vacation *vacanza* ① va·kan·tsa
vaccination *vaccinazione* ①
va·chee·na·tsyo·ne
vagina *vagina* ① va·jee·na

validate *convalidare* kon·va·lee·da·re
valley *valle* ① va·le
valuable *prezioso/a* ⓜ/① pre·tsyo·zo·a
valuables *oggetti* ⓜ pl *di valore* o·je·tee
dee va·lo·re
value (price) *valore* ⓜ va·lo·re
van *furgone* ⓜ foor·go·ne
veal *vitello* ⓜ vee·te·lo
vegetable *verdura* ① ver·doo·ra
vegetarian *vegetariano/a* ⓜ/①
ve·je·ta·rya·no/a
venereal disease *malattia* ① *venerea*
ma·la·tee·a ve·ne·re·a
venue *locale* ⓜ lo·ka·le
very *molto* mol·to
video *videoregistratore* ⓜ
vee·de·o·re·jee·stra·to·re
video camera *videocamera* ①
vee·de·o·ka·me·ra
video tape *videonastro* ⓜ
vee·de·o·nas·tro
view *vista* ① vee·sta
village *villaggio* ⓜ vee·la·jo
vinegar *aceto* ⓜ a·che·to
vineyard *vigneto* ⓜ vee·nye·to
virus *virus* ⓜ vee·roos
visa *visto* ⓜ vee·sto
visit (person) *andare a trovare* an·da·re
a tro·va·re
visit (place) *fare una visita* fa·re oo·na
vee·see·ta
vitamins *vitamine* ① pl vee·ta·mee·ne
voice *voce* ① vo·che
volleyball *pallavolo* ① pa·la·vo·lo
vomit *vomitare* vo·mee·ta·re
vote *votare* vo·ta·re

W

wage *salario* ⓜ sa·la·ryo
wait *aspettare* as·pe·ta·re
waiter *cameriere/a* ⓜ/① ka·mer·ye·re/a
waiting room *sala* ① *d'attesa*
sa·la da·te·sa
wake up *svegliarsi* sve·lyar·see
Wales *Galles* ⓜ ga·les
walk *passeggiata* ① pa·se·ja·ta

walk *camminare* ka·mee·na·re
wall (external) *muro* ⓜ moo·ro
wall (internal) *parete* ⓕ pa·re·te
wallet *portafoglio* ⓜ por·ta·fo·lyo
want *volere* vo·le·re
war *guerra* ⓕ gwe·ra
wardrobe *armadio* ⓜ ar·ma·dyo
warm *tiepido/a* ⓜ/ⓕ tye·pee·do/a
warn *avvertire* a·ver·tee·re
wash (oneself) *lavarsi* la·var·see
wash (something) *lavare* la·va·re
washing machine *lavatrice* ⓕ
  la·va·tree·che
washing powder *detersivo* ⓜ
  de·ter·see·vo
watch *orologio* ⓜ o·ro·lo·jo
watch *guardare* gwar·da·re
water *acqua* ⓕ a·kwa
  boiled water *acqua* ⓕ *bollita*
  a·kwa bo·lee·ta
  still water *acqua* ⓕ *non gassata*
  a·kwa non ga·sa·ta
  tap water *acqua* ⓕ *del rubinetto*
  a·kwa del roo·bee·ne·to
water bottle *borraccia* ⓕ bo·ra·cha
waterfall *cascata* ⓕ kas·ka·ta
watermelon *anguria* ⓕ an·goo·rya
waterproof *impermeabile* ⓜ
  eem·per·me·a·bee·le
water skiing *sci* ⓜ *acquatico* shee
  a·kwa·tee·ko
watersports *sport* ⓜ *acquatici* sport
  a·kwa·tee·chee
wave *onda* ⓕ on·da
way *via* ⓕ vee·a
we *noi* noy
weak *debole* de·bo·le
wealthy *ricco/a* ⓜ/ⓕ ree·ko/a
wear *indossare* een·do·sa·re
weather *tempo* ⓜ tem·po
wedding *matrimonio* ⓜ ma·tree·mo·nyo
wedding present *regalo* ⓜ *di nozze*
  re·ga·lo dee no·tse
week *settimana* ⓕ se·tee·ma·na
weekend *fine settimana* ⓜ fee·ne
  se·tee·ma·na
weight *peso* ⓜ pe·zo

welcome *dare il benvenuto a* da·re eel
  ben·ve·noo·to a
well *in buona salute* een bwo·na
  sa·loo·te
west *ovest* ⓜ o·vest
wet *bagnato/a* ⓜ/ⓕ ba·nya·to/a
wetsuit *muta* ⓕ moo·ta
what *che (cosa)* ke (ko·za)
wheel *ruota* ⓕ rwo·ta
wheelchair *sedia* ⓕ *a rotelle* se·dya a
  ro·te·le
when *quando* kwan·do
where *dove* do·ve
white *bianco/a* ⓜ/ⓕ byan·ko/a
who *chi* kee
why *perché* per·ke
wide *largo/a* ⓜ/ⓕ lar·go/a
widow *vedova* ⓕ ve·do·va
widower *vedovo* ⓜ ve·do·vo
wife *moglie* ⓕ mo·lye
win *vincere* veen·che·re
wind *vento* ⓜ ven·to
window (car, plane) *finestrino* ⓜ
  fee·nes·tree·no
window (general) *finestra* ⓕ fee·nes·tra
windscreen *parabrezza* ⓜ pa·ra·bre·dza
wine *vino* ⓜ vee·no
  red wine *vino* ⓜ *rosso* vee·no ro·so
  sparkling wine *vino* ⓜ *spumante*
  vee·no spoo·man·te
  white wine *vino* ⓜ *bianco*
  vee·no byan·ko
wine cellar *cantina* ⓕ kan·tee·na
wine tasting *degustazione* ⓕ *dei vini*
  de·goos·ta·tsyo·ne day vee·nee
winery *cantina* ⓕ kan·tee·na
wings *ali* ⓕ pl a·lee
winner *vincitore/vincitrice* ⓜ/ⓕ
  veen·chee·to·re/veen·chee·tree·che
winter *inverno* ⓜ een·ver·no
wish *desiderare* de·see·de·ra·re
with *con* kon
within (an hour) *entro (un'ora)*
  en·tro (oon·o·ra)
without *senza* sen·tsa
woman *donna* ⓕ do·na

wonderful *meraviglioso/a* ⓜ/ⓕ
me·ra·vee·*lyo*·zo/a
wood *legno* ⓜ *le*·nyo
wool *lana* ⓕ *la*·na
word *parola* ⓕ pa·*ro*·la
work (occupation) *lavoro* ⓜ la·*vo*·ro
work (of art) *opera* ⓕ *(d'arte)* o·pe·ra
(dar·te)
work *lavorare* la·vo·*ra*·re
workout *allenamento* ⓜ a·le·na·*men*·to
workshop *laboratorio* ⓜ la·bo·ra·*to*·ryo
world *mondo* ⓜ *mon*·do
World Cup *Coppa* ⓕ *del Mondo* *ko*·pa
del *mon*·do
worried *preoccupato/a* ⓜ/ⓕ
pre·o·*koo*·pa·to/a
worship (pray) *pregare* pre·*ga*·re
wrist *polso* ⓜ *pol*·so
write *scrivere* *skree*·ve·re
writer *scrittore/scrittrice* ⓜ/ⓕ
skree·to·re/*skree·tree*·che
wrong *sbagliato/a* ⓜ/ⓕ sba·*lya*·to/a

Y

year *anno* ⓜ *a*·no
  this year *quest'anno* ⓜ kwe·*sta*·no
  last year *l'anno* ⓜ *scorso* *la*·no *skor*·so
yellow *giallo/a* ⓜ/ⓕ *ja*·lo/a
yes *sì* see
yesterday *ieri* ye·ree
(not) yet *(non) ancora* (non) an·*ko*·ra
yogurt *yogurt* ⓜ yo·*goort*
you (inf) *tu* too
you (polite) *Lei* lay
young *giovane* *jo*·va·ne
youth hostel *ostello* ⓜ *della gioventù*
os·*te*·lo *de*·la jo·ven·*too*

Z

zoo *giardino* ⓜ *zoologico* jar·*dee*·no
dzo·o·*lo*·jee·ko
zoom lens *zoom* ⓜ zoom
zucchini *zucchini* ⓜ pl tsoo·*kee*·nee

Nouns in this dictionary, and adjectives affected by gender, have their gender indicated by ⓜ and/or ⓕ. If it's a plural noun, you'll also see pl. Where a word that could be either a noun or a verb has no gender indicated, it's a verb.

A

a a *in • at • to • until • per*
a bordo a *bor*·do *aboard*
abbastanza a·bas·*tan*·tsa *enough*
abbigliamento ⓜ a·bee·lya·men·to *clothing*
abbracciare a·bra·*cha*·re *hug*
abitare a·bee·*ta*·re *live (somewhere)*
abito ⓜ a·bee·to *dress*
aborto ⓜ a·*bor*·to *abortion*
— **spontaneo** spon·*ta*·ne·o *miscarriage*
accanto a·*kan*·to *nearby*
accanto a a·*kan*·to a *next to*
accendino ⓜ a·chen·*dee*·no *(cigarette) lighter*
accetazione ⓕ a·che·ta·*tsyo*·ne *check-in (airport)*
aceto ⓜ a·*che*·to *vinegar*
acqua ⓕ a·kwa *water*
— **bollita** bo·*lee*·ta *boiled water*
— **calda** *kal*·da *hot water*
— **del rubinetto** del roo·bee·*ne*·to *tap water*
— **minerale** mee·ne·*ra*·le *mineral water*
— **non gassata** non ga·*sa*·ta *still water*
adesso a·*de*·so *now*
adulto/a ⓜ/ⓕ a·*dool*·to/a *adult*
aereo ⓜ a·*e*·re·o *plane*
aerobica ⓕ a·e·ro·*bee*·ka *aerobics*
aeroporto ⓜ a·e·ro·*por*·to *airport*
affari ⓜ pl a·*fa*·ree *business*
affascinante a·fa·shee·*nan*·te *charming • attractive*
affilato/a ⓜ/ⓕ a·fee·*la*·to/a *sharp*
affitto ⓜ a·*fee*·to *rent*
affollato/a ⓜ/ⓕ a·fo·*la*·to/a *crowded*

agenda ⓕ a·*jen*·da *diary*
agenzia ⓕ **di viaggio** a·jen·*tsee*·a dee vee·a·jo *travel agency*
agganciare a·gan·*cha*·re *chat up*
aggiustare a·joo·*sta*·re *repair*
aggressivo/a ⓜ/ⓕ a·gre·*see*·vo/a *aggressive*
aglio ⓜ a·lyo *garlic*
agnello ⓜ a·*nye*·lo *lamb*
ago ⓜ a·go *needle (sewing)*
agopuntura ⓕ a·go·poon·*too*·ra *acupuncture*
agricoltore/agricoltrice ⓜ/ⓕ a·gree·kol·*to*·re/a·gree·kol·*tree*·che *farmer*
agricoltura ⓕ a·gree·kol·*too*·ra *agriculture*
AIDS ⓜ a·ee·*dee*·e·se (or a·*eedz*) *AIDS*
aiutare a·yoo·*ta*·re *help*
alba ⓕ *al*·ba *sunrise*
albergo ⓜ al·*ber*·go *hotel*
albero ⓜ *al*·be·ro *tree*
albicocca ⓕ al·bee·*ko*·ka *apricot*
alcuni/e ⓜ/ⓕ pl al·*koo*·nee/al·*koo*·ne *some*
ali ⓕ pl a·lee *wings*
alimentari ⓜ a·lee·men·*ta*·ree *grocery store • convenience store*
alimento ⓜ a·lee·*men*·to *food*
al giorno al *jor*·no *per (day)*
al mare al *ma*·re *seaside*
all'estero a·*les*·te·ro *abroad*
allenamento ⓜ a·le·na·*men*·to *workout*
allergia ⓕ a·ler·*jee*·a *allergy*
alloggio ⓜ a·*lo*·jo *accommodation*
allucinare a·loo·chee·*na*·re *hallucinate*
alpinismo ⓜ al·pee·*neez*·mo *mountaineering*
altare ⓜ al·*ta*·re *altar*

altezza ① al·te·tsa *height*
alto/a ⑩/① al·to/a *high • tall*
altopiano ⑩ al·to·pya·no *plateau*
altro/a ⑩/① al·tro/a *other*
— **ieri** ⑩ ye·ree *day before yesterday*
amaca ① a·ma·ka *hammock*
amante ⑩/① a·man·te *lover*
amare a·ma·re *love*
ambasciata ① am·ba·sha·ta *embassy*
ambasciatore/ambasciatrice ⑩/①
am·ba·sha·to·re/am·ba·sha·tree·che
ambassador
ambiente ⑩ am·byen·te *environment*
ambulanza ① am·boo·lan·tsa *ambulance*
amico/a ⑩/① a·mee·ko/a *friend*
ammazzare a·ma·tsa·re *kill*
amministrazione ①
a·mee·nee·stra·tsyo·ne *administration*
analgesico ⑩ an·al·je·zee·ko *painkillers*
analisi ① **del sangue** a·na·lee·zee del
san·gwe *blood test*
ananas ⑩ a·na·nas *pineapple*
anatra ① a·na·tra *duck*
anche an·ke *also*
ancora an·ko·ra *still • yet*
andare an·da·re *go*
— **a cavallo** a ka·va·lo *horse riding*
— **a vedere** a ve·de·re *visit*
— **in bicicletta** een bee·chee·kle·ta
cycle • ride (a bike)
— **in slitta** een slee·ta *tobogganing*
— **su roccia** soo ro·cha *rock climbing*
andata ① an·da·ta *outward journey*
anello ⑩ a·ne·lo *ring (on finger)*
angolo ⑩ an·go·lo *corner*
anguria ① an·goo·rya *watermelon*
animale ⑩ a·nee·ma·le *animal*
anno ⑩ a·no *year*
annoiato/a ⑩/① a·no·ya·to/a *bored*
annuale a·noo·a·le *annual*
annuncio ⑩ a·noon·cho *advertisement*
antibiotici ⑩ pl an·tee·bee·o·tee·chee
antibiotics
antico/a ⑩/① an·tee·ko/a *ancient*
antinucleare an·tee·noo·kle·a·re
antinuclear
antisettico ⑩ an·tee·se·tee·ko *antiseptic*
antistaminici ⑩ pl an·tee·sta·mee·
nee·chee *antihistamines*

ape ① a·pe *bee*
aperto/a ⑩/① a·per·to/a *open*
apparecchio acustico a·pa·re·kyo
a·koos·tee·ko *hearing aid*
appartamento ⑩ a·par·ta·men·to *flat*
appendice ① a·pen·dee·che *appendix*
appuntamento ⑩ a·poon·ta·men·to
appointment • date
apribottiglie ① a·pree·bo·tee·lye *bottle
opener*
aprire a·pree·re *open*
apriscatole ① a·pree·ska·to·le *can opener*
arachidi ① pl a·ra·kee·dee *peanuts •
groundnuts*
arancia ① a·ran·cha *orange (fruit)*
arancione a·ran·cho·ne *orange (colour)*
arbitro ⑩ ar·bee·tro *referee*
archeologico/a ⑩/① ar·ke·o·lo·jee·ko/a
archaeological
architetto ⑩ ar·kee·te·to *architect*
architettura ① ar·kee·te·too·ra
architecture
argento ⑩ ar·jen·to *silver*
aria ① a·rya *air*
— **condizionata** kon·dee·tsyo·na·ta
air-conditioning
aringa ① a·reen·ga *herring*
armadietti ⑩ pl ar·ma·dye·tee *lockers*
— **per i bagagli** per ee ba·ga·lyee
luggage lockers
armadio ⑩ ar·ma·dyo *wardrobe*
arrabbiato/a ⑩/① a·ra·bya·to/a *angry*
arrestare a·res·ta·re *arrest*
arrivare a·ree·va·re *arrive*
arrivi ⑩ pl a·ree·vee *arrivals*
arte ① ar·te *art*
arti ① pl **marziali** ar·tee mar·tsya·lee
martial arts
artista ⑩&① ar·tee·sta *artist*
ASA a·za *film speed*
ascensore ⑩ a·shen·so·re *elevator*
asciugamano ⑩ a·shoo·ga·ma·no *towel*
asciugare a·shoo·ga·re *dry*
ascoltare as·kol·ta·re *listen*
asilo ⑩ a·zee·lo *kindergarten*
— **nido** nee·do *creche*
asma ① az·ma *asthma*
asparagi ⑩ pl as·pa·ra·jee *asparagus*
aspettare as·pe·ta·re *wait*

aspirina ① as·pee·ree·na *aspirin*
assegno ⓜ a·se·nyo *cheque*
— **di viaggio** dee vee·a·jo *travellers cheque*
assicurazione ① a·see·koo·ra·tsyo·ne *insurance*
assistenza ① **sociale** a·sees·ten·tsa so·cha·le *(social) welfare*
assorbenti ⓜ pl **igienici** as·or·ben·tee ee·je·nee·chee *sanitary napkins*
atletica ① at·le·tee·ka *athletics*
atrio ⓜ a·tryo *foyer*
attesa ① a·te·sa *wait*
attrezzatura ① a·tre·tsa·too·ra *equipment*
attualità ① a·too·a·lee·ta *current affairs*
autobus ⓜ ow·to·boos *bus (city)*
autostop ⓜ ow·to·stop *hitchhiking*
automatico/a ⓜ/① ow·to·ma·tee·ko/a *automatic*
automobilismo ⓜ ow·to·mo·bee·leez·mo *car racing*
autonoleggio ⓜ ow·to·no·le·jo *car hire*
autostrada ① ow·to·stra·da *motorway* • *tollway*
autunno ⓜ ow·too·no *autumn*
a volte a vol·te *sometimes*
avaro/a ⓜ/① a·va·ro/a *stingy*
avena ① a·ve·na *oats*
avere a·ve·re *have*
— **bisogno di** bee·zo·nyo dee *need*
— **fame** ① fa·me *(to be) hungry*
— **fretta** ① fre·ta *(to be) in a hurry*
— **mal di mare** mal dee ma·re *(to be) seasick*
— **sete** ① se·te *(to be) thirsty*
— **sonno** ⓜ so·no *(to be) sleepy*
avocado ⓜ a·vo·ka·do *avocado*
avventura ① a·ven·too·ra *adventure*
avvertire a·ver·tee·re *warn*
avvocato/a ⓜ/① a·vo·ka·to/a *lawyer*
azzurro/a ⓜ/① a·dzoo·ro/a *blue (light)*

B

baby-sitter ⓜ&① be·bee·see·ter *babysitter* • *childminding (private)*
baciare ba·cha·re *kiss*
bacio ⓜ ba·cho *kiss*

bagaglio ⓜ ba·ga·lyo *luggage*
— **a mano** a ma·no *carry-on luggage*
— **consentito** kon·sen·tee·to *baggage allowance*
— **in eccedenza** een e·che·den·tsa *excess bagage*
bagnato/a ⓜ/① ba·nya·to/a *wet*
bagno ⓜ ba·nyo *bath* • *bathroom*
balcone ⓜ bal·ko·ne *balcony*
ballare ba·la·re *dance*
balletto ⓜ ba·le·to *ballet*
ballo ⓜ ba·lo *ball (dancing)* • *dancing*
balsamo ⓜ **per i capelli** bal·sa·mo per ee ka·pe·lee *conditioner*
bambino/a ⓜ/① bam·bee·no/a *child*
bambola ① bam·bo·la *doll*
banca ① ban·ka *bank (money)*
Bancomat ⓜ ban·ko·mat *automatic teller machine (ATM)*
bancone ⓜ ban·ko·ne *counter (at bar)*
banconota ① ban·ko·no·ta *banknote*
bandiera ① ban·dye·ra *flag*
bar ⓜ bar *cafe*
barattolo ① ba·ra·to·lo *jar*
barbabietola ① bar·ba·bye·to·la *beetroot*
barbiere ⓜ bar·bye·re *barber*
barca ① bar·ka *boat*
baseball ⓜ bays·bol *baseball*
basso/a ⓜ/① ba·so/a *low* • *short (height)*
batteria ① ba·te·ree·a *battery (for car)* • *drums*
battesimo ⓜ ba·te·zee·mo *baptism*
batuffoli ⓜ pl **di cotone** ba·too·fo·lee dee ko·to·ne *cotton balls*
bebé ⓜ&① be·be *baby*
bello/a ⓜ/① be·lo/a *beautiful* • *handsome* • *good (weather)*
benessere ⓜ be·ne·se·re *welfare (well-being)*
benzina ① ben·dzee·na *gas (petrol)* • *petrol*
bere be·re *drink*
bevanda ① be·van·da *drink*
biancheria ① **intima** byan·ke·ree·a een·tee·ma *underwear*
bianco/a ⓜ/① byan·ko/a *white*
bibbia ① bee·bya *bible*
bibita ① bee·bee·ta *soft drink*

biblioteca ① beeb·lyo·te·ka *library*
bicchiere ⓜ bee·kye·re *glass (drinking)*
bici ① **(da corsa)** bee·chee (da kor·sa) *(racing) bike*
bicicletta ① bee·chee·kle·ta *bicycle*
bidone ⓜ bee·do·ne *rip-off • bin*
biglietteria ① bee·lye·te·ree·a *ticket office*
biglietto ⓜ bee·lye·to *ticket*
— **di andata e ritorno** dee an·da·ta e ree·tor·no *return ticket*
— **di solo andata** dee so·lo an·da·ta *one-way ticket*
bilancio ⓜ bee·lan·cho *budget*
biliardo ⓜ beel·yar·do *pool (game)*
bimbo/a ⓜ/① beem·bo/a *baby*
binario ⓜ bee·na·ryo *platform*
binocolo ⓜ bee·no·ko·lo *binoculars*
biondo/a ⓜ/① byon·do/a *blonde*
birra ① bee·ra *beer*
— **chiara** kya·ra *lager*
biscotto ⓜ bees·ko·to *biscuit • cookie*
bisogno ⓜ bee·zo·nyo *need • necessity*
bistecca ① bees·te·ka *steak (beef)*
bisticcio ⓜ bees·tee·cho *quarrel*
bloccato/a ⓜ/① blo·ka·to/a *blocked*
blu bloo *blue (dark)*
bocca ① bo·ka *mouth*
boccaglio ⓜ bo·ka·lyo *snorkel*
bollo ⓜ bo·lo *stamp • seal*
— **di circolazione** dee cheer·ko·la·tsyo·ne *car registration*
bordo ⓜ bor·do *edge • border*
borotalco ⓜ bo·ro·tal·ko *baby powder*
borraccia ① bo·ra·cha *water bottle*
borsa ① bor·sa *bag (general)*
borsetta ① bor·se·ta *handbag*
bottiglia ① bo·tee·lya *bottle*
bottiglieria ① bo·tee·lye·ree·a *liquor store*
bottone ⓜ bo·to·ne *button*
braccio ⓜ bra·cho *arm*
Braille ⓜ bray *Braille*
brillante ⓜ/① bree·lan·te *brilliant*
bronchite ① bron·kee·te *bronchitis*
bruciare broo·cha·re *burn*
brutto/a ⓜ/① broo·to/a *ugly*
buca ① boo·ka *hole • pit*
— **delle lettere** de·le le·te·re *mail box*
bucatura ① boo·ka·too·ra *puncture*

buddista ⓜ&① boo·dee·sta *Buddhist*
bugiardo/a ⓜ/① boo·jar·do/a *liar*
buono/a ⓜ/① bwo·no/a *good • nice (meal)*
burro ⓜ boo·ro *butter*
— **per le labbra** per le la·bra *lip balm*
bussola ① boo·so·la *compass*
busta ① **(imbottita)** boo·sta (eem·bo·tee·ta) *(padded) envelope*

C

cabina ① ka·bee·na *cabin • cubicle*
— **telefonica** te·le·fo·nee·ka *phone box*
cacao ⓜ ka·ka·o *cocoa*
caccia ① ka·cha *hunting*
caffè ⓜ ka·fe *coffee*
calcio ⓜ kal·cho *soccer*
calcolatrice ① kal·ko·la·tree·che *calculator*
caldo ⓜ kal·do *heat*
caldo/a ⓜ/① kal·do/a *hot*
calendario ⓜ ka·len·da·ryo *calendar*
calze ① pl kal·tse *stockings*
calzini ⓜ pl kal·tsee·nee *socks*
cambiare kam·bya·re *change*
cambio ⓜ kam·byo *exchange*
— **valuta** va·loo·ta *currency exchange*
camera ① ka·me·ra *room*
— **d'aria** da·rya *tube (tyre)*
— **da letto** da le·to *bedroom*
— **doppia** do·pya *double room*
— **singola** seen·go·la *single room*
cameriere/a ⓜ/① ka·mer·ye·re/a *waiter*
camicia ① ka·mee·cha *shirt*
camion ⓜ ka·myon *truck*
camminare ka·mee·na·re *walk*
camminata ① ka·mee·na·ta *(long) walk*
campagna ① kam·pa·nya *countryside*
campeggiare kam·pe·ja·re *camp*
campeggio ⓜ kam·pe·jo *camp site*
campionato ⓜ kam·pyo·na·to *championships*
campo ⓜ kam·po *field • pitch • court*
— **da golf** da golf *golf course*
— **da tennis** da te·nees *tennis court*
cancellare kan·che·la·re *cancel*
cancello ⓜ kan·che·lo *gate*

cancro ⓜ *kan·*kro *cancer*

candela ⓕ *kan·de·la candle • spark plug*

cane ⓜ *ka·ne dog*
— **guida** *gwee·*da *guide dog*

canottaggio ⓜ *ka·no·ta·jo rowing • canoeing*

canottiera ⓕ *ka·no·tye·ra singlet*

cantante ⓜ/ⓕ *kan·tan·te singer*

cantare *kan·ta·re sing*

cantina ⓕ *kan·tee·na wine cellar • winery*

canzone ⓕ *kan·tso·ne song*

caparra ⓕ *ka·pa·ra deposit (refundable)*

capire *ka·pee·re understand*

capo ⓜ *ka·po leader*

Capodanno ⓜ *ka·po da·no New Year's Day*

cappello ⓜ *ka·pe·lo hat*

cappotto ⓜ *ka·po·to coat*

capra ⓕ *ka·pra goat*

carabinieri ⓜ pl *ka·ra·bee·nye·ree police (military)*

caramelle ⓕ pl *ka·ra·me·le lollies*
— **alla menta** *a·la men·ta mints*

carcere ⓜ *kar·che·re jail*

carino/a ⓜ/ⓕ *ka·ree·no/a pretty • cute*

carne ⓕ *kar·ne meat*
— **tritata** *tree·ta·ta mince meat*

caro/a ⓜ/ⓕ *ka·ro/a expensive*

carota ⓕ *ka·ro·ta carrot*

carpentiere ⓜ *kar·pen·tye·re carpenter*

carrello ⓜ *ka·re·lo trolley*

carrozza ⓕ *ka·ro·tsa carriage*
— **ristorante** *rees·to·ran·te dining car*

carta ⓕ *kar·ta paper*
— **d'identità** *dee·den·tee·ta identification card (ID)*
— **d'imbarco** *deem·bar·ko boarding pass*
— **di credito** *dee kre·dee·to credit card*
— **igienica** *ee·je·nee·ka toilet paper*
— **telefonica** *te·le·fo·nee·ka phone card*

carte ⓕ pl *kar·te cards*

cartolaio ⓜ *kar·to·la·yo stationer*

cartolina ⓕ *kar·to·lee·na postcard*

cartuccia ⓕ *kar·too·cha cartridge*
— **di ricambio del gas** *dee ree·kam·byo del gaz gas cartridge*

casa ⓕ *ka·za house • home*

casalingo/a ⓜ/ⓕ *ka·za·leen·go/a homemaker*

cascata ⓕ *kas·ka·ta waterfall*

casco ⓜ *kas·ko helmet*

casinò ⓜ *ka·zee·no casino*

cassa ⓕ *ka·sa cash register*

cassaforte ⓕ *ka·sa·for·te safe*

cassetta ⓕ *ka·se·ta cassette*

cassiere/a ⓜ/ⓕ *ka·sye·re/a cashier*

castello ⓜ *kas·te·lo castle*

catena ⓕ *ka·te·na chain*
— **di montagne** *dee mon·ta·nye mountain range*

catene ⓕ pl **da neve** *ka·te·ne da ne·ve snow chains*

cattivo/a ⓜ/ⓕ *ka·tee·vo/a bad*

cattolico/a ⓜ/ⓕ *ka·to·lee·ko/a Catholic*

cavalcare *ka·val·ka·re ride (horse)*

cavallino ⓜ *ka·va·lee·no pony*

cavallo ⓜ *ka·va·lo horse*

cavi ⓜ pl **con morsetti** *ka·vee kon mor·se·tee jumper leads*

caviale ⓜ *ka·vya·le caviar*

caviglia ⓕ *ka·vee·lya ankle*

cavo ⓜ *ka·vo cable*

cavoletti ⓜ pl **di Bruxelles** *ka·vo·le·tee dee brook·sel Brussels sprouts*

cavolfiore ⓜ *ka·vol·fyo·re cauliflower*

cavolo ⓜ *ka·vo·lo cabbage*

ceci ⓜ pl *che·chee chickpeas*

celebrazione ⓕ *che·le·bra·tsyo·ne celebration*

celibe ⓜ *che·lee·be single (man)*

cellulare ⓜ *che·loo·la·re mobile phone*

cena ⓕ *che·na dinner*

centesimo ⓜ *chen·te·zee·mo cent*

centimetro ⓜ *chen·tee·me·tro centimetre*

centro ⓜ *chen·tro centre*
— **commerciale** *ko·mer·cha·le shopping centre*
— **storico** *sto·ree·ko old city*
— **telefonico** *te·le·fo·nee·ko telephone centre*

cercare *cher·ka·re look for*

cereali ⓜ pl *che·re·a·lee cereal*

cerotti ⓜ pl *che·ro·tee Band-aids*

certificato ⓜ *cher·tee·fee·ka·to certificate*

cestino ⓜ *ches·tee·no basket*

cetriolo ⓜ *che·tree·o·lo cucumber*

che (cosa) ke (ko·za) *what*

chi kee *who*

chiamata ① kya·ma·ta *phone call*
— **a carico del destinatario** a ka·ree·ko del des·tee·na·ta·ryo *reverse-charges call* • *collect call*

chiaro/a ⓜ/① kya·ro/a *light (colour)*

chiave ① kya·ve *key*

chiesa ① kye·za *church*

chilo ⓜ kee·lo *kilogram*

chilometro ⓜ kee·lo·me·tro *kilometre*

chitarra ① kee·ta·ra *guitar*

chiudere kyoo·de·re *close*

chiuso/a ⓜ/① kyoo·zo/a *closed* • *shut* • *locked*

ciascuno/a ⓜ/① chas·koo·no/a *each*

cibo ⓜ chee·bo *food*
— **da bebè** da be·be *baby food*

ciclismo ⓜ chee·kleez·mo *cycling*

ciclista ⓜ&① chee·klee·sta *cyclist*

ciclopista ① chee·klo·pee·sta *bike path*

cidì ⓜ chee·dee *CD*

cieco/a ⓜ/① chye·ko/a *blind*

cielo ⓜ che·lo *sky*

cima ① chee·ma *peak*

cinema ⓜ chee·ne·ma *cinema*

cinghia ① **della ventola** cheen·gya de·la ven·to·la *fanbelt*

cintura ① **di sicurezza** cheen·too·ra dee see·koo·re·tsa *seatbelt*

cioccolato ⓜ cho·ko·la·to *chocolate*

cipolla ① chee·po·la *onion*

circo ⓜ cheer·ko *circus*

cisti ① **ovarica** chee·stee o·va·ree·ka *ovarian cyst*

cistite ① chees·tee·te *cystitis*

città ① chee·ta *city*

cittadinanza ① chee·ta·dee·nan·tsa *citizenship*

ciucciotto ⓜ choo·cho·to *dummy* • *pacifier*

classe ① kla·se *class*
— **business** beez·nes *business class*
— **turistica** too·ree·stee·ka *economy class*

classico/a ⓜ/① kla·see·ko/a *classical*

cliente ⓜ&① klee·en·te *client*

cocaina ① ko·ka·ee·na *cocaine*

coda ① ko·da *queue*

codice ⓜ **postale** ko·dee·che pos·ta·le *postcode*

cognome ⓜ ko·nyo·me *surname*

coincidenza ① ko·een·chee·den·tsa *coincidence* • *connection (transport)*

collant ① pl ko·lant *pantyhose*

colazione ① ko·la·tsyo·ne *breakfast*

collega ⓜ&① ko·le·ga *colleague*

collegio ⓜ **universitario** ko·le·jo oo·nee·ver·see·ta·ryo *college*

collina ① ko·lee·na *hill*

collirio ⓜ ko·lee·ryo *eye drops*

collo ⓜ ko·lo *neck*

colloquio ⓜ **(selettivo)** ko·lo·kwyo (se·le·tee·vo) *interview*

colore ⓜ ko·lo·re *colour*

colpa ① kol·pa *fault (someone's)*

colpevole kol·pe·vo·le *guilty*

coltello ⓜ kol·te·lo *knife*

come ko·me *how*

cominciare ko·meen·cha·re *begin* • *start*

commedia ① ko·me·dya *play (theatre)*
— **comica** ko·mee·ka *comedy*

commercio ⓜ ko·mer·cho *trade* • *business studies*

commissione ① ko·mee·syo·ne *commission*

comodo/a ⓜ/① ko·mo·do/a *comfortable*

compagno/a ⓜ/① ko·pa·nyo/a *companion* • *partner (intimate)*

compenso ⓜ kom·pen·so *fee*

compleanno ⓜ kom·ple·a·no *birthday*

complesso ⓜ **rock** kom·ple·so rok *rock group*

completo/a ⓜ/① kom·ple·to/a *booked out*

comprare kom·pra·re *buy*

compreso/a ⓜ/① kom·pre·zo/a *included*

computer ⓜ kom·pyoo·ter *computer*
— **portatile** ⓜ por·ta·tee·le *laptop*

comunione ① ko·moo·nyo·ne *communion*

comunista ⓜ&① ko·moo·nee·sta *communist*

con kon *with*
— **filtro** ⓜ feel·tro *filtered*

concerto ⓜ kon·cher·to *concert*

condividere kon·dee·vee·de·re *share (with)*

confermare kon·fer·*ma*·re *confirm (a booking)*

confessione ① kon·fe·*syo*·ne *confession (religious)*

confine ⑩ kon·*fee*·ne *border*

congelare kon·je·*la*·re *freeze*

congelato/a ⑩/① kon·je·*la*·to/a *frozen*

coniglio ⑩ ko·*nee*·lyo *rabbit*

conoscere ko·*no*·she·re *know (a person)*

conservatore/conservatrice ⑩/① kon·ser·va·*to*·re/kon·ser·va·*tree*·che *conservative*

consigliare kon·see·*lya*·re *recommend*

consolato ⑩ kon·so·*la*·to *consulate*

contanti ⑩ pl kon·*tan*·tee *count*

contare kon·*ta*·re *count*

conto ⑩ *kon*·to *bill (account)*
— **in banca** een *ban*·ka *bank account*

contraccettivi ⑩ pl kon·tra·che·*tee*·vee *contraceptives*

contratto ⑩ kon·*tra*·to *contract*

controllare kon·tro·*la*·re *check*

controllore ⑩ kon·tro·*lo*·re *ticket collector*

controllare kon·tro·*la*·re *check*

convalidare kon·va·lee·*da*·re *validate*

convento ⑩ kon·*ven*·to *convent*

coperta ① ko·*per*·ta *blanket*

coperte ① pl **e lenzuola** ① pl ko·*per*·te e len·*zwo*·la *bedding*

coperto ⑩ ko·*per*·to *cover charge (restaurant)*

Coppa ① **del Mondo** *ko*·pa del *mon*·do *World Cup*

coraggioso/a ⑩/① ko·ra·*jo*·zo/a *brave*

corda ① *kor*·da *rope*
— **del bucato** del boo·*ka*·to *clothesline*

corpo ⑩ *kor*·po *body*

corrente ① ko·*ren*·te *current (electricity)*

correre *ko*·re·re *run*

corridoio ⑩ ko·ree·*do*·yo *aisle (in plane, train)*

corrompere ko·*rom*·pe·re *bribe*

corrotto/a ⑩/① ko·*ro*·to/a *corrupt*

corsa ① *kor*·sa *ride • race*

corte ① *kor*·te *court (legal)*

corto/a ⑩/① *kor*·to/a *short (length)*

cosa ① *ko*·za *thing • object • matter*

costa ① *kos*·ta *coast*

costare kos·*ta*·re *cost*

costruire kos·troo·*ee*·re *build*

costruttore/costruttrice ⑩/① kos·troo·*to*·re/ko·stroo·*tree*·che *builder*

costume ⑩ **da bagno** kos·*too*·me da *ba*·nyo *bathing suit*

cotone ⑩ ko·*to*·ne *cotton*

cozza ① *ko*·tsa *mussel*

crema ① *kre*·ma *cream*
— **da barba** da *bar*·ba *shaving cream*
— **solare** so·*la*·re *sunscreen*

crescere *kre*·she·re *grow*

criminalità ① kree·mee·na·*lee*·ta *crime (issue)*

cristiano/a ⑩/① krees·*tya*·no/a *Christian*

croce ① *kro*·che *cross (religious)*

crudo/a ⑩/① *kroo*·do/a *raw*

cucchiaino ⑩ koo·kya·*ee*·no *teaspoon*

cucchiaio ⑩ koo·*kya*·yo *spoon*

cucciolo ⑩ *koo*·cho·lo *puppy*

cucina ① koo·*chee*·na *kitchen*

cucinare koo·chee·*na*·re *cook*

cucire koo·*chee*·re *sew*

culla ① *koo*·la *cot*

cuoco/a ⑩/① *kwo*·ko/a *cook • chef (restaurant)*

cuoio ⑩ *kwo*·yo *leather*

cuore ⑩ *kwo*·re *heart*

curare koo·*ra*·re *look after*

curriculum vitae ⑩ koo·ree·koo·*loom vee*·te *CV • resume*

curry ⑩ *koo*·ree *curry*

cuscino ⑩ koo·*shee*·no *pillow*

D

da da *from • at • to • since*

da solo/a ⑩/① da so·*lo*/a *alone*

danno ⑩ *da*·no *damage*

dare *da*·re *give*
— **il benvenuto a** eel ben·ve·*noo*·to a *welcome*
— **un calcio** oon *kal*·cho *kick*

data ① *da*·ta *date (day)*
— **di arrivo** dee a·*ree*·vo *date of arrival*
— **di nascita** dee *na*·shee·ta *date of birth*
— **di partenza** dee par·*ten*·tsa *date of departure*

datore/datrice ⓜ/ⓕ **di lavoro** da·*to*·re/
da·*tree*·che dee la·*vo*·ro *employer*
dea ⓕ *de*·a *goddess*
debole *de*·bo·le *weak*
degustazione ⓕ **(dei vini)**
de·goos·ta·*tsyo*·ne day *vee*·nee *(wine)
tasting*
delitto ⓜ de·*lee*·to *crime (infringement)*
democrazia ⓕ de·mo·kra·*tsee*·a
democracy
denaro ⓜ de·*na*·ro *money*
dente ⓜ *den*·te *tooth (front)*
denti ⓜ pl *den*·tee *teeth*
dentifricio ⓜ den·tee·*free*·cho *toothpaste*
dentista ⓜ&ⓕ den·*tee*·sta *dentist*
dentro *den*·tro *inside*
deodorante ⓜ de·o·do·*ran*·te *deodorant*
deposito ⓜ de·*po*·zee·to *deposit (bank)*
— **bagagli** ba·ga·*lyee* *left luggage
(office)*
derubare de·roo·*ba*·re *rob*
desiderare de·see·de·*ra*·re *wish • desire*
destinazione ⓕ des·tee·na·*tsyo*·ne
destination
destra *de*·stra *right (direction) • right-
wing*
detersivo ⓜ de·ter·*see*·vo *washing
powder*
di *from • by • of*
— **andata e ritorno** an·*da*·ta e
ree·*tor*·no *return (ticket)*
— **destra** *de*·stra *right-wing*
— **fronte a** *fron*·te a *opposite*
— **lusso** *loo*·so *luxurious*
— **meno** *me*·no *less*
— **nuovo** *nwo*·vo *again*
— **più** *pyoo* *more*
— **recente** re·*chen*·te *recently*
— **seconda mano** se·*kon*·da *ma*·no
second-hand
— **sinistra** see·*nee*·stra *left-wing*
— **solo andata** *so*·lo an·*da*·ta *one-way
ticket*
diabete ⓜ dee·a·*be*·te *diabetes*
diaframma ⓜ dee·a·*fra*·ma *diaphragm*
diapositiva ⓕ dee·a·po·zee·*tee*·va *slide
(film)*
diarrea ⓕ dee·a·*re*·a *diarrhoea*
diesel ⓜ *dee*·zel *diesel*

dieta ⓕ *dye*·ta *diet*
dietro *dye*·tro *behind*
difettoso/a ⓜ/ⓕ dee·fe·*to*·zo/a *faulty*
differente (da) dee·fe·*ren*·te (da) *different*
differenza ⓕ dee·fe·*ren*·tsa *difference*
— **di fuso orario** dee *foo*·zo o·*ra*·ryo
time difference
difficile dee·*fee*·chee·le *difficult*
digitale dee·jee·*ta*·le *digital*
dimensioni ⓕ pl dee·men·*syo*·nee *size
(general)*
dimenticare dee·men·tee·*ka*·re *forget*
dio/dea ⓜ/ⓕ *dee*·o/*de*·a *god (general)*
dipendente ⓜ/ⓕ dee·pen·*den*·te
addicted • dependant
dipingere dee·*peen*·je·re *paint*
dire *dee*·re *say*
diretto/a ⓜ/ⓕ dee·*re*·to/a *direct*
direzione ⓕ dee·re·*tsyo*·ne *direction*
diritti ⓜ pl **umani** dee·*ree*·tee oo·*ma*·nee
human rights
diritto ⓜ dee·*ree*·to/a *straight • right
(prerogative)*
disabile dee·za·*be*·le *disabled*
dischetto ⓜ dees·*ke*·to *disk (computer)*
discriminazione ⓕ
dees·kree·mee·na·*tsyo*·ne
discrimination
disinfettante ⓜ deez·een·fe·*tan*·te
disinfectant
disoccupato/a ⓜ/ⓕ dee·zo·koo·*pa*·to/a
unemployed
distributore ⓜ dee·stree·boo·*to*·re *petrol/
service station*
— **automatico di biglietti**
ow·to·ma·*tee*·ko dee bee·*lye*·tee *ticket
machine*
disturbo ⓜ dees·*toor*·bo *trouble*
disturbi ⓜ pl **da fuso orario** dees·*toor*·bee
da *foo*·zo o·*ra*·ryo *jet lag*
dito ⓜ *dee*·to *finger*
— **del piede** del *pye*·de *toe*
ditta ⓕ *dee*·ta *company (firm)*
diversi/e ⓜ/ⓕ pl dee·*ver*·see/dee·*ver*·se
several
diverso/a dee·*ver*·so/a *different • various*
divertente dee·ver·*ten*·te *funny •
entertaining*
divertimento ⓜ dee·ver·tee·*men*·to *fun*

divertirsi dee·ver·*teer*·see enjoy (oneself)

divorziato/a ⓜ/ⓕ dee·vor·*tsya*·to/a divorced

divisa ⓕ dee·*vee*·za uniform

doccia ⓕ *do*·cha shower

documenti ⓜ pl do·koo·*men*·tee papers

documento ⓜ **d'identità** do·koo·*men*·to dee·den·tee·*ta* identification

dogana ⓕ do·*ga*·na customs

dolce ⓜ *dol*·che sweet • dessert

dolce *dol*·che sweet • soft

dolciumi ⓜ pl dol·*choo*·mee candy

dollaro ⓜ *do*·la·ro dollar

dolore ⓜ do·*lo*·re pain

dolori ⓜ pl **mestruali** do·*lo*·ree me·*stroo*·a·lee period pain

doloroso/a ⓜ/ⓕ do·lo·*ro*·zo/a painful • sore

domanda ⓕ do·*man*·da question

domandare do·man·*da*·re ask (a question)

domani do·*ma*·nee tomorrow
— **mattina** ma·*tee*·na tomorrow morning
— **pomeriggio** po·me·*ree*·jo tomorrow afternoon
— **sera** *se*·ra tomorrow evening

donna ⓕ *do*·na woman
— **d'affari** da·*fa*·ree businesswoman

dopo *do*·po after

dopobarba ⓜ do·po·*bar*·ba aftershave

dopodomani do·po·do·*ma*·nee day after tomorrow

doppio/a ⓜ/ⓕ *do*·pyo/a double

dormire dor·*mee*·re sleep

dose ⓕ *do*·ze dose
— **eccessiva** e·che·*see*·va overdose

dove *do*·ve where

dozzina ⓕ do·*dzee*·na dozen

dramma ⓜ *dra*·ma drama

droga ⓕ *dro*·ga drug/ drugs

drogheria ⓕ dro·ge·*ree*·a grocery

due *doo*·e two
— **letti** *le*·tee twin/two beds
— **volte** *vol*·te twice

duomo ⓜ *dwo*·mo cathedral

durante doo·*ran*·te during

duro/a ⓜ/ⓕ *doo*·ro/a hard (not soft)

E

e e and

ebreo/a ⓜ/ⓕ e·*bre*·o/a Jewish

ecografia ⓕ e·ko·gra·*fee*·a ultrasound

economico/a ⓜ/ⓕ e·ko·no·*mee*·ko/a cheap

eczema ⓜ ek·*dze*·ma eczema

edicola ⓕ e·*dee*·ko·la newsagency

edificio ⓜ e·dee·*fee*·cho building

egoista ⓜ/ⓕ e·go·ee·*sta* selfish

elenco ⓜ **telefonico** e·*len*·ko te·le·fo·nee·ko phone book

elettricista ⓜ&ⓕ e·le·tree·*chee*·sta electrician

elettricità ⓕ e·le·tree·chee·*ta* electricity

elezioni ⓕ pl e·le·*tsyo*·nee elections • polls

email ⓜ e·*mayl* email

emergenza ⓕ e·mer·*jen*·tsa emergency

emicrania ⓕ e·mee·*kra*·nya migraine

emotivo/a ⓜ/ⓕ e·mo·*tee*·vo/a emotional

energia ⓕ **(nucleare)** en·er·*jee*·a (noo·kle·a·re) (nuclear) energy

enorme e·*nor*·me huge

entrare en·*tra*·re enter

entrata ⓕ en·*tra*·ta entry

entro (un'ora) *en*·tro (oon·*o*·ra) within (an hour)

epatite ⓕ e·pa·*tee*·te hepatitis

epilessia ⓕ e·pe·le·*see*·a epilepsy

erba ⓕ *er*·ba grass • pot (dope)

erbe ⓕ pl *er*·be herbs

erborista ⓜ&ⓕ er·bo·*ree*·sta herbalist

eroina ⓕ e·ro·*ee*·na heroin

erotico/a ⓜ/ⓕ e·ro·*tee*·ko/a sexy

errore ⓜ e·*ro*·re mistake

esame ⓜ e·*za*·me test

escluso/a ⓜ/ⓕ es·*kloo*·zo/a excluded

escursione ⓕ es·koor·*syo*·ne excursion • trip
— **a piedi** a *pye*·de hike

escursionismo ⓜ es·koor·syo·*neez*·mo touring
— **a piedi** a *pye*·de hiking

esecuzione ⓕ e·se·koo·*tsyo*·ne performance

esempio ⓜ e·*zem*·pyo example

esperienza ① es·pe·*ryen*·tsa *experience*
esperimenti ⓜ pl **nucleari**
es·pe·ree·*men*·tee noo·kle·a·ree *nuclear testing*
esposimetro ⓜ es·po·zee·me·tro *light meter*
esposizione ① es·po·zee·*tsyo*·ne *exhibition*
espresso/a ⓜ/① es·*pre*·so/a *express*
essere e·se·re *be*
— **d'accordo** da·*kor*·do *agree*
— **raffreddato/a** ⓜ/① ra·fre·*da*·to/a *have a cold*
est ⓜ est *east*
estate ① es·*ta*·te *summer*
estetista ⓜ&① es·te·*tee*·sta *beautician*
estero/a ⓜ/① es·te·ro/a *foreign*
età ① e·*ta* *age*
etichetta ① e·tee·*ke*·ta *luggage tag*
etto ⓜ e·to *100 grams*
euro ⓜ e·oo·ro *euro*
europeo/a ⓜ/① e·oo·ro·*pe*·o/a *European* (adj)
eutanasia ① e·oo·ta·na·*zee*·a *euthanasia*

fabbrica ① fa·*bree*·ka *factory*
faccia ① fa·cha *face*
facile fa·*chee*·le *easy*
fagioli ⓜ pl fa·*jo*·lee *beans*
fame ① fa·me *hunger*
famiglia ① fa·*mee*·lya *family*
famoso/a ⓜ/① fa·*mo*·zo/a *famous*
fango ⓜ *fan*·go *mud*
fantastico/a ⓜ/① fan·*tas*·tee·ko/a *great*
fantino ⓜ fan·*tee*·no *jockey*
fare fa·re *do* • *make*
— **il tifo** eel *tee*·fo *support* (cheer on)
— **l'autostop** *low*·to·stop *hitchhike*
— **la barba** la *bar*·ba *shave*
— **male** *ma*·le *hurt*
— **una camminata** oo·na ka·me·*na*·ta *hike*
— **una foto** oo·na fo·to *take a photo*
farfalla ① far·*fa*·la *butterfly*
fari ⓜ pl fa·ree *headlights*
farina ① fa·*ree*·na *flour*
farmacia ① far·ma·*chee*·a *pharmacy*

farmacista ⓜ&① far·ma·*chee*·sta *chemist*
fascia ① fa·sha *bandage*
fatto/a ⓜ/① fa·to/a *made*
— **a mano** a *ma*·no *handmade*
— **di (cotone)** dee ko·*to*·ne *made of* (cotton)
fattoria ① fa·to·*re*·a *farm*
fax ⓜ faks *fax*
fazzolettini ⓜ pl **di carta** fa·tso·le·*tee*·nee dee *kar*·ta *tissues*
fazzoletto ⓜ fa·tso·*le*·to *handkerchief*
febbre ① fe·bre *temperature (fever)*
— **da fieno** da fye·no *hay fever*
federa ① fe·de·ra *pillowcase*
fegato ⓜ fe·ga·to *liver*
felice ⓜ/① fe·*lee*·che *happy*
ferita ① fe·*ree*·ta *injury*
ferito/a ⓜ/① fe·*ree*·to/a *injured*
fermare fer·*ma*·re *stop*
fermarsi fer·*mar*·see *stay (at a hotel)*
fermata ① fer·*ma*·ta *stop*
fermo ⓜ **posta** *fer*·mo *pos*·ta *poste restante*
ferramenta ① fe·ra·*men*·ta *hardware store*
ferro ⓜ fe·ro *iron*
— **da stiro** da stee·ro *iron (clothes)*
festa ① fes·ta *festival* • *public holiday* • *party (celebration)*
fetta ① fe·ta *slice*
fiammiferi ⓜ pl fya·*mee*·fe·ree *matches*
fico ⓜ fee·ko *fig*
fidanzamento ⓜ fee·dan·tsa·*men*·to *engagement (couple)*
fidanzato/a ⓜ/① fee·dan·*tsa*·to/a *fiance(e)*
figlia ① fee·lya *daughter*
figlio ⓜ fee·lyo *son*
film ⓜ feelm *movie*
filo ⓜ fee·lo *thread (sewing)*
— **dentario** den·ta·ree·o *dental floss*
fine ① fee·ne *end*
fine settimana ⓜ fee·ne se·tee·*ma*·na *weekend*
finestra ① fee·*nes*·tra *window (general)*
finestrino ⓜ fee·nes·*tree*·no *window (car, plane)*
finire fee·*nee*·re *end* • *finish* • *run out of*

finito/a ⓜ/ⓕ fee·nee·to finished

fino a (giugno) fee·no a (joo·nyo) until
(June)

fiocchi ⓜ pl di mais fyo·kee dee ma·ees
cornflakes

fioraio ⓜ&ⓕ fyo·ra·yo florist

fiore ⓜ fyo·re flower

firma ⓕ feer·ma signature

fiume ⓜ fyoo·me river

flash ⓜ flesh flash (camera)

fluido ⓜ idratante floo·ee·do
ee·dra·tan·te hydrating fluid

foglia ⓕ fo·lya leaf

fondo ⓜ fon·do bottom

fondo/a ⓜ/ⓕ fon·do·a deep

footing ⓜ foo·teeng jogging • running
(sport)

forbici ⓕ pl for·bee·chee scissors

forchetta ⓕ for·ke·ta fork

foresta ⓕ fo·res·ta forest

forma ⓕ for·ma shape

formaggio ⓜ for·ma·jo cheese
— fresco fres·ko cream cheese

formica ⓕ for·mee·ka ant

forno ⓜ for·no oven
— a microonde a mee·kro·on·de
microwave (oven)

forse for·se maybe

forte ⓜ/ⓕ for·te strong • loud

fortuna ⓕ for·too·na chance • luck

fortunato/a ⓜ/ⓕ for·too·na·to/a lucky

foto ⓕ fo·to photo

fotografia ⓕ fo·to·gra·fee·a photography

fotografo ⓜ fo·to·gra·fo photographer •
camera shop

fra fra between
— poco po·ko soon

fragile fra·jee·le fragile

fragola ⓕ fra·go·la strawberry

francobollo ⓜ fran·ko·bo·lo stamp

fratello ⓜ fra·te·lo brother

freccia ⓕ fre·cha indicator (car)

freddo/a ⓜ/ⓕ fre·do·a cold

freno ⓜ fre·no brake

fresco/a ⓜ/ⓕ fres·ko·a fresh

fretta ⓕ fre·ta hurry

friggere free·je·re fry

frigo ⓜ free·go fridge

frigobar ⓜ free·go·bar bar fridge •
mini-bar

frigorifero ⓜ free·go·ree·fe·ro refrigerator

frizione ⓕ free·tsyo·ne clutch

frutta ⓕ froo·ta fruit
— secca se·ka dried fruit

fruttivendolo/a ⓜ/ⓕ
froo·tee·ven·do·lo/a greengrocer

fumare foo·ma·re smoke

fumato/a ⓜ/ⓕ foo·ma·to/a smoked •
stoned (drugged)

funerale ⓜ foo·ne·ra·le funeral

fungo ⓜ foon·go mushroom

funivia ⓕ foo·nee·vee·a cable car

fuoco ⓜ fwo·ko fire

fuori fwo·ree outside

furgone ⓜ foor·go·ne van

futuro ⓜ foo·too·ro future

G

gabinetto ⓜ (pubblico) ga·bee·ne·to
(poo·blee·ko) (public) toilet

galleria ⓕ d'arte ga·le·ree·a dar·te art
gallery

Galles ⓜ ga·les Wales

gamba ⓕ gam·ba leg (body part)

gambero ⓜ gam·be·ro prawn

gara ⓜ ga·ra race (sport) • competition

garage ⓜ ga·raj garage

gas ⓜ gaz gas (for cooking)

gasolio ⓜ ga·zo·lyo diesel

gastroenterite ⓕ gas·tro·en·te·ree·te
gastroenteritis

gattino ⓜ ga·tee·no kitten

gatto ⓜ ga·to cat

gay gei gay

gelateria ⓕ je·la·te·ree·a ice-cream
parlour

gelato ⓜ je·la·to ice cream

geloso/a ⓜ/ⓕ je·lo·zo/a jealous

gemelli/e ⓜ/ⓕ pl je·me·lee/je·me·le
twins

generale je·ne·ra·le general

gengiva ⓕ jen·jee·va gum (mouth)

genitori ⓜ pl je·nee·to·ree parents

gente ⓕ jen·te people

gentile jen·tee·le kind • nice (person)

germogli ⓜ pl (di soia) jer·mo·lyee (dee
so·ya) beansprouts

gettone ⓜ je·to·ne token

ghiaccio ⓜ *gya·cho ice*
già *ja already*
giacca ⓕ *ja·ka jacket*
giallo/a ⓜ/ⓕ *ja·lo/a yellow*
Giappone ⓜ *ja·po·ne Japan*
giardinaggio ⓜ *jar·dee·na·jo gardening*
giardino ⓜ *jar·dee·no garden*
— **zoologico** *dzo·o·lo·jee·ko zoo*
ginecologo/a ⓜ/ⓕ *jee·ne·ko·lo·go/a gynaecologist*
ginnastica ⓕ *jee·nas·tee·ka gymnastics*
ginocchio ⓜ *jee·no·kyo knee*
giocare *jo·ka·re play*
— **a calcio** *a kal·cho play soccer*
gioco ⓜ *jo·ko game (play)*
— **elettronico** *e·le·tro·nee·ko computer game*
gioielli ⓜ pl *jo·ye·lee jewellery*
giornale ⓜ *jor·na·le newspaper*
giornalista ⓜ&ⓕ *jor·na·lee·sta journalist*
giorno ⓜ *jor·no day*
giovane *jo·va·ne young*
girare *jee·ra·re turn*
gita ⓕ *jee·ta tour • trip*
giù *joo down*
giubbotto ⓜ **di salvataggio** *joo·bo·to dee sal·va·ta·jo life jacket*
giudice ⓜ *joo·dee·che judge*
giudò *joo·do judo*
giusto/a ⓜ/ⓕ *joo·sto/a right (correct)*
gola ⓕ *go·la throat*
gomma ⓕ *go·ma tyre*
— **da masticare** *da ma·stee·ka·re (chewing) gum*
gonfiore ⓜ *gon·fyo·re swelling*
gonna ⓕ *go·na skirt*
governo ⓜ *go·ver·no government*
grammi ⓜ pl *gra·mee grams*
grande *gran·de big • large*
grande magazzino ⓜ *gran·de ma·ga·dzee·no department store*
grandinata ⓕ *gran·dee·na·ta hailstorm*
grandine ⓕ *gran·dee·ne hail*
grasso/a ⓜ/ⓕ *gra·so/a fat*
gratuito/a ⓜ/ⓕ *gra·too·ee·to/a free (gratis) • complimentary (free)*
grigio/a ⓜ/ⓕ *gree·jo/a grey*
grotta ⓕ *gro·ta cave*

gruppo ⓜ *groo·po band (music)*
— **sanguigno** *san·gwee·nyo blood group*
guanti ⓜ *gwan·tee gloves*
guardare *gwar·da·re look • watch*
— **le vetrine** *le ve·tree·ne go window-shopping*
guardaroba ⓜ *gwar·da·ro·ba cloakroom*
guastarsi *gwas·tar·see break down*
guastato/a ⓜ/ⓕ *gwas·ta·to/a broken down*
guasto/a ⓜ/ⓕ *gwa·sto/a off (food)*
guerra ⓕ *gwe·ra war*
guida ⓕ *gwee·da guide (person) • guidebook*
— **agli spettacoli** *a·lyee spe·ta·ko·lee entertainment guide*
— **audio** *ow·dyo guide (audio)*
— **turistica** *too·ree·stee·ka guidebook*
guidare *gwee·da·re drive*
gustoso/a ⓜ/ⓕ *goo·sto·zo/a tasty*

H

halal *a·lal halal*
hashish ⓜ *a·sheesh hash*
hockey ⓜ *o·kee hockey*
— **su ghiaccio** *soo gya·cho ice hockey*

I

idiota ⓜ&ⓕ *ee·dyo·ta idiot*
idratante ⓜ *ee·dra·tan·te moisturiser*
ieri *ye·ree yesterday*
illegale *ee·le·ga·le illegal*
imbarazzato/a ⓜ/ⓕ *eem·ba·ra·tsa·to/a embarrassed*
imbrogliare *eem·bro·lya·re cheat*
immersione ⓕ *ee·mer·syo·ne submersion • dive*
— **in apnea** *een ap·ne·a snorkelling*
— **subacquea** *soo·ba·kwe·a scuba diving*
immigrazione ⓕ *ee·mee·gra·tsyo·ne immigration*
imparare *eem·pa·ra·re learn*
impermeabile ⓜ *eem·per·me·a·bee·le waterproof*
impermeabile *eem·per·me·a·bee·le waterproof*

impiegato/a ⓜ/ⓕ eem·pye·ga·to/a
employee • office worker
importante eem·por·tan·te *important*
impossibile eem·po·see·bee·le *impossible*
in een *in • to*
— **bianco e nero** byan·ko e ne·ro *B&W*
— **buona salute** bwo·na sa·loo·te *in good health*
— **fondo** fon·do *at the bottom • after all*
— **fretta** fre·ta *in a hurry*
— **lista d'attesa** lee·sta da·te·za *standby (ticket)*
— **omaggio** o·ma·jo *complimentary (free gift)*
— **ritardo** ree·tar·do *late (adv)*
— **salita** sa·lee·ta *uphill*
— **sciopero** ⓜ sho·pe·ro *on strike*
— **vendita** ven·dee·ta *on sale*
inalatore ⓜ ee·na·la·to·re *inhaler*
incidente ⓜ een·chee·den·te *accident • crash*
incinta een·cheen·ta *pregnant*
incontrare een·kon·tra·re *meet*
incrocio ⓜ een·kro·cho *intersection*
indicare een·dee·ka·re *point*
indigestione ⓕ een·dee·je·styo·ne *indigestion*
indirizzo ⓜ een·dee·ree·tso *address*
indossare een·do·sa·re *wear*
indù ⓜ&ⓕ een·doo *Hindu*
industria ⓕ een·doos·trya *industry*
infermiere/a ⓜ/ⓕ een·fer·mye·re/a *nurse*
infezione ⓕ een·fe·tsyo·ne *infection*
infiammazione ⓕ een·fya·ma·tsyo·ne *inflammation*
influenza ⓕ een·floo·en·tsa *flu • influenza*
informatica ⓕ een·for·ma·tee·ka *IT*
informazioni ⓕ pl een·for·ma·tsyo·nee *information*
infortunato/a ⓜ/ⓕ een·for·too·na·to/a *injured*
ingegnere ⓜ&ⓕ een·je·nye·re *engineer*
Inghilterra ⓕ een·geel·te·ra *England*
inglese een·gle·ze *English*
ingorgo ⓜ een·gor·go *traffic jam*
ingrediente ⓜ een·gre·dyen·te *ingredient*

ingresso ⓜ een·gre·so *cover charge (venue) • entrance*
iniezione ⓕ ee·nye·tsyo·ne *injection*
inizio ⓜ ee·nee·tsyo *start (beginning)*
innocente ee·no·chen·te *innocent*
inquinamento ⓜ een·kwee·na·men·to *pollution*
insalata ⓕ een·sa·la·ta *salad*
insegnante ⓜ&ⓕ een·sen·yan·te *teacher (general)*
insetto ⓜ een·se·to *insect*
insieme een·sye·me *together*
insolito/a ⓜ/ⓕ een·so·lee·to/a *unusual*
interessante een·te·re·san·te *interesting*
internazionale een·ter·na·tsyo·na·le *international*
Internet (point) ⓜ een·ter·net (poynt) *Internet (cafe)*
interprete ⓜ/ⓕ een·ter·pre·te *interpreter*
interurbano/a ⓜ/ⓕ een·ter·oor·ba·no/a *long-distance (bus)*
intervallo ⓜ een·ter·va·lo *intermission*
intervento ⓜ een·ter·ven·to *operation (medical) • intervention (police) • speech*
intossicazione ⓕ **alimentare** een·to·see·ka·tsyo·ne a·lee·men·ta·re *food poisoning*
inverno ⓜ een·ver·no *winter*
invitare een·vee·ta·re *invite*
io ee·o *I*
isola ⓕ ee·zo·la *island*
istruttore/istruttrice ⓜ/ⓕ ee·stroo·to·re/ ee·stroo·tree·che *instructor (general)*
istruzione ⓕ ees·troo·tsyo·ne *education*
itinerario ⓜ ee·tee·ne·ra·ryo *itinerary • route*
— **escursionistico** es·koor·syo·nee·stee·ko *hiking route*
IVA ⓕ ee·va *sales tax*

J

jeans ⓜ pl jeens *jeans*

K

kiwi ⓜ kee·wee *kiwifruit*
kosher ka·sher *kosher*

L

là la *there*
labbra ① pl *la·bra lips*
laboratorio ⑩ la·bo·ra·to·ryo *workshop*
ladro/a ⑩/① *la·dro/a thief*
lago ⑩ *la·go lake*
lamentarsi la·men·tar·see *complain*
lamette ① pl **(da barba)** la·me·te (da bar·ba) *razor blades*
lampadina ① lam·pa·dee·na *light bulb*
lampone ⑩ lam·po·ne *raspberry*
lana ① *la·na wool*
lardo ⑩ *lar·do lard*
largo/a ⑩/① *lar·go/a wide*
lassativi ⑩ pl la·sa·tee·vee *laxatives*
lato ⑩ *la·to side*
latte ⑩ *la·te milk*
 — **di soia** dee so·ya *soy milk*
 — **scremato** skre·ma·to *skimmed milk*
lattuga ① la·too·ga *lettuce*
lavaggio ⑩ **a secco** la·va·jo a se·ko *dry cleaning*
lavanderia ① la·van·de·ree·a *laundry (room)*
 — **a gettone** je·to·ne *laundrette*
lavare la·va·re *wash (something)*
lavarsi la·var·see *wash (oneself)*
lavatrice ① la·va·tree·che *washing machine*
lavorare la·vo·ra·re *work*
 — **in proprio** een pro·pryo *(to be) self-employed*
lavoratore/lavoratrice ⑩/① la·vo·ra·to·re/la·vo·ra·tree·che *worker*
lavoro ⑩ *la·vo·ro job • occupation • work*
forza ① *for·tsa strength • force*
forze ① pl **armate** *for·tse ar·ma·te military*
legale le·ga·le *legal*
legge ① *le·je law*
leggere *le·je·re read*
leggero/a ⑩/① *le·je·ro/a light (not heavy)*
legna ① **(da ardere)** *le·nya (da ar·de·re) (fire)wood*
legno ⑩ *le·nyo wood*
legume ⑩ *le·goo·me legume*

lei lay *she*
Lei pol lay *you (polite)*
lentamente len·ta·men·te *slowly*
lenti ① pl **a contatto** *len·tee a kon·ta·to contact lenses*
lenticchia ① len·tee·kya *lentil*
lento/a ⑩/① *len·to/a slow*
lenzuolo ⑩ len·tswo·lo *sheet (bed)*
lesbica ① *lez·bee·ka lesbian*
lettera ① *le·te·ra letter*
letto ⑩ *le·to bed*
 — **matrimoniale** ma·tree·mo·nya·le *double bed*
libero/a ⑩/① *lee·be·ro/a free (not bound) • vacant*
libreria ① lee·bre·ree·a *bookshop*
libretto ⑩ lee·bre·to *booklet*
 — **di circolazione** dee cheer·ko·la·tsyo·ne *car owner's title*
libro ⑩ *lee·bro book*
licenza ① lee·chen·tsa *permit*
limetta ① lee·me·ta *lime (fruit) • nail file*
limite ⑩ **di velocità** lee·me·te dee ve·lo·chee·ta *speed limit*
limonata ① lee·mo·na·ta *lemonade*
limone ⑩ lee·mo·ne *lemon*
linea ① *lee·ne·a line*
 — **aerea** a·e·re·a *airline*
lingua ① *leen·gwa tongue • language*
lista ① *lee·sta list*
 — **d'atteza** da·te·za *waiting list*
lite ① *lee·te fight*
litigare lee·tee·ga·re *argue*
litro ⑩ *lee·tro litre*
livello ⑩ lee·ve·lo *level (tier)*
livido ⑩ *lee·vee·do bruise*
locale ⑩ lo·ka·le *bar • venue*
locale lo·ka·le *local*
lontano/a ⑩/① lon·ta·no/a *far*
loro *lo·ro they*
Loro *lo·ro you* pl pol
lozione ① lo·tsyo·ne *lotion*
 — **abbronzante** a·bron·dzan·te *tanning lotion*
lubrificante ⑩ loo·bree·fee·kan·te *lubricant*
lucchetto ⑩ loo·ke·to *bike lock • padlock*
luce ① *loo·che light*
lucertola ① loo·cher·to·la *lizard*

lui *loo·ee he*

lumaca ① *loo·ma·ka snail*

luminoso/a ⑩/① *loo·meen·o·zo/a light (not dark)*

luna ① *loo·na moon*
— **di miele** *dee mye·le honeymoon*
— **piena** *pye·na full moon*

lungo/a ⑩/① *loon·go/a long*

luogo ⑩ *lwo·go place (location)*
— **di nascita** *dee na·shee·ta place of birth*

lusso ⑩ *loo·so luxury*

M

M

ma *ma but*

macchina ① *ma·kee·na car • machine*
— **fotografica** *fo·to·gra·fee·ka camera*

macelleria ① *ma·che·le·ree·a butcher's shop*

madre ① *ma·dre mother*

maestro/a ⑩/① *ma·es·tro/a teacher (primary school or music) • instructor (skiing)*

maglietta ① *ma·lye·ta T-shirt*

maglione ⑩ *ma·lyo·ne jumper • sweater*

magro/a ⑩/① *ma·gro/a thin • lean*

mai *mai never*

maiale ⑩ *ma·ya·le pig • pork*

maionese ① *ma·yo·ne·ze mayonnaise*

male ⑩ *ma·le pain • harm • evil*

mal ⑩ *mal*
— **di aereo** *dee a·e·re·o travel sickness (air)*
— **di denti** *dee den·tee toothache*
— **di macchina** *dee ma·kee·na travel sickness (car)*
— **di mare** *dee ma·re travel sickness (sea)*
— **di pancia** *dee pan·cha stomach ache*
— **di testa** *dee tes·ta headache*

malato/a ⑩/① *ma·la·to/a ill • sick*

malattia ① *ma·la·tee·a disease*
— **venerea** *ve·ne·re·a venereal disease*

mamma ① *ma·ma mum*

mammografia ① *ma·mo·gra·fee·a mammogram*

manager ⑩ *me·nee·je manager*

mancare *man·ka·re miss • be lacking*

mancia ① *man·cha tip (gratuity)*

mandare *man·da·re send*

mandarino ⑩ *man·da·ree·no mandarin*

mandorla ① *man·dor·la almond*

mangiare *man·ja·re eat*

mango ⑩ *man·go mango*

manifestazione ① *ma·nee·fes·ta·tsyo·ne demonstration (protest)*

mano ① *ma·no hand*

manovale ⑩&① *ma·no·va·le manual worker*

manuale *ma·noo·a·le manual*

manubrio ⑩ *ma·noo·bryo handlebars*

manzo ⑩ *man·dzo beef*

marciapiede ⑩ *mar·cha·pye·de footpath*

mare ⑩ *ma·re sea*

marea ① *ma·re·a tide*

margarina ① *mar·ga·ree·na margarine*

marijuana ① *ma·ree·wa·na marijuana*

marito ⑩ *ma·ree·to husband*

marmellata ① *mar·me·la·ta jam*
— **d'arance** *da·ran·che marmalade*

marmo ⑩ *mar·mo marble*

marrone ⑩/① *ma·ro·ne brown*

martello ⑩ *mar·te·lo hammer*

massaggio ⑩ *ma·sa·jo massage*

materasso ⑩ *ma·te·ra·so mattress*

matita ① *ma·tee·ta pencil*

matrimonio ⑩ *ma·tree·mo·nyo marriage*

mattina ① *ma·tee·na morning*

mazzuolo ⑩ *ma·tswo·lo mallet*

meccanico ⑩&① *me·ka·nee·ko mechanic*

medicina ① *me·dee·chee·na medicine*

medicinale ⑩ *me·dee·chee·na·le drug (medicinal)*

medico ⑩ *me·dee·ko doctor*

meditazione ① *me·dee·ta·tsyo·ne meditation*

mela ① *me·la apple*

melanzana ① *me·lan·dza·na aubergine • eggplant*

melodia ① *me·lo·dee·a tune*

melone ⑩ *me·lo·ne melon*

membro ⑩ *mem·bro member*

mendicante ⑩&① *men·dee·kan·te beggar*

meno *me·no less*

menù ⓜ me·noo *menu*
meraviglioso/a ⓜ/ⓕ me·ra·vee·*lyo*·zo/a *wonderful*
mercato ⓜ mer·*ka*·to *market*
merletto ⓜ mer·*le*·to *lace*
mescolare mes·ko·*la*·re *mix*
mese ⓜ me·ze *month*
messa ⓕ me·sa *Mass*
messaggio ⓜ me·*sa*·jo *message*
mestiere ⓜ mes·*tye*·re *craft (trade)* • *occupation (work)*
mestruazione ⓕ me·stroo·a·*tsyo*·ne *menstruation*
metallo ⓜ me·*ta*·lo *metal*
metro ⓜ *me*·tro *metre (distance)*
metropolitana ⓕ me·tro·po·lee·*ta*·na *subway*
mettere *me*·te·re *put*
mezzanotte ⓕ me·*dza* no·te *midnight*
mezzi ⓜ pl **di comunicazione** me·tsee dee ko·moo·nee·ka·*tsyo*·ne *media*
mezzo ⓜ *me*·dzo *half*
mezzogiorno ⓜ me·dzo·*jor*·no *noon*
microonda ⓕ mee·kro·on·da *microwave*
miele ⓜ *mye*·le *honey*
migliore mee·*lyo*·re *better* • *best*
millimetro ⓜ mee·*lee*·me·tro *millimetre*
minestra ⓕ mee·*nes*·tra *soup*
minibar ⓜ *mee*·nee·bar *mini-bar* • *bar fridge*
minuto ⓜ mee·*noo*·to *minute*
minuto/a ⓜ/ⓕ mee·*noo*·to/a *tiny*
mobili ⓜ pl *mo*·bee·lee *furniture*
moda ⓕ *mo*·da *fashion*
modem ⓜ *mo*·dem *modem*
moderno/a ⓜ/ⓕ mo·*der*·no/a *modern*
moduli ⓜ pl mo·*doo*·lee *paperwork*
modulo ⓜ *mo*·doo·lo *form (paper)*
moglie ⓕ *mo*·lye *wife*
molestia ⓕ mo·*les*·tya *harassment*
molto *mol*·to *very*
molto/a ⓜ/ⓕ *mol*·to/a *a lot (of)* • *many*
monastero ⓜ mon·as·*te*·ro *monastery*
mondo ⓜ *mon*·do *world*
monete ⓕ pl mo·*ne*·te *coins*
mononucleosi ⓜ mo·no·noo·kle·o·zee *glandular fever*
montagna ⓕ mon·*ta*·nya *mountain*
monumento ⓜ mo·noo·*men*·to *monument*

morbillo ⓜ mor·*bee*·lo *measles*
morire mo·*ree*·re *die*
morso ⓜ *mor*·so *bite (dog)*
morto/a ⓜ/ⓕ *mor*·to/a *dead*
mosca ⓕ *mos*·ka *fly*
moschea ⓕ mos·*ke*·a *mosque*
mostrare mos·*tra*·re *show*
moto ⓕ *mo*·to *motorbike*
motore ⓜ mo·*to*·re *engine*
motoscafo ⓜ mo·to·*ska*·fo *motorboat*
mouse ⓜ mows *computer mouse*
mucca ⓕ *moo*·ka *cow*
muesli ⓜ *moos*·lee *muesli*
mughetto ⓜ moo·*ge*·to *thrush (medical)*
multa ⓕ *mool*·ta *fine (payment)*
muro ⓜ *moo*·ro *wall (outer)*
muscolo ⓜ *moo*·sko·lo *muscle*
museo ⓜ moo·*ze*·o *museum*
musica ⓕ *moo*·zee·ka *music*
musicista ⓜ&ⓕ moo·zee·*chee*·sta *musician*
  — **di strada** dee *stra*·da *busker*
musulmano/a ⓜ/ⓕ moo·sool·*ma*·no/a *Muslim*
muta ⓕ **di subacqueo** *moo*·ta dee soo·ba·*kwe*·o *wetsuit*
muto/a ⓜ/ⓕ *moo*·to/a *mute*

N

narrativa ⓕ na·ra·*tee*·va *fiction*
naso ⓜ *na*·zo *nose*
Natale ⓜ na·*ta*·le *Christmas*
natura ⓕ na·*too*·ra *nature*
nausea ⓕ *now*·ze·a *nausea*
  — **mattutina** ma·too·*tee*·na *morning sickness*
nave ⓕ *na*·ve *ship* • *boat*
nazionale na·tsyo·*na*·le *national*
nazionalità ⓕ na·tsyo·na·*lee*·ta *nationality*
nebbioso/a ⓜ/ⓕ ne·*byo*·zo/a *foggy*
necessario/a ⓜ/ⓕ ne·che·*sa*·ryo/a *necessary*
negozio ⓜ ne·*go*·tsyo *shop*
  — **da campeggio** da kam·*pe*·jo *camping store*
  — **di abbigliamento** dee a·bee·lya·*men*·to *clothing store*

— di articoli sportivi dee ar·*tee*·ko·lee spor·*tee*·vee *sports store*

— di giocattoli dee jo·ka·to·lee *toyshop*

— di scarpe dee *skar*·pe *shoe shop*

— di souvenir dee *soo*·ve·neer *souvenir shop*

nero/a ⓜ/ⓕ *ne*·ro/a *black*

nessuno/a dei due ⓜ/ⓕ ne·*soo*·no/a day *doo*·e *neither*

neve ⓕ *ne*·ve *snow*

nido ⓜ *nee*·do *nest* • *childminding (group)*

niente *nyen*·te *nothing* • *none*

nipote ⓜ&ⓕ nee·*po*·te *grandchild*

no no *no*

noce ⓕ *no*·che *nut* • *walnut*

— di acagiù dee a·ka·*joo* *cashew*

nodulo ⓜ *no*·doo·lo *lump*

noi noy *we*

noioso/a ⓜ/ⓕ no·yo·zo/a *boring*

noleggiare no·le·*ja*·re *hire*

nome ⓜ *no*·me *name*

non non *no* • *not*

— ancora an·*ko*·ra *not yet*

— fumatore foo·ma·*to*·re *non-smoking*

— diretto/a ⓜ/ⓕ dee·*re*·to/a *non-direct*

nonna ⓕ *no*·na *grandmother*

nonno ⓜ *no*·no *grandfather*

nord ⓜ nord *north*

normale nor·*ma*·le *regular*

notizie ⓕ pl no·*tee*·tsye *news*

notte ⓕ *no*·te *night*

nubile ⓕ *noo*·bee·le *single (woman)*

numero ⓜ *noo*·me·ro *number*

— di camera dee *ka*·me·ra *room number*

— di targa dee *tar*·ga *licence plate number*

— di telefono dee te·*le*·fo·no *telephone number*

nuotare nwo·*ta*·re *swim*

nuoto ⓜ *nwo*·to *swimming*

Nuova Zelanda ⓕ nwo·va dze·*lan*·da *New Zealand*

nuovo/a ⓜ/ⓕ *nwo*·vo/a *new*

nuvola ⓕ *noo*·vo·la *cloud*

nuvoloso/a ⓜ/ⓕ noo·vo·*lo*·zo/a *cloudy*

O

obiettivo ⓜ o·bye·*tee*·vo *lens* • *objective*

occhiali ⓜ pl o·*kya*·lee *glasses (spectacles)*

— da sci da shee *goggles (skiing)*

— da sole da *so*·le *sunglasses*

occhio ⓜ *o*·kyo *eye*

oceano ⓜ o·*che*·a·no *ocean*

odore ⓜ o·*do*·re *smell*

oggetti ⓜ pl o·*je*·tee *articles* • *things*

— d'artigianato dar·tee·ja·*na*·to *handicrafts*

— di valore dee va·*lo*·re *valuables*

— in ceramica een che·*ra*·mee·ka *pottery*

oggi o·jee *today*

olio ⓜ o·*lyo* *oil*

— d'oliva do·*lee*·va *olive oil*

oliva ⓕ o·*lee*·va *olive*

ombra ⓕ *om*·bra *shadow* • *shade*

ombrello ⓜ om·*bre*·lo *umbrella*

omeopatia ⓕ o·me·o·pa·*tee*·a *homeopathy*

omosessuale ⓜ&ⓕ o·mo·se·*swa*·le *homosexual*

onda ⓕ *on*·da *wave*

opera ⓕ *o*·pe·ra *work (of art)*

— lirica *lee*·ree·ka *opera*

operaio/a ⓜ/ⓕ o·pe·*ra*·yo/a *factory worker*

operatore/operatrice ⓜ/ⓕ o·pe·ra·*to*·re/ o·pe·ra·*tree*·che *operator*

opinione ⓕ o·pee·*nyo*·ne *opinion*

oppure o·*poo*·re *or* • *otherwise* • *or else*

ora ⓕ o·ra *hour*

orario ⓜ o·*ra*·ryo *timetable*

— di apertura dee a·per·*too*·ra *opening hours*

— ridotto ree·*do*·to *part-time*

orchestra ⓕ or·*kes*·tra *orchestra*

ordinare or·dee·*na*·re *order*

ordinario/a ⓜ/ⓕ or·dee·*na*·ryo/a *ordinary*

ordine ⓜ or·*dee*·ne *order*

orecchini ⓜ pl o·re·*kee*·nee *earrings*

orecchio ⓜ o·*re*·kyo *ear*

originale ⓕ o·ree·jee·*na*·le *original*

oro ⓜ *o*·ro *gold*

orologio m o·ro·lo·jo *clock • watch*
orrendo/a m/f o·ren·do/a *awful*
ospedale m os·pe·da·le *hospital*
ospitalità f os·pee·ta·lee·ta *hospitality*
ossigeno m o·see·je·no *oxygen*
osso m o·so *bone*
ostello m **della gioventù** os·te·lo de·la jo·ven·too *youth hostel*
osteria f os·te·ree·a *pub*
ostrica f o·stree·ka *oyster*
ottimo/a m/f o·tee·mo/a *excellent • great*
ovest m o·vest *west*

P

pacchetto m pa·ke·to *parcel • packet • package*
pace f pa·che *peace*
padella f pa·de·la *frying pan*
padre m pa·dre *father*
padrone/padrona m/f **di casa** pa·dro·ne/pa·dro·na dee ka·za *landlord/landlady*
paese m pa·e·ze *country (nation)*
Paesi Bassi pl pa·e·zee ba·see *Netherlands*
pagamento m pa·ga·men·to *payment*
pagare pa·ga·re *pay*
pagina f pa·jee·na *page*
paio m pa·yo *pair (couple)*
palazzo m pa·la·tso *palace*
palcoscenico m pal·ko·she·nee·ko *stage*
palestra f pa·le·stra *gym*
palla f pa·la *ball (sports)*
pallacanestro f pa·la·ka·ne·stro *basketball*
pallamuro m pa·la·moo·ro *handball*
pallavolo f pa·la·vo·lo *volleyball*
pallone m pa·lo·ne *ball (inflated)*
pancetta f pan·che·ta *bacon*
pane m pa·ne *bread*
— **a pasta acida** a pas·ta a·chee·da *sourdough bread*
— **di segala** dee se·ga·la *rye bread*
— **integrale** een·te·gra·le *wholemeal bread*
— **tostato** tos·ta·to *toast*
panetteria f pa·ne·te·ree·a *bakery*

panino m pa·nee·no *roll (bread)*
panna f pa·na *cream (food)*
— **acida** a·chee·da *sour cream*
pannolino m pa·no·lee·no *diaper • nappy*
pantaloncini m pl pan·ta·lon·chee·nee *shorts*
pantaloni m pl pan·ta·lo·nee *pants • trousers*
pap test pap test *pap smear*
papà m pa·pa *dad*
parabrezza f pa·ra·bre·dza *windscreen*
parcheggio m par·ke·jo *carpark*
parco m par·ko *park*
— **nazionale** na·tsyo·na·le *national park*
— **giochi** jo·kee *playground*
parlamentare m&f par·la·men·ta·re *member of parliament*
parlamento m par·la·men·to *parliament*
parlare par·la·re *speak • talk*
parola f pa·ro·la *word*
parrucchiere m pa·roo·kye·re *beauty salon*
parrucchiere/a m/f pa·roo·kye·re/a *hairdresser*
parte f par·te *part*
partenza f par·ten·tsa *departure*
partire par·tee·re *depart • leave*
partita f par·tee·ta *game • match*
partito m par·tee·to *party (politics)*
Pasqua f pas·kwa *Easter*
passaggio m pa·sa·jo *pass (sport) • passage*
passaporto m pa·sa·por·to *passport*
passatempo m pa·sa·tem·po *hobby*
passato m pa·sa·to *past*
passeggero/a m/f pa·se·je·ro/a *passenger*
passeggiata f pa·se·ja·ta *walk*
passo m pa·so *pass (mountain)*
pasta f pa·sta *pasta • noodles*
pasticceria f pa·stee·che·ree·a *cake shop*
pasto m pa·sto *meal*
— **freddo** fre·do *buffet (meal)*
patata f pa·ta·ta *potato*
paté m pa·te *paté (food)*
patente f **(di guida)** pa·ten·te (dee gwee·da) *drivers licence*

pavimento ⓜ pa·vee·*men*·to *floor*
pazzo/a ⓜ/ⓕ *pa*·tso/a *crazy*
pecora ⓕ *pe*·ko·ra *sheep*
pedale ⓜ pe·*da*·le *pedal*
pedone ⓜ pe·*do*·ne *pedestrian*
pelle ⓕ *pe*·le *skin*
pellicola ⓕ pe·*lee*·ko·la *film (for camera)*
pene ⓜ *pe*·ne *penis*
penicillina ⓕ pe·nee·chee·*lee*·na *penicillin*
penna (a sfera) *pe*·na (a *sfe*·ra) *pen (ballpoint)*
pensare pen·*sa*·re *think*
pensionato/a ⓜ/ⓕ pen·syo·*na*·to/a *pensioner • retired*
pensione ⓕ pen·*syo*·ne *guesthouse • boarding house*
pentola ⓕ *pen*·to·la *pan*
pepe ⓜ *pe*·pe *pepper*
peperoncino ⓜ pe·pe·ron·*chee*·no *chilli*
peperone ⓜ pe·pe·*ro*·ne *capsicum*
per per *for • to • through • by*
— **esempio** e·*zem*·pyo *for example*
— **sempre** *sem*·pre *forever*
pera ⓕ *pe*·ra *pear*
percentuale ⓕ per·chen·*twa*·le *percentage*
perché per·*ke* *why • because*
perdere *per*·de·re *lose*
perdonare per·do·*na*·re *forgive*
pericoloso/a ⓜ/ⓕ pe·ree·ko·*lo*·zo/a *dangerous • unsafe*
permanente ⓜ/ⓕ per·ma·*nen*·te *permanent*
permesso ⓜ per·*me*·so *permission • permit*
perso/a ⓜ/ⓕ *per*·so/a *lost*
persona ⓕ per·so·na *person*
personale ⓜ/ⓕ per·so·*na*·le *personal*
pesante pe·*zan*·te *heavy*
pesca ⓕ *pe*·ska *fishing • peach*
pesce ⓜ *pe*·she *fish (food)*
pesce/pesci ⓜ sg/pl *pe*·she/*pe*·shee *fish (alive)*
pescheria ⓕ pe·ske·*ree*·a *fish shop*
peso ⓜ *pe*·zo *weight*
petizione ⓕ pe·tee·*tsyo*·ne *petition*
pettine ⓜ *pe*·tee·ne *comb*
petto ⓜ *pe*·to *chest*

pezzo ⓜ *pe*·tso *piece*
— **di antiquariato** dee an·tee·kwa·*rya*·to *antique*
— **d'artigianato** dar·tee·ja·*na*·to *craft (product)*
piacere pya·*che*·re *like*
pianeta ⓜ pya·*ne*·ta *planet*
piano ⓜ *pya*·no *floor (storey)*
pianta ⓕ *pyan*·ta *map • plant*
piatto ⓜ *pya*·to *plate*
— **fondo** *fon*·do *bowl*
piatto/a ⓜ/ⓕ *pya*·to/a *flat*
piazza ⓕ *pya*·tsa *square (town)*
picchetti ⓜ pl pee·*ke*·tee *pegs (tent)*
piccolo/a ⓜ/ⓕ *pee*·ko·lo/a *small*
piccone ⓜ pee·*ko*·ne *pickaxe*
piccozza ⓕ pee·*ko*·tsa *ice axe*
picnic ⓜ *peek*·neek *picnic*
pidocchi ⓜ pl pee·*do*·kee *lice*
piede ⓜ *pye*·de *foot*
pieno/a ⓜ/ⓕ *pye*·no/a *full*
pietra ⓕ *pye*·tra *stone*
pignatta ⓕ pee·*nya*·ta *pot (ceramics)*
pigro/a ⓜ/ⓕ *pee*·gro/a *lazy*
pila ⓕ *pee*·la *battery*
pillola ⓕ *pee*·lo·la *pill • the Pill*
— **anticoncezionale** an·tee·kon·che·tsy o·*na*·le *the Pill*
— **del mattino dopo** del ma·*tee*·no *do*·po *morning after pill*
ping-pong ⓜ peeng·*pong* *table tennis*
pinzette ⓕ pl peen·*tse*·te *tweezers*
pioggia ⓕ *pyo*·ja *rain*
piombo ⓜ *pyom*·bo *lead*
piscina ⓕ pee·*shee*·na *swimming pool*
pisello ⓜ pee·*ze*·lo *pea*
pista ⓕ *pee*·sta *trail • track (sports) • racetrack • slope*
pistacchio ⓜ pee·*sta*·kyo *pistachio*
pittore/pittrice ⓜ/ⓕ pee·*to*·re/ pee·*tree*·che *painter*
pittura ⓕ pee·*too*·ra *painting (the art)*
più *pyoo* *more*
plastica ⓕ *pla*·stee·ka *plastic*
un po' oon po *(a) little*
poco/a ⓜ/ⓕ *po*·ko/a *few*
poesia ⓕ po·e·*zee*·a *poetry*
politica ⓕ po·*lee*·tee·ka *politics*
politico ⓜ po·*lee*·tee·ko *politician*

polizia ① po·lee·tsee·a police (civilian)
polline ⑩ po·lee·ne pollen
pollo ⑩ po·lo chicken
polmoni ⑩ pl pol·mo·nee lungs
polso ⑩ pol·so wrist
polvere ① pol·ve·re powder
pomeriggio ⑩ po·me·ree·jo afternoon
pomodoro ⑩ po·mo·do·ro tomato
pompa ① pom·pa pump
pompelmo ⑩ pom·pel·mo grapefruit
ponte ⑩ pon·te bridge
popolare po·po·la·re popular
porro ⑩ po·ro leek
porta ① por·ta door
portacenere ⑩ por·ta·che·ne·re ashtray
portafoglio ⑩ por·ta·fo·lyo wallet
portare por·ta·re bring • carry
portatile ⑩ por·ta·tee·le laptop
portatile por·ta·tee·le portable
porto ⑩ por·to harbour • port
posate ① pl po·za·te cutlery
possibile po·see·bee·le possible
posta ① pos·ta mail
— **elettronica** e·le·tro·nee·ka email
— **ordinaria** or·dee·na·rya surface mail
— **prioritaria** pree·o·ree·ta·rya
express mail
— **raccomandata** ① ra·ko·man·da·ta
registered mail
posteggio di tassi po·ste·jo dee ta·see
taxi stand
posto ⑩ pos·to place • seat
— **di polizia** dee po·lee·tsee·a police
station
potabile po·ta·bee·le drinkable
potere ⑩ po·te·re power (strength)
potere po·te·re can
povero/a ⑩/① po·ve·ro/a poor
povertà ① po·ver·ta poverty
pranzo ⑩ pran·dzo lunch
praticare pra·tee·ka·re play (sport)
— **il surf** eel soorf surf
prima colazione ① pree·ma ko·la·tsyo·ne
breakfast
preferire pre·fe·ree·re prefer
preferito/a ⑩/① pre·fe·ree·to/a favourite
pregare pre·ga·re worship (pray)
preghiera ① pre·gye·ra prayer

prendere pren·de·re take
— **in affitto** een a·fee·to rent
— **in prestito** een pres·tee·to borrow
prenotare pre·no·ta·re book (make a
booking)
prenotazione ① pre·no·ta·tsyo·ne
reservation
preoccupato/a ⑩/① pre·o·koo·pa·to/a
worried
preparare pre·pa·ra·re prepare
preservativo ⑩ pre·zer·va·tee·vo condom
presidente ⑩/① pre·zee·den·te president
pressione ① pre·syo·ne pressure
— **del sangue** del san·gwe blood
pressure
presto ⑩/① pre·sto early
prete ⑩ pre·te priest
prezioso/a ⑩/① pre·tsyo·zo/a valuable
prezzemolo ⑩ pre·tse·mo·lo parsley
prezzo ⑩ pre·tso price
— **d'ingresso** deen·gre·so admission
price
prigione ① pree·jo·ne prison
prigioniero/a ⑩/① pree·jo·nye·ro/a
prisoner
prima pree·ma before
— **classe** ① kla·se first class
— **colazione** ① ko·la·tsyo·ne breakfast
primavera ① pree·ma·ve·ra spring
(season)
primo ministro ⑩/① pree·mo
mee·nee·stro prime minister
primo/a ⑩/① pree·mo/a first
principale preen·chee·pa·le main
privato/a ⑩/① pree·va·to/a private
problema ⑩ pro·ble·ma problem
— **cardiaco** kar·dee·a·ko heart
condition
produrre pro·doo·re produce
profesore/profesoressa ⑩/①
pro·fe·so·re/pro·fe·so·re·sa
teacher (general)
profitto ⑩ pro·fee·to profit
profondo/a ⑩/① pro·fon·do/a deep
profumo ⑩ pro·foo·mo perfume
programma ⑩ pro·gra·ma program
proiettore ⑩ pro·ye·to·re projector
promessa ① pro·me·sa promise
pronto/a ⑩/① pron·to/a ready

pronto soccorso ⓜ *pron·*to so·*kor·*so *first-aid*

proprietario/a ⓜ/ⓕ pro·prye·*ta·*ryo/a *owner*

proroga ⓕ *pro·*ro·ga *extension (visa)*

prosciutto ⓜ **(cotto)** pro·*shoo·*to (*ko·*to) *ham (boiled)*

prossimo/a ⓜ/ⓕ *pro·*see·mo/a *next*

proteggere pro·*te·*je·re *protect*

protetto/a ⓜ/ⓕ pro·*te·*to/a *protected*

protestare pro·tes·*ta·*re *protest*

provare pro·*va·*re *try (attempt)*

provviste ⓕ pl pro·*vee·*ste *provisions • supplies*

— **alimentari** a·lee·men·*ta·*ree *food supplies*

prugna ⓕ *proo·*nya *plum • prune*

prurito ⓜ proo·*ree·*to *itch*

pub ⓜ *pub* *pub*

pugilato ⓜ poo·jee·*la·*to *boxing*

pulce ⓕ *pool·*che *flea*

pulito/a ⓜ/ⓕ poo·*lee·*to/a *clean*

pulizia ⓕ poo·lee·*tsee·*a *cleaning*

pullman ⓜ *pool·*man *bus (coach)*

punteggio ⓜ poon·*te·*jo *score*

punto ⓜ *poon·*to *point*

puntura ⓕ poon·*too·*ra *bite (insect)*

puro/a ⓜ/ⓕ *poo·*ro/a *pure*

Q

quaderno ⓜ kwa·*der·*no *notebook*

quadro ⓜ *kwa·*dro *painting (canvas)*

qualcosa kwal·*ko·*za *something*

qualcuno/a ⓜ/ⓕ kwal·*koo·*no/a *someone*

qualità ⓕ kwa·lee·*ta* *quality*

quando *kwan·*do *when*

quantità ⓕ kwan·tee·*ta* *amount • quantity*

quanto/a ⓜ/ⓕ *kwan·*to/a *how much*

quarantena ⓕ kwa·ran·*te·*na *quarantine*

quaresima ⓕ kwa·*re·*zee·ma *Lent*

quartiere ⓜ kwar·*tye·*re *suburb*

quarto ⓜ *kwar·*to *quarter*

questo/a ⓜ/ⓕ *kwe·*sto/a *this (one)*

questura ⓕ kwes·*too·*ra *police headquarters*

qui kwee *here*

quota ⓕ *kwo·*ta *altitude*

R

racchetta ⓕ ra·*ke·*ta *racquet*

raccogliere ra·ko·*lye·*re *pick (up)*

raccomandare ra·ko·man·*da·*re *recommend*

raccomandata ⓕ ra·ko·man·*da·*ta *registered mail*

raccontare ra·kon·*ta·*re *tell*

racconto ⓜ ra·*kon·*to *story*

radiatore ⓜ ra·dya·*to·*re *radiator*

rafano ⓜ *ra·*fa·no *horseradish*

raffreddore ⓜ ra·fre·*do·*re *cold (illness)*

ragazza ⓕ ra·*ga·*tsa *girl(friend)*

ragazzo ⓜ ra·*ga·*tso *boy(friend)*

ragione ⓕ ra·*jo·*ne *reason*

ragno ⓜ *ra·*nyo *spider*

rapido/a ⓜ/ⓕ *ra·*pee·do/a *quick*

rapinare ra·pee·*na·*re *rob*

rapporti ⓜ pl **protetti** ra·*por·*tee pro·*te·*tee *safe sex*

rapporto ⓜ ra·*por·*to *relationship*

raro/a ⓜ/ⓕ *ra·*ro/a *rare*

rasatura ⓕ ra·za·*too·*ra *shave*

rasoio ⓜ **(elettrico)** ra·zo·yo (e·*le·*tree·ko) *razor*

ravanello ⓜ ra·va·*ne·*lo *radish*

razzismo ⓜ ra·*tseez·*mo *racism*

re ⓜ re *king*

realistico/a ⓜ/ⓕ re·a·lee·*stee·*ko/a *realistic*

recente re·*chen·*te *recent*

recinzione ⓕ re·cheen·*tsyo·*ne *fence*

regalo ⓜ re·*ga·*lo *present (gift)*

— **di nozze** dee *no·*tse *wedding present*

reggiseno ⓜ re·jee·*se·*no *bra*

regina ⓕ re·*jee·*na *queen*

regione ⓕ re·*jo·*ne *region*

regista ⓜ&ⓕ re·*jee·*sta *director (films)*

registrazione ⓕ re·jee·stra·*tsyo·*ne *check-in (hotel)*

regolare re·go·*la·*re *regular*

regole ⓕ pl *re·*go·le *rules*

religione ⓕ re·lee·*jo·*ne *religion*

religioso/a ⓜ/ⓕ re·lee·*jo·*zo/a *religious*

reliquia ⓕ re·*lee·*kwee·a *relic*

remoto/a ⓜ/ⓕ re·*mo·*to/a *remote*

respirare res·pee·*ra·*re *breathe*

resto ⓜ *res·*to *change (money)*

rete ① re·te *net*
ricco/a ⓜ/① *ree·ko/a rich (wealthy)*
ricetta ① *ree·che·ta prescription*
ricevere *ree·che·ve·re receive*
ricevuta ① *ree·che·voo·ta receipt*
richiedere *ree·kye·de·re ask (for something)*
riciclabile *ree·chee·kla·bee·le recyclable*
riciclare *ree·chee·kla·re recycle*
ricordino ⓜ *ree·kor·dee·no souvenir*
ridere *ree·de·re laugh*
rifiutare *ree·fyoo·ta·re refuse*
rifugiato/a ⓜ/① *ree·foo·gya·to/a refugee*
rifiuti ⓜ pl *ree·fyoo·tee rubbish*
rilassarsi *ree·la·sar·see relax*
rimborso ⓜ *reem·bor·so refund*
ringraziare *reen·gra·tsya·re thank*
riparare *ree·pa·ra·re repair*
ripido/a ⓜ/① *ree·pee·do/a steep*
riposare *ree·po·za·re rest*
riscaldamento ⓜ *rees·kal·da·men·to heating*
　— centrale *chen·tra·le central heating*
rischio ⓜ *rees·kyo risk*
riscuotere un assegno *ree·skwo·te·re oon a·se·nyo cash a cheque*
riso ⓜ *ree·zo rice*
　— integrale *een·te·gra·le brown rice*
risposta ① *rees·pos·ta answer*
ristorante ⓜ *rees·to·ran·te restaurant*
ritardo ⓜ *ree·tar·do delay*
ritiro bagagli *ree·tee·ro ba·ga·lyee baggage claim*
ritmo ⓜ *reet·mo rhythm*
ritornare *ree·tor·na·re return*
ritorno ⓜ *ree·tor·no return*
rivista ① *ree·vee·sta magazine*
roba ① *ro·ba stuff (belongings)* • *dope (drugs)*
roccia ① *ro·cha rock* • *rock climbing*
romantico/a ⓜ/① *ro·man·tee·ko/a romantic*
romanzo ⓜ *ro·man·dzo novel*
rompere *rom·pe·re break*
rosa ⓜ/① *ro·za pink*
rossetto ⓜ *ro·se·to lipstick*
rosso/a ⓜ/① *ro·so/a red*
rotonda ⓜ *ro·ton·da roundabout*
rotondo/a ⓜ/① *ro·ton·do/a round*

rotto/a ⓜ/① *ro·to/a broken*
roulotte ① *roo·lot caravan*
rovine ① pl *ro·vee·ne ruins*
rubare *roo·ba·re steal*
rubato/a ⓜ/① *roo·ba·to/a stolen*
rubinetto ⓜ *roo·bee·ne·to faucet*
rugby ⓜ *roog·bee rugby*
rullino ⓜ *roo·lee·no film (roll for camera)*
rumoroso/a ⓜ/① *roo·mo·ro·zo/a noisy*
ruota ① *rwo·ta wheel*
ruscello ⓜ *roo·she·lo stream*

S

sabato ⓜ *sa·ba·to saturday* • *Sabbath*
sabbia ① *sa·bya sand*
sacchetto ⓜ *sa·ke·to bag (shopping)*
sacco ⓜ *sa·ko sack* • *bag*
　— a pelo *a pe·lo sleeping bag*
sala ① *sa·la room* • *hall*
　— di transito *dee tran·zee·to transit lounge*
　— d'aspetto *das·pe·to waiting room*
salame ⓜ *sa·la·me salami*
salario ⓜ *sa·la·ryo wage*
saldi ⓜ pl *sal·dee sales*
saldo ⓜ *sal·do balance (account)*
sale ⓜ *sa·le salt*
salire *sa·lee·re climb* • *go up*
　— su *su board (a plane, ship)*
salmone ⓜ *sal·mo·ne salmon*
salsa ① *sal·sa sauce*
salsiccia ① *sal·see·cha sausage*
saltare *sal·ta·re jump*
salumeria ① *sa·loo·me·ree·a delicatessen*
salute ① *sa·loo·te health*
salva slip ⓜ pl *sal·va sleep panty liners*
san Silvestro ⓜ *san seel·ves·tro New Year's Eve*
sandali ⓜ pl *san·da·lee sandals*
sangue ⓜ *san·gwe blood*
santo/a ⓜ/① *san·to/a saint*
santuario ⓜ *san·too·a·ryo shrine*
sapere *sa·pe·re know (how to)*
sapone ⓜ *sa·po·ne soap*
sardine ① pl *sar·dee·ne sardines*
sarto/a ⓜ/① *sar·to/a tailor*
sauna ① *sow·na sauna*
sbagliato/a ⓜ/① *sba·lya·to/a wrong*

sbaglio ⓜ *sba·lyo mistake*
scacchi ⓜ pl *ska·kee chess*
scala ⓕ **mobile** *ska·la mo·bee·le escalator*
scalare *ska·la·re climb*
scale ⓕ pl *ska·le stairway*
scanner ⓜ *ska·ner scanner*
scarafaggio ⓜ *ska·ra·fa·jo cockroach*
scarpe ⓕ pl *skar·pe shoes*
scarpette ⓕ pl *skar·pe·te boots (soccer)*
scarponi ⓜ pl *skar·po·nee boots (hiking, ski)*
scatola ⓕ *ska·to·la box • carton • can • tin*
scatoletta ⓕ *ska·to·le·ta tin • can*
scheda ⓕ **telefonica** *ske·da te·le·fo·nee·ka phone card*
scherma ⓕ *sker·ma fencing (sport)*
scherzo ⓜ *sker·tso joke*
schiena ⓕ *skye·na back (body)*
sci ⓜ *shee skiing • ski(s)*
— **acquatico** *a·kwa·tee·ko waterskiing*
sciare *shee·a·re ski*
sciarpa ⓕ *shar·pa scarf*
scienza ⓕ *shen·tsa science*
sciopero ⓜ *sho·pe·ro strike*
sciovia ⓕ *shee·o·vee·a ski-lift*
sciroppo ⓜ *shee·ro·po syrup*
— **per la tosse** *per la to·se cough medicine*
scogliera ⓕ *sko·lye·ra cliff*
scommessa ⓕ *sko·me·sa bet*
scomodo/a ⓜ/ⓕ *sko·mo·do/a uncomfortable*
sconosciuto/a ⓜ/ⓕ *sko·no·shoo·to/a stranger*
sconto ⓜ *skon·to discount*
scorie ⓕ pl *sko·rye waste (rubbish)*
— **radioattive** *ra·dyo·a·tee·ve nuclear waste*
— **tossiche** *to·see·che toxic waste*
scottatura ⓕ *sko·ta·too·ra sunburn*
Scozia ⓕ *sko·tsya Scotland*
scrittore/scrittrice ⓜ/ⓕ *skree·to·re/ skree·tree·che writer*
scrivere *skree·ve·re write*
scultura ⓕ *skool·too·ra sculpture*
scuola ⓕ *skwo·la school*
— **superiore** *soo·pe·ryo·re high school*
scuro/a ⓜ/ⓕ *skoo·ro/a dark*

se *se if*
seccato/a ⓜ/ⓕ *se·ka·to/a cross (angry)*
secchio ⓜ *se·kyo bucket*
secco/a ⓜ/ⓕ *se·ko/a dry*
seconda classe ⓕ *se·kon·da kla·se second class*
di seconda mano ⓜ/ⓕ *dee se·kon·da ma·no second-hand*
secondo *se·kon·do second*
secondo/a ⓜ/ⓕ *se·kon·do/a second*
sedere *se·de·re sit*
sedia ⓕ *se·dya chair*
— **a rotelle** *a ro·te·le wheelchair*
sedile ⓜ *se·dee·le seat (chair)*
seggiolino ⓜ *se·jo·lee·no child seat*
seggiovia ⓕ *se·jo·vee·a chairlift (skiing)*
segnale ⓜ *se·nya·le signal • dial tone*
— **acustico** *a·koos·tee·ko dial tone*
segnare *se·nya·re score*
segno ⓜ *se·nyo sign*
segretario/a ⓜ/ⓕ *se·gre·ta·ryo/a secretary*
seguire *se·gwee·re follow*
sella ⓕ *se·la saddle*
semaforo ⓜ *se·ma·fo·ro traffic lights*
semplice ⓜ/ⓕ *sem·plee·che simple*
sempre *sem·pre always*
senape ⓕ *se·na·pe mustard*
seno ⓜ *se·no breast*
sensuale ⓜ/ⓕ *sen·soo·a·le sensual*
sentiero ⓜ *sen·tye·ro path • track • trail*
— **di montagna** *dee mon·ta·nya mountain path*
sentimenti ⓜ pl *sen·tee·men·tee feelings*
sentire *sen·tee·re feel • hear*
senza *sen·tsa without*
— **piombo** *pyom·bo unleaded*
senzatetto ⓜ&ⓕ *sen·tsa·te·to homeless*
separato/a ⓜ/ⓕ *se·pa·ra·to/a separate*
sera ⓕ *se·ra evening*
serie ⓕ **(televisiva)** *se·ree·e (te·le·vee·see·va) (TV) series*
serio/a ⓜ/ⓕ *se·ryo/a serious*
serpente ⓜ *ser·pen·te snake*
serratura ⓕ *se·ra·too·ra lock (door)*
servizi ⓜ pl **igienici** *ser·vee·tse ee·je·nee·chee toilets*

servizio ⓜ ser·*vee*·tsyo *service • service-charge*

— **militare** mee·lee·*ta*·re *military service*

sessismo ⓜ se·*seez*·mo *sexism*

sesso ⓜ se·so *sex*

seta ⓕ *se*·ta *silk*

settimana ⓕ se·tee·*ma*·na *week*

— **santa** san·ta *Holy Week*

sfogo ⓜ *sfo*·go *rash*

— **da pannolino** da pa·no·*lee*·no *nappy rash*

sfruttamento ⓜ sfroo·ta·*men*·to *exploitation*

shampoo ⓜ sham·poo *shampoo*

sì see *yes*

sicuro/a ⓜ/ⓕ see·*koo*·ro/a *safe*

sidro ⓜ *see*·dro *cider*

sieropositivo/a ⓜ/ⓕ sye·ro·po·zee·*tee*·vo/a *HIV positive*

sigaretta ⓕ see·ga·*re*·ta *cigarette*

sigaro ⓜ *see*·ga·ro *cigar*

simile ⓜ *see*·mee·le *similar*

simpatico/a ⓜ/ⓕ seem·*pa*·tee·ko/a *nice (person)*

sinagoga ⓕ see·na·*go*·ga *synagogue*

sindaco ⓜ *seen*·da·ko *mayor*

sinistra ⓕ see·*nee*·stra *left (direction)*

sintetico/a ⓜ/ⓕ seen·*te*·tee·ko/a *synthetic*

siringa ⓕ see·*reen*·ga *syringe*

slitta ⓕ *slee*·ta *sleigh • toboggan*

soccorso ⓜ so·*kor*·so *help • aid*

socialista ⓜ&ⓕ so·cha·*lee*·sta *socialist*

socio/a ⓜ/ⓕ so·cho/a *member*

soffice ⓜ/ⓕ *so*·fee·che *soft*

sognare so·*nya*·re *dream*

sogno ⓜ *so*·nyo *dream*

soldato ⓜ sol·*da*·to *soldier*

soldi ⓜ pl *sol*·dee *money • cash*

sole ⓜ *so*·le *sun*

soleggiato/a ⓜ/ⓕ so·le·*ja*·to/a *sunny*

solo *so*·lo *only*

— **andata** ⓕ an·*da*·ta *one-way*

sonniferi ⓜ pl so·*nee*·fe·ree *sleeping pills*

sonno ⓜ *so*·no *sleep • sleepiness*

sopra *so*·pra *above • over*

soprannome ⓜ so·pra·*no*·me *nickname*

sordo/a ⓜ/ⓕ *sor*·do/a *deaf*

sorella ⓕ so·*re*·la *sister*

sorpresa ⓕ sor·*pre*·sa *surprise*

sorridere so·*ree*·de·re *smile*

sostenitore/sostenitrice ⓜ/ⓕ sos·te·nee·*to*·re/sos·te·nee·*tree*·che *supporter*

sotto *so*·to *below*

sottoaceti ⓜ pl so·to·a·*che*·tee *pickles*

sottotitoli ⓜ pl so·to·*tee*·to·lee *subtitles*

spacciatore/spacciatrice ⓜ/ⓕ spa·cha·*to*·re/spa·cha·*tree*·che *drug dealer*

Spagna ⓕ *spa*·nya *Spain*

spago ⓜ *spa*·go *string*

spalla ⓕ *spa*·la *shoulder*

spazio ⓜ *spa*·tsyo *space*

spazzatura ⓕ spa·tsa·*too*·ra *rubbish • garbage*

spazzolino ⓜ **da denti** spa·tso·*lee*·no da *den*·tee *toothbrush*

specchio ⓜ *spe*·kyo *mirror*

speciale spe·*cha*·le *special*

specialista ⓜ&ⓕ spe·cha·*lee*·sta *specialist*

specie ⓕ *spe*·che *species • type*

— **in via di estinzione** een *vee*·a dee es·teen·*tsyo*·ne *endangered species*

— **protetta** pro·*te*·ta *protected species*

spermicida ⓜ sper·mee·*chee*·da *spermicide*

spesso *spe*·so *often*

spesso/a ⓜ/ⓕ *spe*·so/a *thick*

spettacolo ⓜ spe·*ta*·ko·lo *show • performance*

spiaggia ⓕ *spya*·ja *beach*

spiccioli ⓜ pl *spee*·cho·lee *loose change*

spina ⓕ *spee*·na *plug (electricity)*

— **multipla** *mool*·tee·pla *adaptor*

spinaci ⓜ pl spee·*na*·chee *spinach*

spingere *speen*·je·re *push*

spirale ⓕ spee·*ra*·le *IUD*

spogliatoio ⓜ spo·lya·*to*·yo *change room (sport)*

sporco/a ⓜ/ⓕ *spor*·ko/a *dirty*

sport ⓜ sport *sport*

sportivo/a ⓜ/ⓕ spor·*tee*·vo/a *sportsperson*

sposalizio ⓜ spo·za·*lee*·tsyo *wedding*

sposare spo·*za*·re *marry*

sposato/a ⓜ/ⓕ spo·za·to/a *married*
spremuta ⓕ spre·moo·ta *fruit juice (fresh)*
— **d'arancia** da·ran·cha *orange juice (fresh)*
spuntino ⓜ spoon·tee·no *snack*
squadra ⓕ skwa·dra *team*
stadio ⓜ sta·dyo *stadium*
stagione ⓕ sta·jo·ne *season*
stampante ⓕ stam·pan·te *printer (computer)*
stanco/a ⓜ/ⓕ stan·ko/a *tired*
stanza ⓕ stan·tsa *room*
stasera sta·se·ra *tonight*
Stati Uniti d'America ⓜ pl sta·tee oo·nee·tee da·me·ree·ka *USA*
stato ⓜ **civile** sta·to chee·vee·le *marital status*
statua ⓕ sta·too·a *statue*
stazione ⓕ sta·tsyo·ne *(train) station*
— **d'autobus** dow·to·boos *bus station*
— **della metropolitana** de·la me·tro·po·lee·ta·na *metro station*
— **di servizio** dee ser·vee·tsyo *petrol station • service station*
— **ferroviaria** fe·ro·vyar·ya *train station*
stelle ⓕ pl ste·le *stars*
stendersi sten·der·see *lie (not stand)*
sterlina ⓕ ster·lee·na *pound (money)*
stesso/a ⓜ/ⓕ ste·so/a *same*
stile ⓜ stee·le *style*
stipendio ⓜ stee·pen·dyo *salary*
stitichezza ⓕ stee·tee·ke·tsa *constipation*
stivali ⓜ pl stee·va·lee *boots*
stoffa ⓕ sto·fa *fabric*
stomaco ⓜ sto·ma·ko *stomach*
stordito/a ⓜ/ⓕ stor·dee·to/a *dizzy*
storia ⓕ sto·rya *history • story*
storico/a ⓜ/ⓕ sto·ree·ko/a *historical*
storta ⓕ stor·ta *sprain*
strada ⓕ stra·da *road • street*
straniero/a ⓜ/ⓕ stra·nye·ro/a *foreign*
strano/a ⓜ/ⓕ stra·no/a *strange*
strato ⓜ **d'ozono** stra·to do·dzo·no *ozone layer*
stretto/a ⓜ/ⓕ stre·to/a *tight*
studente/studentessa ⓜ/ⓕ stoo·den·te/stoo·den·te·sa *student*

stufa ⓕ stoo·fa *heater • stove*
— **a gas** a gaz *gas stove*
stupido/a ⓜ/ⓕ stoo·pee·do/a *stupid*
stupro ⓜ stoo·pro *rape*
stuzzicadenti ⓜ stoo·tsee·ka·den·te *toothpick*
su soo *on • up*
succo ⓜ soo·ko *juice*
— **d'arancia** da·ran·cha *orange juice (bottled)*
— **di frutta** dee froo·ta *fruit juice (bottled)*
sud ⓜ sood *south*
sugo ⓜ soo·go *sauce*
suocera ⓕ swo·che·ra *mother-in-law*
suocero ⓜ swo·che·ro *father-in-law*
suonare (la chitarra) swo·na·re (la kee·ta·ra) *play (guitar)*
suora ⓕ swo·ra *nun*
supermercato ⓜ soo·per·mer·ka·to *supermarket*
superstizione ⓕ soo·per·stee·tsyo·ne *superstition*
surf ⓜ **da neve** soorf da ne·ve *snow boarding*
surgelati ⓜ pl soor·je·la·tee *frozen foods*
sussidio ⓜ **di disoccupazione** soo·see·dyo dee dee·zo·koo·pa·tsyo·ne *unemployment benefit*
sveglia ⓕ sve·lya *alarm clock*
svegliarsi sve·lyar·see *wake up*
Svizzera ⓕ svee·tse·ra *Switzerland*

T

tabaccheria ⓕ ta·ba·ke·ree·a *tobacconist*
tabacco ⓜ ta·ba·ko *tobacco*
tabellone ⓜ **segnapunti** ta·be·lo·ne se·nya·poon·tee *scoreboard*
tacchino ⓜ ta·kee·no *turkey*
tachimetro ⓜ ta·kee·me·tro *speedometer*
taglia ⓕ ta·lya *size (clothes)*
tagliare ta·lya·re *cut*
tagliaunghie ⓜ ta·lya·oon·gye *nail clippers*
taglio ⓜ **di capelli** ta·lyo dee ka·pe·lee *haircut*
tamponi ⓜ pl tam·po·nee *tampons*

tappa ① *ta·pa leg (in race or journey)* • *stage (in race)*

tappeto ⓜ *ta·pe·to mat* • *rug*

tappi ⓜ pl **per le orecchie** *ta·pee per le o·re·kye earplugs*

tappo ⓜ *ta·po plug (bath)*

tardi *tar·dee late (adj)*

targa ① *tar·ga number plate*

tariffa ① **postale** *ta·ree·fa pos·ta·le postage*

tasca ① *tas·ka pocket*

tassa ① *ta·sa tax*

tassì ⓜ *ta·see taxi*

tasso ⓜ **di cambio** *ta·so dee kam·byo exchange rate*

tastiera ① *tas·tye·ra keyboard*

tavola ① *ta·vo·la table*

— **da surf** *da soorf surfboard*

tazza ① *ta·tsa cup*

tè ⓜ *te tea*

teatro ⓜ *te·a·tro theatre*

— **dell'opera** *del·o·per·a opera house*

telecomando ⓜ *te·le·ko·man·do remote control*

telefonare *te·le·fo·na·re telephone*

telefonata ① *te·le·fo·na·ta phone call*

telefono ⓜ *te·le·fo·no telephone*

— **cellulare** *che·loo·la·re mobile/cell phone*

— **diretto** *dee·re·to direct-dial*

— **pubblico** *poo·blee·ko public telephone*

telegramma ⓜ *te·le·gra·ma telegram*

telenovela ① *te·le·no·ve·la soap opera*

teleobiettivo ⓜ *te·le·o·bye·tee·vo telephoto lens*

telescopio ⓜ *te·le·sko·pyo telescope*

televisione ① *te·le·vee·zyo·ne television*

temperatura ① *tem·pe·ra·too·ra temperature (weather)*

temperino ⓜ *tem·pe·ree·no penknife*

tempio ⓜ *tem·pyo temple*

tempo ⓜ *tem·po time* • *weather*

— **pieno** *pye·no full-time*

temporale ⓜ *tem·po·ra·le storm*

tenda ① *ten·da tent*

tensione ① **premestruale** *ten·syo·ne pre·me·stroo·a·le premenstrual tension*

Terra ① *te·ra Earth*

terra ① *te·ra land*

terremoto ⓜ *te·re·mo·to earthquake*

terribile ⓜ/① *te·ree·bee·le terrible*

terzo/a ⓜ/① *ter·tso/a third*

tessera ① *te·se·ra pass (document)*

test ⓜ **di gravidanza** *test dee gra·vee·dan·tsa pregnancy test kit*

testa ① *tes·ta head*

tiepido/a ⓜ/① *tye·pee·do/a warm*

tifoso/a ⓜ/① *tee·fo·zo/a fan (person)* • *supporter*

timido/a ⓜ/① *tee·mee·do/a shy*

tipico/a ⓜ/① *tee·pee·ko/a typical*

tipo ⓜ *tee·po type*

tirare *tee·ra·re pull*

titolo ⓜ *tee·to·lo title*

titoli ⓜ pl **di studio** *tee·to·lee dee stoo·dee·o qualifications*

toboga ⓜ *to·bo·ga toboggan* • *sledge*

toccare *to·ka·re touch*

tofu ⓜ *to·foo tofu*

tomba ① *tom·ba grave*

tonno ⓜ *to·no tuna*

topo ⓜ *to·po mouse (rodent)* • *rat*

torcia ① **elettrica** *tor·cha e·le·tree·ka torch (flashlight)*

torre ① *to·re tower*

torta ① *tor·ta cake* • *pie*

tossico/a ⓜ/① *to·see·ko/a toxic*

tossicodipendenza ① *to·see·ko·dee·pen·den·tsa drug addiction*

tossire *to·see·re cough*

tostapane ⓜ *tos·ta·pa·ne toaster*

tovaglia ① *to·va·lya tablecloth*

tovagliolo ⓜ *to·va·lyo·lo napkin*

tradurre *tra·doo·re translate*

traffico ⓜ *tra·fee·ko traffic*

traghetto ⓜ *tra·ge·to ferry*

tram ⓜ *tram tram*

tramezzino ⓜ *tra·me·dzee·no sandwich*

tramonto ⓜ *tra·mon·to sunset*

tranquillo/a ⓜ/① *tran·kwee·lo/a quiet*

trasporto ⓜ *tras·por·to transport*

travestito ⓜ *tras·ves·tee·to drag queen*

treno ⓜ *tre·no train*

triste *tree·ste sad*

troppo (caro/a) *tro·po ka·ro/a too (expensive)*

troppo/a ⓜ/① *tro·po/a too much* • *too many*

trovare tro·va·re *find*
trucco ⓜ *troo·*ko *make-up*
tu too *you (inf)*
tubo ⓜ di scappamento *too·*bo dee ska·pa·*men·*to *exhaust (car)*
tuffi ⓜ pl *too·*fee *diving (in pool)*
turista ⓜ&ⓕ too·*ree·*sta *tourist*
tutti/e ⓜ/ⓕ *too·*tee/*too·*te *all (plural)*
tutto *too·*to *everything*
tutto/a ⓜ/ⓕ *too·*to/a *all (singular)*
TV ⓕ tee·*voo* *TV*

U

ubriaco/a ⓜ/ⓕ oo·bree·*a·*ko/a *drunk*
uccello ⓜ oo·*che·*lo *bird*
ufficio ⓜ oo·*fee·*cho *office*
— del turismo del too·*reez·*mo *tourist office*
— oggetti smarriti o·*je·*tee sma·*ree·*tee *lost property office*
— postale pos·*ta·*le *post office*
ultimo/a ⓜ/ⓕ *ool·*tee·mo/a *last*
un po' oon po *(a) little*
una volta *oo·*na *vol·*ta *once*
università oo·nee·ver·see·*ta* *university*
universo ⓜ oo·nee·*ver·*so *universe*
uomo ⓜ *wo·*mo *man*
— d'affari da·fa·ree *businessman*
uovo ⓜ *wo·*vo *egg*
urgente ⓜ/ⓕ oor·*jen·*te *urgent*
urlare oor·*la·*re *shout*
usare oo·*za·*re *use*
usa e getta *oo·*za e *je·*ta *disposable*
uscire con oo·*shee·*re kon *go out with • date*
uscita ⓕ oo·*shee·*ta *exit*
utile *oo·*tee·le *useful*
uva ⓕ pl *oo·*va *grapes*
— passa *pa·*sa *raisin*

V

vacanza ⓕ va·*kan·*tsa *holiday • vacation*
vacanze ⓕ pl va·*kan·*tse *holidays*
vaccinazione ⓕ va·chee·na·*tsyo·*ne *vaccination*
vagina ⓕ va·*jee·*na *vagina*

vagone ⓜ va·*go·*ne *carriage • wagon*
— letto *le·*to *sleeping car*
valigetta ⓕ va·lee·*je·*ta *briefcase*
— del pronto soccorso del *pron·*to so·*kor·*so *first-aid kit*
valigia ⓕ va·*lee·*ja *suitcase*
valle ⓕ *va·*le *valley*
valore ⓜ va·*lo·*re *value (price)*
vanga ⓕ *van·*ga *spade*
vecchio/a ⓜ/ⓕ *ve·*kyo/a *old*
vedere ve·*de·*re *see*
vedovo/a ⓜ/ⓕ *ve·*do·vo/a *widower/ widow*
veduta ⓕ ve·*doo·*ta *lookout*
vegetariano/a ⓜ/ⓕ ve·je·ta·*rya·*no/a *vegetarian*
velenoso/a ⓜ/ⓕ ve·le·*no·*zo/a *poisonous*
veloce ve·*lo·*che *fast*
velocità ⓕ ve·lo·chee·*ta* *speed*
vendere *ven·*de·re *sell*
vendita ⓕ *ven·*dee·ta *sale*
venire ve·*nee·*re *come*
ventilatore ⓜ ven·tee·la·*to·*re *fan (machine)*
vento ⓜ *ven·*to *wind*
verde *ver·*de *green*
verdura ⓕ ver·*doo·*ra *vegetable*
vero/a ⓜ/ⓕ *ve·*ro/a *true*
vescica ⓕ ve·*shee·*ka *blister*
vetro ⓜ *ve·*tro *glass*
via ⓕ *vee·*a *way*
— aerea a·e·re·a *airmail*
viaggiare vee·a·*ja·*re *travel*
viaggio ⓜ vee·*a·*jo *trip*
— d'affari da·*fa·*ree *business trip*
viale ⓜ vee·*a·*le *avenue*
vicino/a ⓜ/ⓕ vee·*chee·*no/a *close • nearby*
vicino (a) vee·*chee·*no *(a) near (to)*
vicolo ⓜ *vee·*ko·lo *lane*
videocamera ⓕ vee·de·o·*ka·*me·ra *videocamera*
videonastro ⓜ vee·de·o·*nas·*tro *video tape*
videoregistratore ⓜ vee·de·o·re·jee·stra·*to·*re *video*
vigna ⓕ *vee·*nya *vineyard • wine cellar*
vigneto ⓜ vee·*nye·*to *vineyard*
villaggio ⓜ vee·*la·*jo *village*

vincere *veen·che·re* win
vincitore/vincitrice m/f *veen·chee·to·re/ veen·chee·tree·che* winner
vino m *vee·no* wine
— **bianco** *byan·ko* white wine
— **rosso** *ro·so* red wine
— **spumante** *spoo·man·te* sparkling wine
viola *vee·o·la* purple
virus m *vee·roos* virus
visita f *vee·zee·ta* visit • tour • medical examination
— **guidata** *gwee·da·ta* guided tour
vista f *vee·sta* view
visto m *vee·sto* visa
vita f *vee·ta* life
vitamine f pl *vee·ta·mee·ne* vitamins
vitello m *vee·te·lo* veal
vitto m *vee·to* food
vivere *vee·ve·re* live
vocabolarietto m *vo·ka·bo·la·rye·to* phrasebook
vocabolario m *vo·ka·bo·la·ryo* dictionary
voce f *vo·che* voice

volare *vo·la·re* fly
volere *vo·le·re* want
volo m *vo·lo* flight
volta f *vol·ta* time • turn
volume m *vo·loo·me* volume
vomitare *vo·mee·ta·re* vomit
votare *vo·ta·re* vote
vuoto/a m/f *vwo·to/a* empty

Y

yogurt m *yo·goort* yogurt

Z

zaino m *dzai·no* backpack • knapsack
zanzara f *tsan·tsa·ra* mosquito
zenzero m *dzen·dze·ro* ginger
zia f *tsee·a* aunt
zoom m *zoom* zoom lens
zucca f *tsoo·ka* pumpkin
zucchero m *tsoo·ke·ro* sugar
zucchini m pl *tsoo·kee·nee* courgette • zucchini

Y

DICTIONARY

254

What kind of traveller are you?

A. You're eating chicken for dinner *again* because it's the only word you know.

B. When no one understands what you say, you step closer and shout louder.

C. When the barman doesn't understand your order, you point frantically at the beer.

D. You're surrounded by locals, swapping jokes, email addresses and experiences
– other travellers want to borrow your phrasebook or audio guide.

If you answered A, B, or C, you NEED Lonely Planet's language products ...

- **Lonely Planet Phrasebooks** – for every phrase you need in every language
you want

- **Lonely Planet Language & Culture** – get behind the scenes of English as it's
spoken around the world – learn and laugh

- **Lonely Planet Fast Talk & Fast Talk Audio** – essential phrases for short trips and
weekends away – read, listen and talk like a local

- **Lonely Planet Small Talk** – 10 essential languages for city breaks

... and this is why

- **Talk to everyone everywhere**
Over 120 languages, more than any other publisher

- **The right words at the right time**
Quick-reference colour sections, two-way dictionary, easy pronunciation,
every possible subject – and audio to support it

Lonely Planet Offices

Australia
90 Maribyrnong St, Footscray,
Victoria 3011
☎ 03 8379 8000
fax 03 8379 8111
✉ talk2us@lonelyplanet.com.au

USA
150 Linden St, Oakland,
CA 94607
☎ 510250 6400
fax 510 896 8572
✉ info@lonelyplanet.com

UK
2nd fl, 186 City Rd,
London EC1V 2NT
☎ 020 7106 2100
fax 020 7106 2101
✉ go@lonelyplane

lonelyplanet.com